Forgotten Genocides

Pennsylvania Studies in Human Rights

Bert B. Lockwood, Jr., Series Editor

A complete list of books in the series is available from the publisher.

Forgotten Genocides

Oblivion, Denial, and Memory

Edited by
René Lemarchand

UNIVERSITY OF PENNSYLVANIA PRESS

PHILADELPHIA

Published by
University of Pennsylvania Press
Philadelphia, Pennsylvania 19104-4112
www.upenn.edu/pennpress

Printed in the United States of America on acid-free paper
10 9 8 7 6 5 4 3 2 1

Library of Congress Cataloging-in-Publication Data
Forgotten genocides : oblivion, denial, and memory / edited by René Lemarchand.
    p.   cm.—(Pennsylvania studies in human rights)
    Includes bibliographical references and index.
    ISBN: 978-0-8122-4335-2 (hardcover : alk. paper)
    1. Genocide.   2. Ethnic conflict.   3. Political violence.   4. Crimes against humanity.   5. War crimes.
I. Pennsylvania studies in human rights.
HV6322.7 .F67   2011
364.15′1

                                                            2011011293

Contents

Preface

My main motivation for putting this book together stems from my life-long immersion in the tragic destinies of Rwanda and Burundi. No two other countries in the continent have experienced genocidal bloodshed on a comparable scale. That they happen to share much the same ethnic map, a mutually understandable language, and were once traditional kingdoms before they became republics make their divergent paths to modernity all the more intriguing. And while genocide is the overarching theme of their blood-stained trajectories, the parallel should not mask the differences: the victims in each state belonged to different communities (Tutsi in Rwanda, Hutu in Burundi) and, unlike what happened in Rwanda in 1994, the perpetrators in Burundi won the day, insuring that the story be told from the victor's point of view. Hence the paradox inscribed in their agonies: while Rwanda suddenly emerged from decades of obscurity to become a synonym for a tropical version of the Holocaust, very few in the United States or elsewhere outside Africa have the faintest awareness of the scale of human loss suffered by Burundi twenty-two years earlier. That about three times as many people died in Rwanda is no reason to ignore the fate of its "false twin" to the south.

Because of its even more appalling reenactment in Rwanda, and the connection between them, my early encounter with the Burundi slaughter stays in my mind as if it happened yesterday. I am still haunted by visions of school children being rounded up and ordered to get into trucks, like sheep taken to the abattoir, only to be bayoneted to death or their skulls crushed with rifle butts on their way to the mass graves. Compounding the moral revulsion I felt in the face of the first genocide recorded in independent Africa was the death of many close friends, a loss I would experience again, twenty-two years later in Rwanda. Notwithstanding the retributive character of the killings, the vehement denial by

Burundi officials at the time that anything even remotely resembling a genocide had happened is what I found particularly difficult to swallow. All genocides have their deniers, and Burundi is no exception. Retrospectively, what made denial in this case so unusual is that it went virtually unchallenged. Equally astonishing is the manipulation of the facts, not just by Burundi officials but by Western scholars and journalists, with a view to shifting the onus of genocidal guilt to the victim group, while presenting the state-sanctioned killings as a legitimate repression.

As I read the essays in this volume I came to realize there is nothing exceptional about the misrepresentations surrounding the Burundi tragedy. Every genocide is unique in terms of circumstances and motives, but the deliberate concealment or manipulation of the facts by the perpetrators is more often the rule than the exception. This is not to exonerate survivors from similar distortions, only to emphasize the difficulties involved in getting at the truth.

To reiterate a commonplace observation, many more genocides have been committed through history than is recorded in human memory. Although the cases discussed here are but a limited sample in a litany of abominations going back to biblical times, they give us is a sense of the diversity of contexts out of which emerged the same hideous reality. The Holocaust will forever remain the archetypal frame of reference for taking the measure of human perversity. But as readers of Cathie Carmichael's splendid inquest into *Genocide Before the Holocaust* (2009) must surely realize, fixation on the Holocaust is likely to deflect our attention from the similarly horrendous crimes that preceded (and followed) the Jewish apocalypse, as if each generation needed to be reminded of the horrors of the past. This is only one of the many lessons to be learned from these essays.

I am willing to concede a touch of hyperbole in the title of this book. Needless to say, none of the events it seeks to illuminate have been forgotten by the descendants of the victims. Nor are they likely to be forgotten by those readers who came across the rare accounts of such cases that have appeared in academic publications, notably those on the Gypsies, on Anfal, and Burundi, in the edited volume by Samuel Totten and William S. Parsons, *Century of Genocide* (2009). Some may wonder, with reason, whether it is at all appropriate to describe the tragedy of the Herero as a forgotten genocide; my principal motive for doing so is that in the course of his research Dominik Schaller has unearthed a rich trove of new materials, which cast a singularly lurid light on the genocidal enterprise of the colonial state. Furthermore, there can be little doubt that the killings of the Herero, like the other tales of horror discussed in this book, are scarcely remembered by the wider public or ever entered the consciousness of some prospective readers.

Although my interest in the comparative study of genocide is insepa-
rable from my work on Central Africa, I have derived enormous intellectual profit, and no little stimulation, from the seminars I taught from
1998 to 2003 at the University of California at Berkeley, Smith College,
Brown, Concordia (Montreal), and in Europe at the Universities of Bordeaux, Copenhagen, and Antwerp, all of them centered on the analysis
of genocide from a broad historical perspective. I would like to take up
this occasion to express my sincere gratitude to those colleagues of mine
who made it possible for me to expand my horizons, geographically and
intellectually. Among others, Jacques Sémelin, Research Director at the
Paris-based Centre National pour la Recherche Scientifique CNRS) and
Director of the Online Encyclopedia of Mass Violence, has been particularly generous of his time in sharing with me his insights and critical
commentaries on issues related to this book. I also owe a huge debt to
my seminar students here and abroad for inviting me to bounce ideas
off them and forcing me to call into question many of the assumptions
I once took for granted, including the notion that genocide is just as
straightforward a concept as the circumstances that bring about the tec-
tonic slide of intergroup enmities into the abyss of mass murder.

Over the years Helen Fein has been a major source of inspiration in
everything I have written on this dreadful theme. The introduction to
this volume bears testimony to my indebtedness to her pioneering work.
But if there is any one person who, more than anyone else, played a part
in awakening my interest in the subject at hand it is the late Leo Kuper.
Years ago, when I was a graduate student at UCLA, his help and encouragement while I tried to make sense of the complexities of ethnic politics in Rwanda and Burundi, at a time when neither one evoked the
faintest interest among most scholars and Africanists, has been invaluable.

I thank each of the contributors for their patience while the manuscript was going through many revisions and painful surgical cuts, some
accompanied by much gnashing of the teeth. No one is more deserving
of my gratitude than Margaret Joyner, an accomplished editor, for her
exemplary skills in giving final shape to each of the chapters. I also thank
Cambridge University Press for permission to reproduce the maps
included in Chapter 1, which first appeared in Filip Reytjens, *The Great
African War: Congo and Regional Geopolitics 1996–2006*, Copyright 2009
Filip Reyntjens.

Introduction

René Lemarchand

None of the appalling stories told in this book is a household name. Unlike the better known cases—the Holocaust, Armenia, Cambodia, and Rwanda—most have been consigned to oblivion, by design or by indifference. This is nothing new. For mass murders to be "airbrushed out of history," in Milan Kundera's pithy phrasing, is a common phenomenon, even for the most uncommon of crimes. "Who, after all, speaks today about the annihilation of the Armenians?" Hitler famously said in 1939 while addressing a group of Nazi followers. In a similar vein one might ask how many today remember the genocide of the Assyrians, simultaneous to that of the Armenians in Ottoman Turkey? Or the genocide of the Herero in what was then German-controlled South-West Africa (now Namibia) in 1904, at a time when the killings of Christian communities in Turkey had already reached alarming proportions? More recently how many in the West recall the wholesale massacre, code-named Anfal, of the Kurds by Saddam Hussein, during the Iran-Iraq war (1987–1988)? Or the systematic cleansing of Hutu refugees in eastern Congo in 1996–1997 by Kagame's army? Or the 1972 extermination of tens if not hundreds of thousands of Hutu in Burundi, causing President Nixon to exclaim, in a response to the State Department's subdued stance on the issue, "this is one of the most cynical, callous reaction of a great government to a terrible human tragedy I have seen!" Nixon's outburst found little resonance outside the Oval Office.

The aim of this book, then, is to drag out of the shadows a number of searing human dramas in Africa, Asia, Europe, and the Middle East, in hope that they will be remembered for what they are, that is, massive violations of human rights that, whether or not they fit into any particular definition of genocide, cry out for sustained attention. Not just because of the scale of the crimes, but because of the questions they raise about how and why the past is so often ignored, manipulated, or denied.

That there are theoretical dividends to be drawn from this exercise seems reasonably clear. Including such seldom-remembered tragedies in our field of vision expands the range of variance beyond the cases most frequently selected for analysis, what Scott Straus calls the Big Five (the Armenian genocide, the Holocaust, Cambodia, the former Yugoslavia, and Rwanda).[1] It brings into view a broad spectrum of contextual differences in space and time, suggesting that very different sets of historical circumstances may generate broadly similar outcomes.

Contextual Diversities

More than a century and a half separates the total genocide of the Aborigine population in Tasmania (the last woman of her race, as Shayne Breen reports, died in 1876) and the hunting down of Hutu refugees in eastern Congo. During this time, tens of millions of human beings were exterminated. To the extent that numbers can be trusted, and within the limits of this discussion, they vary widely—from about 6,000 in Tasmania to anywhere from one-half to a million Gypsies killed between 1940 and 1945, and 250,000 to 300,000 in the case of the Assyrians in Ottoman Turkey. So do the circumstances that determined their fates.

The murderous effects of colonial rule are nowhere more cruelly evident than in the total physical extermination of the indigenous people of Tasmania (to say nothing of the killings perpetrated in other parts of Australia) and the genocide of the Herero people in South-West Africa, which resulted in the deaths of about 60,000. Following the violent 1959 Tibetan uprising, the forceful incorporation of Tibet into the boundaries of Communist China clearly stands as another example of colonial genocide. Even though the cultural differences between colonizer and colonized are not as salient as between Europeans and "natives," Chinese colonization has been no less repressive in thwarting the efforts of the Tibetan people to assert their cultural and political sovereignty.

About the time the genocide of the Herero revealed the full extent of colonial brutality, the rising tide of Turkish nationalism on the ruins of the Ottoman Empire was to prove even more lethal. The wholesale eradication of Christian minorities and Assyrians (or Nestorians) as well as Armenians and Greeks bears testimony to the appalling backlash provoked by the sudden disintegration of the Ottoman Empire, and the revanchist attitude generated by the violent expulsion of Muslim communities from many parts of the Balkans and the Caucasus. As Hannibal Travis's contribution shows, the killings that took place in the 1890s and the first decade of the last century were harbingers of much worse to come. As the anti-Assyrian campaign reached its climax in the summer of 1915, its genocidal proportions had become clear: "ultimately about 250,000 Assyrians died in the massacres and related famines and outbreaks of disease. But the number of victims nears 500,000 once the massacres of the 1890s and the Yezidi communities are included."

The 1988 Anfal campaign against Iraq's Kurdish minority is illustrative of a very different context, where the war between Iran and Iraq, coupled with the collaborative ties between Iraqi Kurds and their kinsmen in Iran, led to the dreadful retribution exacted by the use of chemical gas against Kurdish civilians, killing some 100,000. Although the eradication of the Gypsies in Central Europe also occurred in wartime, and continued even after the cessation of hostilities, their tragic fate, as Michael Stewart compellingly demonstrates, had more to do with racial prejudice than security risks.

Security, on the other hand, was certainly a key consideration behind President Paul Kagame's decision in October 1996 to send his army into eastern Congo to wipe out not just the remnants of the Rwandan *génocidaires*, but tens of thousands of innocent Hutu refugees. The same could be said of the motives behind the deliberate massacre of at least 200,000 Hutu in Burundi in the wake of a peasant insurrection that took the lives of many Tutsi. Fear of yet another Hutu-led uprising was a key factor, yet in both instances security concerns swiftly morphed into a wholesale eradication of civilian populations. What began as ethnic cleansing led inexorably to genocide. The table captures some of the characteristics of these litanies of horrors.

Given this diversity of contexts and circumstances, sometimes referred to as "unit heterogeneity," it is hardly surprising that the cases above fall into different analytic categories. The most useful for our purpose refers to the classic distinction drawn by Helen Fein between developmental, retributive, despotic, and ideological genocides having as their goals, respectively, "to acquire economic wealth, to eliminate a real or potential threat, to spread terror among real or potential enemies, and to implement a belief, a theory or an ideology."[2] While these are better seen as "ideal types" than mirrors of reality, they bring into relief the political dynamics at work in the cases at hand.

Although the mass murder of Aborigines and Herero clearly fits into the category of developmental genocides—their rationale was the acquisition of wealth and control over land—the ideological element is equally plain. Consider the Social-Darwinist arguments advanced by

Genocides

Country/Region	Target Group	Perpetrators	Number of Victims[a]	Time Period
Tasmania	Aborigines	British settlers	6,000	1803–1876
Ottoman Turkey	Assyrians	Turks/Kurds	30,000–250,000	1905–1915
South-West Africa	Herero	Germans	60,000	1904–1905
Germany	Gypsies/Roma	Germans et al.	0.5–1 million	1941–1945
Iraq/Kurdistan	Kurds	Iraqi Arabs	100,0001988	
China/Tibet	Tibetans	Chinese	N/A	1959–2008
Burundi	Hutu	Tutsi	200,000–300,000	1972
Eastern Congo[b]	Rwandan Hutu	Rwandan Tutsi	300,000–350,000	1976–1977

[a] The true number of victims in each case is impossible to determine. As a rule, the more disputed the genocide, the greater the likelihood of discrepancies in estimates. Burundi is a case in point, with conservative estimates claiming 100,000 dead as against 300,000 by some Burundi analysts. Even in the best of circumstances, the numbers vary widely. Consider the case of Rwanda: on closer inspection the standard figure of 800,000, sometimes inflated to more than one million, has been downsized to approximately 507,000. Again, the genocide of Assyrians is claimed by some to have taken the lives of 750,000 (*Encyclopedia of the Modern Middle East and North Africa*, vol. 1 [New York: Macmillan, 2004], p. 326) and from 20,000 to 30,000 by others (Donald Bloxham, *The Great Game of Genocide* [New York: Oxford University Press, 2005], p. 98). In many instances discrepancies hinge around differences between the direct and secondary effects of violence, that is, displacement, disease, hunger. The most reliable (though not infallible) guide to estimates of victims of genocide is Helen Fein, *Human Rights and Wrongs: Slavery, Terror, Genocide* (Boulder, Colo.: Paradigm Publishers, 2007), pp. 28–130.

[b] Included in the victim group in eastern Congo were thousands of Hutu, also known as *génocidaires* or *interahamwe* in Kinyarwanda, involved in the Rwanda genocide, as well as a far greater number of civilian refugees, consisting mostly of women and children. Although the principal perpetrators were Rwandan soldiers, they were joined by a fair number of so-called Banyamulenge, that is, Tutsi-related elements indigenous to eastern Congo acting as auxiliaries to the Rwandan army. The number of Hutu victims may be largely guesswork, but there can be little doubt that the vast majority were unarmed civilians.

Paul Rohrbach, identified by Dominik Schaller as "an influential public intellectual at the time of the Empire and Weimar Republic," to justify the killings of "Bantus": "The idea that the Bantus would have the right to live and die according to their own fashion is absurd." To proceed on that assumption, we are told, would scarcely be "an advantage for the evolution of humankind in general or the German people in partic-ular." Speaking of General von Trotha's take on the disposition of natives, Schaller writes, "His view of history was straightforwardly Dar-winist: Europeans, as member of a 'superior race' ought to conquer and populate the world."

Echoes of the same theme resonate in Shayne Breen's portrayal of "social-Darwinist myth-makers" in the context of nineteenth-century Tasmania. Tibet is another case of overlap. That there is every reason to view its coercive inclusion into China as a colonial genocide is made unambiguously clear by Claude Levenson, but she also shows the impor-tance of strategic goals behind the control of mineral wealth and land. Nor can one leave out the ideological (i.e., anti-religious) under-pinnings of the Chinese assault against the "feudalistic" forces of

Buddhism. Some of the same ambivalence can be detected in the motivations that led to the killings of Assyrians combining despotic and ideological motives. Seen from another perspective, however, and in light of the massive violations of human rights among Muslim populations by czarist Russia's expanding *imperium* in the Caucasus,[3] the retributive motive in the form of a revanchist reaction against Christian minorities cannot be ignored. In other cases, notably Burundi and eastern Congo, this dimension is frighteningly clear. The wanton killings of Hutu in Burundi did not just happen. It came about in response to the threat posed to the Burundi state, and specifically to the Tutsi elites running that state, by a Hutu-led peasant revolt that took the lives of anywhere from 1,000 to 3,000 lives. To an even greater extent, security concerns were paramount in Kagame's mind as he unleashed his army against Rwandan Hutu in eastern Congo. Nonetheless, in both instances the perfectly legitimate objective of warding off security threats quickly morphed into genocidal butcheries. The tragic and continuingly precarious fate of the European Gypsies, by contrast, has evidently more to do with a straightforward ideological mass murder, where belief in the inherent inferiority of the victims was the motivating force behind the attempt to exterminate them.

With these considerations in mind, what new insights can one gain from the essays in this volume? Contrary to what is often assumed, genocide is not always state-sponsored. That the initiative may indeed come from below, with little or no pressure from above, emerges with striking clarity in the essays by Shayne Breen and Michael Stewart on the Aborigines of Tasmania and the Gypsies, respectively. As Breen explains, "random killings were apparently common. . . . 'We shot them whenever we find them' [one visiting missionary was told]. . . . Pursuit killings were perpetrated under order by official parties of troops and colonists, by groups of colonist who took matter into their own hands, and by groups of men who hunted and killed Aborigines for sport." Unlike the Aborigines, the Gypsies were not killed for sport or at random or so overtly, but the fact remains that many were sent to their graves through what Michael Stewart describes as "local, individual" initiatives. He warns us against the danger of reading a central plan behind the "invisible" genocide. "If we try to read all the local initiatives and approaches as the unfolding of some central plan, or the inevitable consequence of structural features of Nazi rule we will never make sense of what happened."

In other instances, the role of the state is undeniable, while its motives and strategies may change over time, as when the success of preemptive measures, however brutal, may inspire more drastic action. This is one of the conclusions to be drawn from the essays on Burundi, eastern

Congo, and South-West Africa. As noted above in the first two cases, limited retaliation arising from security concerns swiftly evolved into a massive preemptive strike against all members of the victim group; in the third, as Dominik Schaller demonstrates, the German quest for *Lebensraum* overseas went far beyond the initial goal, in Lemkin's words, of "settling the surplus of German population in Africa and turn[ing] it into a German white empire." Not content to use force against traditional authorities in order to appropriate their land and cattle, violent resistance led to a swift and ruthless retaliation. The failure of Governor Leutwein's "divide and rule policy" quickly led to annihilation followed by concentration camps and slave labor. Elsewhere, while the motive remained basically unchanged, the methods varied. Breen's gruesome depiction of "techniques of extermination" in nineteenth-century Tasmania makes the point in graphic terms: land seizure, abduction, murder, massacre, and war of extermination, along with capture, incarceration, and exile.

Viewed through the prism of history, the roles of victims and perpetrators become blurred. That these are sometimes assumed by the same communities, albeit in different settings and in different epochs, is indeed the subtext of several chapters. Illustrative of this paradox is the case of the Assyrians, the target of horrendous bloodletting before and during World War I, and whose reputation, Rummel reminds us, "would be transmitted down the ages as one of particular savagery."[4] The Kurds are another example. In view of the terrible punishment they suffered during the Iran-Iraq War for their pro-Iranian stance, it is difficult to imagine that members of the same ethnic group took an active part in the killing of Assyrians and Armenians in the early 1900s. Similarly double-edged has been the role of the Hutu in Burundi: the staggering toll exacted in 1972 did not prevent some of their members twenty years later from committing atrocious crimes against Tutsi civilians in response to the assassination of Burundi's first elected Hutu president, Melchior Ndadaye. Only by reference to the historical context can one explicate such contradictions, which in the case of Burundi takes us back to 1972. The perverse logic at work here is not unlike the one described by Cathie Carmichael in her analysis of how the genocide of Muslim minorities by Christians in the Balkans paved the way for a replay of similar atrocities by Muslims against Christians in Ottoman Turkey.[5]

The notion of "genocide by attrition," set forth by Fein to describe situations involving the "interdiction and social reproduction of group members,"[6] though implicit in the 1948 UN Convention on the Prevention and Punishment of Genocide (UNGC), has not received nearly as much attention by genocide scholars as it deserves. This volume helps reestablish its relevance. It is central to an understanding of the humanitarian catastrophes that have accompanied these genocidal massacres and helps account for the discrepancies between direct and indirect human losses. As several chapters, in particular those dealing with the Assyrians in Ottoman Turkey, the Herero of Southwest Africa, the Kurds of Iraq, Tibet, and the killings in eastern Congo, poignantly demonstrate, the terrible losses caused by the appalling conditions imposed on survivors are no less tragic than those resulting from the blows of the perpetrators.

A last point concerns social structure as an incubator of genocidal violence. Although the significance of ethnic stratification as an independent variable is open to debate, the evidence at hand, whether it be from Rwanda, Burundi, Australia, or Ottoman Turkey, , strongly suggests that where divisions among groups are vertically structured, standing in a ranked relationship to each other, the result is to greatly enhance the likelihood of genocidal violence once the existing social system faces a frontal challenge. One is reminded in this connection of Leo Kuper's pioneering insights in his discussion of the plural context of genocide. Speaking of "the plural society in its extreme form," where "the same sections are dominant or subordinate, favored or discriminated against, in the political structure, in the economy, in opportunities for education, in human rights, in access to amenity . . . these structural conditions," he concludes "are likely to be conducive to genocidal conflict."[7] Despite the criticisms voiced by new generations of genocide scholars, there is much in this volume that would seem to substantiate his views.

Genocide, Mass Murder, or War Crimes?

The title of this book raises another question: In what sense can one describe these massive human rights violations, horrendous as they are, as genocides? To this query there are no satisfactory answers. Much depends on one's definition of what Churchill called "this crime without a name." Long after Lemkin gave it a name as well as a definition—"A coordinated plan of action aimed at the destruction of essential foundations of the life of national groups, with the aim of annihilating the groups completely"[8]—disagreements persist about these and other attributes. Although the definition offered by the UNGC is widely accepted in international law, it is by no means problem-free.[9] As has been noted time and time again by genocide scholars, it provides no quantitative threshold beyond which massacres mutate into genocides; it leaves out of the accounting collective identities other than racial, ethnic, or religious to describe the targeting of victims; and the question of intent behind the killings remains moot.[10] These are by no means trivial issues. They show the limitations of a legal/normative definition and how the debates it has engendered over its applicability is likely to hamper policy initiatives to "prevent and punish."[11]

One way of circumventing this problem is to expand the definition of genocide to make it more inclusive. An extreme example is the drastic recasting of the concept offered by Ben Kiernan in his weighty 724-page tome bearing the equally ponderous title of *Blood and Soil: A World History of Genocide and Extermination from Sparta to Darfur* (2007) that draws from just about every conceivable intra- and interstate conflict from ancient Greece to modern Sudan.[12] Exactly where to draw the line between genocide and other types of conflict is up to the reader. Much the same kind of definitional promiscuity afflicts Daniel Jonah Goldhagen's latest effort to reconsider the meaning of "eliminationism," a catch-all concept to designate not just genocide, but "five forms of elimination," namely "transformation, repression, expulsion, prevention of reproduction, or extermination."[13] Although there is much to be learned from his wide-ranging discussion of eliminationist violence, and no little to disagree with, the singularity of genocide ends up being the principal casualty of his all-embracing, moralizing discourse. No longer is genocide seen as a rare and distinctive phenomenon; it emerges as a quasi-ubiquitous trait of our past and contemporary universe.

The same criticism might be leveled on Benjamin Valentino's suggestion that genocide be subsumed under the broader concept of mass crimes so as to take into account those groups that are left out of the UNCG because of their nonethnic characteristics. Although the rationale behind his argument is persuasive, more problematic is his somewhat arbitrary setting of the number of victims required before a massacre qualifies as a mass killing: only when a minimal number of 50,000 civilians are killed over a five-year period can one legitimately speak of mass killing. Just as puzzling is his explanation that "selecting these relatively high thresholds helps establish with a greater degree of confidence that massive violence did in fact occur, and that the killing was intentional."[14] Just how intention relates to the scale of the killings and why a threshold of 30,000 or 40,000 would not suffice to establish massive violence remains unclear. By this yardstick many of the massacres, including Tasmania and Srebenica, called genocides would fail to qualify even as mass killings.

No less problematic is Israel Charny's effort to remedy "the ills of definitionalism," which he describes as "a damaging style of intellectual inquiry based on a perverse, fetishistic involvement with definitions to the point at which the reality of the subject under discussion is lost,"[15] through a "generic" reconceptualization that would include "all known types of mass murder and mass deaths that are brought about by the hand of man."[16] To sort out the wide range of crimes covered by his definition, Charny makes a laudable, though self-defeating, attempt to arrive at analytic clarity through a complex variety of subcategories. A limited sample would include such criminal acts as ethnocide, linguicide, and omnicide ("simultaneous intentional genocide against numerous races, nations, religions, etc."), genocidal massacres, intentional genocide (specific and multiple), genocide as a result of ecological destruction and abuse, and war crimes against humanity. One wonders whether the gratuitousness of this semantic exercise is the most useful antidote to the ills of definitionalism.

Considering that four of the cases examined here occurred during wartime (Assyrians, Gypsies, Kurds, and eastern Congo), the concept of war crimes inevitably comes to mind as a substitute for genocide or mass murder. Article 1 of the UNGC stipulates that "genocide whether committed in time of peace or in time of war is a crime under international law." Thus in describing the killings of Hutu refugees in eastern Congo in 1996–1997, the UN commission of investigation stated that the Rwandan army had committed large-scale war crimes and crimes against humanity,[17] while at the same time recognizing that genocide could not be ruled out. The distinction between war crimes and genocide is by no means self-evident. In a number of cases, war becomes a pretext for eradicating a community that had already been identified as a potential target for elimination. This was certainly the case for the Armenians and Assyrians during World War I and the Kurds during the Iran-Iraq War. One can only agree with Fein's observation that "although all poison gas attacks in war are war crimes, because they are attacks with a banned weapon, purposeful attacks on civilians (in this case civilians of the attacked state) they are more than war crimes—they are crimes against humanity if not genocide."[18] The same could be said of the wholesale eradication of Hutu refugees in eastern Congo, the Assyrians in Ottoman Turkey, and Gypsies in Germany during World War II.

Despite all its flaws, the UNGC definition still has considerable merit in helping us identify genocide as a crime unlike all others by its scale, intentionality, and target. No one has argued the case for its usefulness more convincingly than Fein, who writes, "I employ the UNGC definition because I believe that it is useful to maintain a common universe of discourse among genocide scholars, international lawyers and human rights monitors; to discriminate between victims of genocide and the violations of life integrity; and to recognize related violations in international law, such as war crimes and crimes against humanity."[19]

Oblivion

That so few appear to remember the human dramas resurrected in this book is both disturbing and puzzling. Disturbing because, in George Santayana's well-known aphorism, those who do not remember the past are doomed to repeat it; puzzling because there are no obvious answers as to why this should be so, except for the fact that some of these atrocities happened a long time ago in faraway places. This is certainly the case with regard to the fate that befell the Aborigines of Tasmania, to which might be added that of the Assyrians. But what of the more recent cases of genocide?

Endorsement, as distinct from enforcement, of human rights has a long pedigree, going back to the French Declaration of the Rights of Man and Citizen of 1789 (massively violated four years later during the Terror). The emergence of human rights as an issue of international concern, legitimized by international jurisdictions and conventions, and backed by influential international NGOs, is a much more recent phenomenon, traceable to the last decades of the previous century. An early precursor was the Carnegie Endowment for International Peace, founded in 1910, whose report on "the causes and conduct of the Balkan Wars" of 1912 and 1913 contributed in no small way to alert public opinion to the atrocities committed by all parties to the conflict. In a retrospective commentary on the Carnegie report, George Kennan ruefully noted that its warnings about "the megalomania of the national ideal" did little to alter the tragic course of events nearly a century later.[20]

Some of the most egregious cases covered in this book occurred at a time when the notion of human rights—as natural (inherent in human beings), equal (the same for all) and universal (applicable everywhere)—had yet to enter the conscience if not the consciousness of humanity. Reflecting on the history of human rights, Lynn Hunt convincingly argues that such rights "are best defended in the end by the feelings, convictions and actions of multitudes of individuals, who demand responses that accord with their inner sense of outrage."[21] The absence of this inner sense of outrage goes far to explain the ease with which past genocides tend to be forgotten.

A major contributing factor is the efforts made by criminal states to impede investigations. Invoking national sovereignty to keep the lid on the atrocities committed by the perpetrators has been a frequent occurrence, even where their claims to sovereignty seemed very much in doubt. The sinister comedy of Laurent Kabila, reluctantly playing the role of Kagame's obedient client and leaning over backward to obstruct the UN investigation into "crimes against humanity" in eastern Congo, is one obvious example. Or take the case of Burundi in 1972, where every effort was made by what was left of the state to prevent journalists from traveling into the country. Tibet is even more cruelly pertinent. Very few outside observers were allowed into the country to observe firsthand the devastating retribution exacted by China in the wake of the 1959 rebellion, resulting in the deaths of hundreds of thousands. Even as recently as 2008, when Tibetan claims for autonomy reached a new pitch of intensity, crippling restrictions were placed on travel to Lhasa and its vicinity.

Where the evidence is lacking or difficult to obtain, chances are that some genocides will claim a monopoly on public attention, ensuring that others will remain shrouded in obscurity. This phenomenon is brilliantly brought to light by Timothy Snyder's discussion of why the atrocities of Auschwitz have all but eclipsed the even more appalling crimes committed in Treblinka, Belzec, and Sobibor in occupied Poland. He writes, "Auschwitz, generally taken to be an adequate or even a final symbol of the evil of mass killing, is in fact only the beginning of knowledge, a hint of the true reckoning with the past still to come." He goes on to explain that "we know about Auschwitz because there were survivors, mostly West European Jews, who were able to write and publish as they liked, whereas East European Jewish survivors, if caught behind the iron curtain, could not."[22] In the same way that "Auschwitz as symbol of the Holocaust excludes those who were at the center of the historical event,"[23] one might argue that Rwanda is a symbol of a "tropical Holocaust," which, while giving due prominence to the Hutu perpetrators, all too often excludes those who were at the center of the historical event, the Tutsi refugee warriors who fought their way into the country from Uganda. In a more general sense what might be called the "Auschwitz effect" is directly relevant to the cases explored in this book.

Whereas some genocides have gained considerable public attention, others have not. The result has been to eclipse the latter. Thus while the Rwanda genocide continues to attract the concerns of journalists, social scientists, and policy-makers, its Burundi counterpart is largely ignored. The Armenian genocide is at the heart of the controversies raging among politicians, policy makers, and social scientists, which helps explain why it has been the subject of an enormous amount of outstanding academic research,[24] but the systematic eradication of tens if not hundreds of thousands of Assyrians receives little or no attention. Again, consider the marginal attention paid to the martyrdom of the Gypsy victims of the Holocaust. How the Auschwitz effect reduced their agonies to near-footnotes is well described by the late Sybil Milton: "Despite the similarity and simultaneity of persecuting, the disparity between the vast quantity of secondary literature about Nazi Judeophobia and the limited number of studies about the fate of Roma and Sinti has inevitably influenced current historical analyses, in which Gypsies are at most an afterthought."[25]

Explaining "Why Anfal has nearly fallen into oblivion" Choman Hardi notes a somewhat similarly elusive phenomenon: if so many have forgotten the mass extermination of the Kurds this is in no small part because "it is overshadowed in public opinion by the dramatic events that followed in the wake of the 2003 invasion of Iraq" and because "it is all too often seen as a sideshow in the larger drama of the Iran-Iraq War."

That so many of these abominations have been consigned to oblivion is not just happenstance. As the preceding discussion suggests, it is rooted in a number of factors, some having to do with historical circumstances and moral indifference, others with the role of the state in obstructing the search for truth. But even more important to the concealing of their hideous reality has been the combination of denial and myth-making surrounding the debate about "what really happened."

Denial and Myth-Making

All genocides have been contested. Each has found its Robert Faurisson or David Irving willing to deny the undeniable. The cases examined here are no exception, but few fit into the same mold. It is one thing for former Tasmanian Premier Ray Groom to assert that "there had been no killing in the island state," thus making him, writes Colin Tatz, "Australia's foremost genocide denialist in the 1990s,"[26] and quite another to admit the existence of such killings while questioning their characterization as genocide. This is the position taken by Henry Reynolds, "the most prominent historian of Tasmania," writes Shayne Breen, "[who] while unequivocally demonstrating the widespread destruction, has argued that genocide did not occur," the reason being the absence of "demonstrable intent on the part of the state to exterminate."

If denialism is an extreme form of myth-making, mythologies can also promote revisionist assessments that stop short of denial. The distinction between revisionism and denial emerges with striking clarity from Breen's discussion of the Tasmanian tragedy, to which might be adduced the cases of eastern Congo, Burundi, and the Gypsies. Rather than contesting the reality of violence, revisionism puts a radically new construction on the motivations and circumstances of genocidal violence. More often than not the presumed victims turn out to be the génocidaires, or else there are perpetrators on both sides, the result being a double genocide.

Reversing the roles of perpetrators and victims so as to shift blame to the victimized community has a long pedigree in the history of mass crimes. In Tasmania it is traceable to 1830, when an Aborigines Committee was set up to inquire into the causes of the natives' hostility toward the colonists: "In a piece of blame-the-victims reasoning characteristic of *génocidaires*," Breen informs us, "the Committee concluded that Aboriginal treachery and violence were the primary causes of violence against them." And this, he adds, despite the fact that "three earlier governors had publicly warned colonists against their habit of wantonly killing and abduction of Aborigines."

This blame-the-victims construction is one of the most bizarre aspects of the ongoing debate surrounding the multiple bloodbaths that have ravaged the Great Lakes region of Central Africa. As the chapter on Burundi shows, this role reversal is typical of the discourse of certain Tutsi intellectuals, who, to this day, insist that only the killings of Tutsi civilians by Hutu insurgents, the precipitating factor behind the 1972 bloodbath, qualify as genocide, whereas the far more devastating slaughter of Hutu can best be seen as a legitimate repression, excessive perhaps, but by no means genocidal. Something of the same reasoning can be detected in the official assessments offered by Rwandan authorities of the results achieved by the destruction of the refugee camps in eastern Congo and the follow-up search-and-destroy operations. The Rwandan army, we are told, was never involved in the killing of civilians; the purpose of its foray into eastern Congo was basically prophylactic in nature, aimed at cleansing the nests of Hutu génocidaires, an interpretation that, though deserving of the strongest reservations, was fully endorsed by the U.S. ambassador at the time. In both instances, the aim was to shift the onus of genocidal guilt to the victim group, and to view retribution as a strategy designed to stop further bloodshed.

The double genocide thesis introduces a major variation on this theme. It received a semblance of respectability from French President François Mitterrand when he described the Rwandan bloodbath in precisely such terms, not without hurting many sensibilities in France and elsewhere, not least among them the Rwandan survivors. This thesis finds an echo in other contexts, some going as far back in history as the accusations launched against Russia at the time of the Armenian and Assyrian slaughters: if anything resembling a genocide had been committed against Christian minorities, presumably much the same atrocities had been perpetrated by Czarist Russia against Muslim minorities in the course of Russia's imperial expansion into the Caucasus. Although the terrible price exacted by Russia cannot be ignored, to equate the killings of Muslims with the far more sustained and systematic elimination of Christian minorities of Anatolia is hardly convincing. It implies a symmetry in criminal behavior that, in fact, is wholly unwarranted. The same holds for other contexts in which the dogma of equivalence has been applied. As the Burundi chapter tries to explain, this is the main flaw behind the double genocide thesis adumbrated by French historian Jean-Pierre Chrétien and his co-author the Belgian journalist Jean-François Dupaquier in a book misleadingly titled *Burundi 1972: Au bord des génocides* (Burundi 1972: On the brink of genocides [2007]). The implication, strange as it may sound to most Burundi scholars, is that the country experienced two "near genocides," one by the Hutu and another by the Tutsi. Rather than reiterating the critique set forth elsewhere in this book, suffice it to note that the evidence marshaled by the authors leaves a great deal to be desired.

Denial, like revisionism, involves the manipulation of historical facts in order to promote a political agenda. The aim is to leave out some crucial episodes and magnify others so as to exonerate the butchers and denounce the victims as provocateurs. Nowhere is this sleight of hand more evident than in the relentless efforts displayed by Turkish authorities to deny responsibility for the genocides of Armenians, Assyrians, and Greeks. Turkish aspirations to join the European Union have given renewed urgency to this agenda. The "provocation thesis," as Bloxham argues, has been the stock in trade of Turkish nationalists and pro-Turkish commentators eager to demonstrate the involvement of Armenians on the side of Russia during World War I so as to project the deportation of Armenians as a matter of military necessity.[27] Much the same argument has been used to explain away the mass murder of Assyrians. As Travis points out, among the historical myths surrounding their extermination lies the "hoary notion that the Ottoman Empire was an innocent victim of the British and Russian empires during World War I" and that "there is no objective or verifiable evidence of an official policy to endorse massacres, enslavement, rapes, or cultural devastation." As with the Armenian genocide, the reconstructed version of the Assyrian case is backed by an impressive display of propaganda and scholarly rewards for "willing interpreters."

The provocation argument looms equally large in Kagame's brief to explain his murderous incursion into eastern Congo. The reasoning in this case is not without foundation, at least as far as the initial phase of the intervention was concerned. No one familiar with the history of the region can deny the security threats posed to Rwanda by the presence of Hutu extremists at its doorstep. Just as plain, however, is Kagame's skill in manipulating the facts when confronted with the mass slaughter of Hutu refugees. Although the argument can be made that there were plausible reasons of state to destroy the refugee camps, there were none for the mass murder of anywhere from 200,000 to 300,000 innocent

Hutu men, women, and children. To do so with some pretence of justification, the official version of the facts ran as follows: (a) all civilians had walked back to Rwanda after the destruction of the refugee camps in late 1996, (b) those who remained behind were the murderers (*interahamwe*) and their supporters, and (c) the military operations of the Rwandan Patriotic Army (RPA) effectively cleansed the Congo of its génocidaires. On each of these counts the evidence plainly suggests otherwise, yet by twisting the evidence, Kagame was able to convince international public opinion, including the U.S. Ambassador to Rwanda, of the righteousness of his claims and eventually thwart a painstakingly planned international intervention designed to save innocent lives.

The less-than-edifying role played by the U.S. Embassy in Kigali during the "events" in eastern Congo finds a parallel of sorts in the U.S. government's stance during the Anfal crisis. As Choman Hardi reports, while tens of thousands of Kurds were being wiped out by "Chemical Ali," the stance of the U.S. government is best captured by Samantha Power's terse formula, "official knowledge, official silence," in effect denying what Peter Galbraith, in his 1998 report to the U.S. Senate Foreign Relations Committee, described as an act of genocide. One only needs to remember that the United States was Iraq's closest ally during the Iran-Iraq war (an alliance immortalized by the photo of Rumsfeld shaking hands with Saddam Hussein) to grasp the principal motive, among many others, behind the deafening silence of the State Department. As for the Iraqi authorities, their official position was that the fate that befell the Kurds was amply merited; not only were they seen as religiously suspect and culturally different, but also and most importantly as a political liability.

Nor is China exempt from responsibility in manipulating historical facts. To conceal its genocidal role and strengthen its territorial claims to the "autonomous region" of Tibet, the Chinese version of history greatly magnifies the "ties that bind" the Roof of the World to the Middle Kingdom at the expense of their distinctive cultural differences. By the same token, undue lip service is paid by Beijing to the blessings of Chinese overrule. While the propaganda spotlight is turned on the social and economic benefits derived from the "liberation of Tibet from the constraints of its feudal past," not the slightest mention is made of the extremely bloody repression visited upon the Tibetans in the wake of the 1959 uprising, the wholesale destruction of their temples and shrines, the severe restrictions placed on religious practice, and the massive transfer of Han Chinese to the autonomous region so as to hasten the pace of assimilation of the indigenous Tibetan population.

The propensity of genocidal states to mask or deny the evidence is not so much, as some might claim, a by-product of contested histories as it is the result of a deliberate attempt to rewrite history. The aim is to legitimize the present by falsifying the past. This political dimension is central to an understanding of why conflicting views of the past have a major stake in the continuing debate about who killed whom, where, and why.

Memory

Memory matters not just for what it says about the past, but for what it forgets to tell us. In his pioneering work on collective memory, Maurice Halbwachs goes to great lengths to stress the selectivity of individual and social memories.[28] The same is true of official memory. Nowhere is this bias more obvious than in post-genocidal contexts. As many of the cases in this book demonstrate, what to forget and what to remember is a political choice, more often than not dictated by the need to erase the past to legitimize the present. A dominant narrative thus emerges that projects the victor's version of history and silences dissenting voices.

It is not every day that an academic is taken to task by an African head of state for his erroneous take on how to heal the wounds of genocide, yet this is precisely what happened when President Kagame was impelled to turn a critical eye to my essay "The Politics of Memory in Post-Genocide Rwanda" in a recently published collaborative volume.[29] Drawing on the insights of Paul Ricoeur and Eva Hoffman, I made a case for reconciliation between Hutu and Tutsi through the sharing of ethnic memories. Hutu memories, I argued, are "thwarted memories" that instead of being repressed by a pro-Tutsi dominant discourse, should be given voice and "equal time" with Tutsi memories. I went on to suggest a path to reconciliation, that is, a joint effort to undertake a shared memory project, what Ricoeur calls a *travail de mémoire*, this would involve sharing narratives about *the sufferings experienced by both communities* as a major step toward an understanding of the twofold relationship between history and memory and memory and recognition.[30] In his preface to the book, President Kagame used the predictable argument that there is no such thing as a thwarted Hutu memory, much less a clash of memories, writing, "Lemarchand is wrong to suggest that the memory of the Hutu victims of genocide have been thwarted. . . . The premise on which Lemarchand's chapter is based is mistaken. . . . It is also wrong for Lemarchand to assume that there has been a global criminalization of the Hutu community, etc." This is not the place to challenge Kagame's stance on ethnic memories, but suffice it to note that the validity of his claims will be difficult to test as long as references to ethnic identities are strictly forbidden by the Rwandan Constitution. What better way to erase the collective memories of a group than to deny its distinctive identity?

Kagame's take on the subject reminds one of the remarks of the African American woman in Studs Terkel's book on race relations in the United States. "They never let you forget their history, but they want you to forget yours."[31] Although Rwanda is an extreme case, it is not unique. Burundi is another example of a post-genocidal state where collective memories have been obstructed and manipulated. Unlike what happened in Rwanda, ethnic identities have never been legislated out of existence, yet much the same result was achieved out of fear during the years following the 1972 bloodbath. What the case of Burundi illuminates is the propensity of traumatized populations, in this case the Hutu, to greatly magnify the horrors they suffered at the hands of the Tutsi perpetrators, a phenomenon closely linked to the proliferation of what Liisa Malkki calls "mythico-histories."[32] As we tried to demonstrate, the recasting of mythico-histories through a political discourse aimed at mobilizing ethnic loyalties is a key element in the persistence of Hutu radicalism. To this day, however, and in spite of the coming to power of a Hutu president, ethnic memories have yet to find a proper outlet to engage in a constructive *travail de mémoire.* Herein lies yet another disquieting parallel with Rwanda.

Other examples can be cited of how collective memories are selectively retrieved. Consider how the history of the Aborigines, tragic as it is, has been virtually erased from the collective consciousness of white Australians. Shayne Breen shows how the "myth of inevitable extinction," bolstered by "the theories of Social-Darwinist ideologues" helped propagate the idea of "a hybrid people with no history, no culture, and no future apart from total assimilation into mainstream Tasmanian society and culture." Colin Tatz for his part perceptively notes the contrast between events that speak to the white Australians' heroic past, notably their display of extraordinary valor at Gallipoli during World War I, and the silence surrounding the agony of native peoples. This is how he describes the symbolic meaning of Gallipoli: "Australians scrutinize, magnify, exhibit, venerate, and strive to remember every square inch of Gallipoli, every wound, act of valor and every death in that 'birth of the nation,'" and then adds, "on matters concerning Gallipoli the striving is ever more toward 'moving back.' But on matters Aboriginal, the catchphrase is that time has come 'to move on.'"[33]

The Assyrians are another example of what Pierre Vidal-Naquet called "assassinated memories."[34] Their tragic destiny has been thoroughly excised from the record of crimes committed by the Ottoman Turks, and this, as in the case of the Armenians, with the active cooperation of

Western intellectuals all too willing to succumb to the enticements of the Turkish state. Bloxham's commentary on the part played by Turkey in promoting denial of the Armenian genocide applies equally well to the Assyrians. Denial in both instances has been backed "by the full force of a Turkish state machinery that has pumped substantial funding into public relations firms and American university endowments to provide a slick and superficially plausible defense of its position."[35] Perhaps to an even greater extent than the Armenians, the collective memory of the Assyrians has been "airbrushed out of history." As Travis shows, specific measures by the governments of Turkey and Iraq also contributed to the memorial assassination: "They eliminated the Assyrian category from the census, replacing it with Christian Kurds, Turks, or Arabs. In Turkey even Assyrian personal names and towns and village designations were outlawed. The Turkish and Iraqi governments claimed Assyrian land, cultural monuments and artifacts as property of the state." Meanwhile, "revisionist histories inverted every pertinent event between 1894 and 1925 to argue that the Turks were the victim and the tyrannical Christian nationalists were the aggressors." Not until recently, thanks to the initiative of genocide scholars, has a concerted attempt been made to break the silence surrounding the planned extermination of the Assyrians and other forgotten minorities. Thea Halo's commentary—in reponse to the International Genocide Scholars Association (IGSA)'s overwhelming approval of a resolution to recognize the genocides inflicted on Assyrian and Greek populations of the Ottoman Empire between 1914 and 1923—is worth quoting: "In a victory for historical accuracy and inclusion, the International Association of Genocide Scholars (IAGS), an organization of some of the world's foremost experts on genocide, overwhelmingly affirmed that, between 1914–1993, Christians, Assyrians and Pontian and other Anatolian [Asia Minor] Greeks, suffered a genocide that was qualitatively and quantitatively similar to the genocide suffered by the Armenian Christians."[36] Equally deserving notice, however, are the strong reservations to the IAGS initiative expressed by reputable scholars, for the most part on highly dubious grounds.

The claims of memory assert themselves in a variety of ways. One of these is restitution. The link between memory and restitution finds an intriguing illustration in the Herero Day ceremony described by Dominik Schaller: "Every last weekend in August the Herero gather in Okahandja to celebrate 'Herero Day.' They make a procession to the graves of their old chiefs and remember the murder of their ancestors by the German colonizers. In recent years 'Herero Day' has become the forum for restitution claims. Because of their iron-willed determination to survive, and their persistent demand for historical justice, the immense sufferings visited upon their ancestors are still widely remembered, enshrined as it were in their collective memory." Unlikely though it is that the Herero demands for redress will be met in the foreseeable future, that they happen to be so insistently and formally articulated bears testimony to their determination to resist collective amnesia. That there are limits, however, to what restitution can accomplish is well captured by the German term *Wiedergutmachung*, "making good again," as if the dead could be resurrected.

Restitution may assuage the consciences of those who have inherited the burden of guilt; it cannot make whole again what has been so thoroughly destroyed. Not just the lives of tens of millions of innocent human beings, but the trust that their surviving relatives and descendants may have had in humankind. Little wonder if, in many parts of the world where the earth has been soaked in genocidal blood, appeals to forgive and forget seem cruelly illusory. And yet, the way in which the past is remembered, how narratives are shared, how ethnic memories are filtered through the prism of common sufferings, all of this in may help the healing process. "Remembering to forget" is how one close observer of post-genocide Rwanda describes the path to ethnic coexistence.[37] A more hopeful agenda is remembering to forgive. Such indeed is the ultimate purpose of this book.

Chapter 1

Mass Murder in Eastern Congo, 1996–1997

Filip Reyntjens and René Lemarchand

> A story as macabre as any other, involving genocidal attacks against refugees some of whom were guilty of genocide themselves; mercenaries of the traditional "dogs of war" variety; the smashing of refugee encampments and the perversion of humanitarian assistance; Western businessmen with mobile telephones and an intense desire to follow the victors and fix new contracts for exploiting Zaïre's diamond and copper mines; and the defeat of a dying old dictator. All of these and more were involved in a vicious game of pursuit through the steaming jungles of eastern Zaïre.
> —William Shawcross, *Deliver Us from Evil*

Of the countless human rights violations committed by President Paul Kagame's army before, during, and after the Rwanda genocide, the systematic extermination of tens of thousands of Hutu civilians in eastern Congo (then known as Zaïre) between October 1996 and September 1997 can only be described as a case of mass murder. Some would not hesitate to call it a genocide—a term used by a UN panel to describe what it perceived as a distinct possibility.[1] Very few outside Central Africa remember the horrendous scale of this human tragedy, let alone the complicated circumstances behind it. Nonetheless, the disastrous sequel of these events continues to plague the relations between Kigali and Kinshasa, and to mortgage the prospects for a durable peace in eastern Congo.

Although the exact number of victims will never be known, several things are reasonably well established. One is that, contrary to official

Rwandan propaganda, the victims included a majority of civilians rather than being made up exclusively of *génocidaires*. Another is that the number of refugees who chose to return to their homeland—or had no other option—after the destruction of their camps must not have exceeded half a million.[2] This means that of the 1.1 million refugees who fled to the Congo in the wake of the genocide, more than half remained unaccounted for. Tens of thousands died of hunger, disease, and sheer exhaustion as they fled the avenging arm of the Rwanda Patriotic Army (RPA); others, mostly former *interahamwe* (civilians) and ex-Forces Armées Rwandaises (FAR), managed to survive the manhunt, thanks to their weapons and physical stamina; the remainder, consisting mainly of women, children, and the elderly, fell under the blows of the RPF.

Estimates of the number of refugees killed by RPF soldiers vary widely. In an interview with the news agency Congopolis on October 15, 1997, former U.S. Assistant Secretary of State for Africa Herman Cohen came up with what seems a wildly exaggerated figure: "I believe that the Rwanda Patriotic Army (RPA, ex-RPF) massacred as many as 350,000 Hutu refugees in eastern Congo." Stephen Smith's "guesstimate" of "200,000 Hutu killed by Rwandan troops during Laurent Kabila's march to power" could be closer to the mark.[3] On the basis of a careful scrutiny of the evidence another observer, K. Emizet, arrives at a death toll of about 233,000.[4]

That such massive bloodshed should have made so little impact on Western consciousness is due in no small part to the deliberate efforts of the Kagame government to conceal the truth by a sustained campaign of disinformation—a task in which it received considerable assistance from the U.S. Embassy in Kigali. What Lionel Rosenblatt, president of Refugees International (RI), refers to as "a reverse form of the CNN factor" suggests another explanation: "Because the current humanitarian catastrophe in eastern Zaïre is not on television, many don't believe it's happening (or feel that, politically, they can afford to ignore it)."[5] Not unnaturally, public attention was largely focused on the more widely publicized dimension of the war in eastern Congo. The triumphant march of the Rwanda-backed rebels to Kinshasa all but eclipsed public attention to the horrendous crimes that have accompanied its victory. Philip Gourevitch aptly described the image that impressed itself most forcefully on the minds of casual observers: "The Congolese rebellion," he averred, "offered Africa the opportunity to rid itself of its greatest homegrown political evil, and to supplant the West as the arbiter of its own political destiny."[6] As we now realize, Kagame's Rwanda—the central orchestrator of Kabila's victory—emerged as the real arbiter of the Congo's destiny, but at horrendous cost to the Congolese and to many of its own citizens.

The Roots of Disaster: Security Threats and Minorities at Risk

Before going any further something must be said of the potentially explosive regional situation that came into existence in the wake of the Rwanda genocide. In the context of an increasingly tense relationship among the three principal actors—Mobutu's Congo (then known as Zaïre), ethnic Tutsi communities of eastern Congo, and the new rulers of Rwanda—the provocations of Hutu (and Congolese) extremists can best be seen as the fuse that ignited the wider conflict.

At the root of the crisis lay the existential threat posed to Rwanda's security by the presence of thousands of Hutu hard-liners in the refugee camps. Of some forty camps strung along the border with Rwanda and Burundi, the two largest, Katale and Mugunga, both in North Kivu and sheltering 202,566 and 156,115, respectively, accounted for nearly one-third of the total refugee population of 1.1 million registered by the UNHCR in June 1996.[7] The camps' strategic locations, the control exercised by armed extremists over the civilian refugee population, the refugees' widespread support of the radical opposition movement in exile, the *Rassemblement pour le retour des réfugies et la démocratie au Rwanda* (RDR), the substantial military assistance Hutu hardliners received from Mobutu, and the cross-border raids organized from the campsites—all this made the Rwandan authorities acutely conscious of the clear and present danger looming on their doorstep.[8]

Insecurity inside the camps only served to magnify the external threats posed to Rwanda. In most cases, recourse to violence was the work of Hutu extremists trying to assert their control over civilians. In response to mounting criticisms of the international community for its inability to rein in the extremists, Sadako Ogata, the head of UNHCR, decided to turn to Mobutu's troops to maintain security in the camps, a step that turned out to be totally counterproductive. What became known as the Contingent Zairois Chargé de la Sécurité des Camps (CZSC)—consisting of some 1,500 subcontracted Zairian soldiers—proved even more dangerous than the troublemakers they were sent to control, as many reportedly went about stealing refugee property, raping women, and even selling weapons to those they were supposed to disarm. Most of them ran away when confronted with units of the Rwandan army.

A matter of equal concern for Kigali was the menacing tone of the provincial authorities in North and South Kivu toward the ethnic Tutsi minorities indigenous to each province. Although most of them consider the Congo their homeland and trace their ancestry to long-established immigrant communities, the so-called Banyamulenge of South Kivu ("the people of Mulenge") and the ethnic Tutsi of North Kivu claim strong cultural and psychological affinities to the Tutsi of Rwanda. That many volunteered to join the ranks of the RPF in the early 1990s as it fought its way into Rwanda testifies to their sense of solidarity with their kinsmen in exile. As Congolese politicians intensified their anti-Tutsi rhetoric through much of 1995 and 1996, threatening to expel all Tutsi and Banyamulenge residents—now globally seen as foreigners collaborating with their Rwandan kinsmen—Rwanda's sympathy for "the near abroad" only strengthened its sense of revulsion toward the Mobutist state and its provincial satraps.

Eastern Congo has a long history of anti-Rwandan sentiment going back to the years immediately following independence when Kinyarwanda-speaking elements were viewed with mounting hostility by local Congolese politicians. There was no precedent, however, for the intense anti-Tutsi hostility triggered by the outpouring of Hutu refugees from Rwanda to North and South Kivu. Until then, Hutu and Tutsi were objects of equal distrust by self-styled "native Congolese," being lumped together as they were into a single "Banyarwanda" (or "Rwandophone") entity. Now the Tutsi were singled out as the prime cause of the problems facing the Congo. Hatred of the Tutsi found expression in countless acts of aggression and a ratcheting up of threats, culminating with officially supported anti-Tutsi public demonstrations in Bukavu and Uvira. A number of Tutsi were killed in Bukavu during a "march of anger" on September 18, 1996; a week earlier, according to Amnesty International (AI), dozens of Tutsi were arrested in Uvira. Illustrative of the venomous mood among "native" Congolese is the statement of a local civil society organization in South Kivu comparing the Banyamulenge to "disloyal snakes who have abused Zaïrian hospitality and must be sent back to Rwanda, where they come from."[9] Ethnic tension reached its peak after the South Kivu governor called for "all Bayamulenge to leave Zaïre within a week," adding that "those remaining would be considered as rebels and would be treated as such."[10]

In what turned out to be a self-fulfilling prophecy many of the Banyamulenge subsequently joined Kabila's rebel organization, the Alliance of Democratic Forces for the Liberation of Congo/Zaïre (AFDL), a broad-based coalition of anti-Mobutist forces stitched together through the joint efforts of Kagame and Museveni. Long before its existence became known ethnic Tutsi were being actively recruited by President Kagame to beef up his armed forces. As early as 1995, according to President Yoweri Museveni of Uganda, some 2,000 joined the RPA in anticipation of a major strike against the refugee camps, later to be joined by an additional 2,000. By June 1996, many Banyamulenge "rebels" were being trained in northwestern Burundi, under the protection of the predominantly Tutsi Burundi army. Among the truckloads of soldiers that crossed the Burundi border into eastern Congo in September 1996 many were Banyamulenge, eager to serve the RPA units as their scouts and auxiliaries in their march to the campsites.[11]

Securing Eastern Congo

What began as concerted attacks against urban communities—Uvira fell on October 24, Bukavu on October 30, and Goma on November 1—quickly mutated into a systematic "clean-up" of the refugee camps and immediately thereafter into a wide-ranging manhunt directed against all refugees, be they civilians, interahamwe, or ex-FAR. The largest of the camps, Mugunga, now home to 200,000 refugees, was attacked on November 14, two weeks after the fall of Goma. During those two weeks frantic efforts were made by the UNHCR, with the active support of France and Canada—and against the strenuous opposition of the United States and the United Kingdom—to open up safe corridors that would "simultaneously allow delivery of relief in one direction, and the secure passage of refugees back to Rwanda in the other."[12] No less important was the assembling of a multinational force of some 10,000 to 12,000 troops to ensure the safety of the operation, a task entrusted to Maurice Barril, senior military adviser to UN Secretary General Boutros Boutros-Ghali (of which more later). Meanwhile, in clear disagreement with the Franco-Canadian initiative, U.S. Assistant Secretary of State for Population, Refugees, and Migration Phyllis Oakley flatly suggested cutting off all assistance to the refugees in order to force them back into Rwanda, a country where, in her words, "we have seen a great improvement."[13]

As has become painfully clear, the destruction of Mugunga on November 14 was a move carefully calculated by Kagame, and presumably with the full approval of the United States,[14] to ensure the failure of the UNHCR's humanitarian strategy and at the same time present France and Canada with a fait accompli. In Samantha Power's blunt assessment, "They decided to strike a knockout blow before the international troops had time to assemble."[15]

After a sustained shelling of the campsites, units of the AFDL and RPA moved in from the west, leaving the refugees no other option but to walk back to Rwanda. As noted earlier, as many as one-half million poured back into Rwanda. Pointing to the massive return of refugees, Kagame made the argument that those who stayed behind could safely be presumed to be génocidaires—their refusal to come home being cited as proof of their culpability. In such circumstances, there was no need for either the safe corridors or the MNF. What Kagame failed to

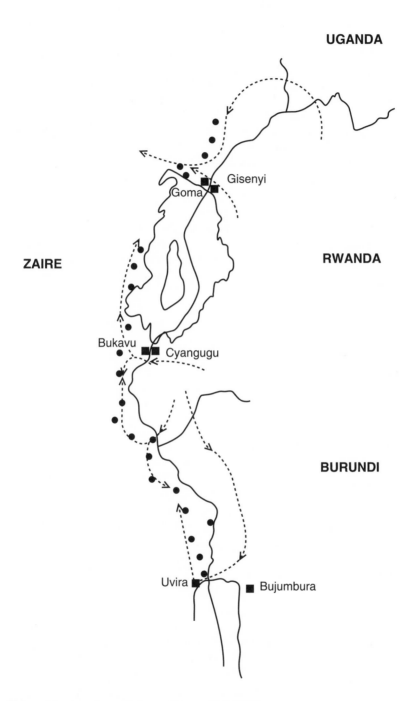

UGANDA

ZAIRE

RWANDA

Gisenyi
Goma

Bukavu
Cyangugu

BURUNDI

Uvira
Bujumbura

Figure 1.1. Attacks on Refugee Camps (Fall 1996)

recognize is that, in addition to thousands of interahamwe and ex-FAR, hundreds of thousands of civilians were now on the run, desperately trying to evade the tightening noose of the search-and-destroy operations conducted by the RPA, who quickly caught up with the huge flow of refugees from other camps, also desperate to outpace their pursuers.

The Rwandan army played the key role in the destruction of the camps, as it would in the next few weeks in the wanton slaughter of innocent civilians. Long before the attack on Mugunga, the Voice of America made clear the implication of the RPA: on October 28, Rwandan authorities, speaking on condition of anonymity, admitted that "the Rwandan government was sympathetic to the Banyamulenge and that some officers from the Rwandan army had helped organize rebel groups." The participation of Rwandan troops was particularly clear in the capture of Goma after attack units were sent in from Rwanda by land and across Lake Kivu. By early November the borders between the Congo and neighboring Rwanda and Burundi had been secured by a buffer zone stretching along 250 kilometers from Goma in the north to Uvira in the south.

The next phase was now about to begin. In addition to the countless men, women, and children who died of hunger, disease, and sheer exhaustion in a murderous game of hide-and-seek, tens of thousands were savagely murdered.

The Manhunt

As the exodus of refugees wound its way toward Kisangani and ultimately to Mbandaka, the last station on their Golgotha, new camps were hastily assembled in hopes that their inhabitants would be spared. For survivors of the ordeal, the names Shanji, Lula, Ubundu, Kasese, and Tingi-Tingi are not just geographical references to temporary campsites; they are evocative of collective agonies that have been virtually obliterated from the rest of the world's memory.

This is how Howard French, one of the rare journalists to visit the camps, described what he saw at Tingi-Tingi as his old DC-3 landed nearby:

> I looked out the window as we banked for the descent and discovered a scene worthy of *The Ten Commandments*. On either side of the road, pressed to its very edges and sometimes spilling onto the highway itself, was a sea of refugees—150,000 people or more, dressed in tatters and jumping with excitement over the arrival of a special visitor bearing desperately needed relief supplies. . . . As we touched down the sea of people parted in a feat of just-in-time reactions. . . . Wide-eyed refugees swamped me as I plunged into the crowd. Many were desperate to tell me their stories but could

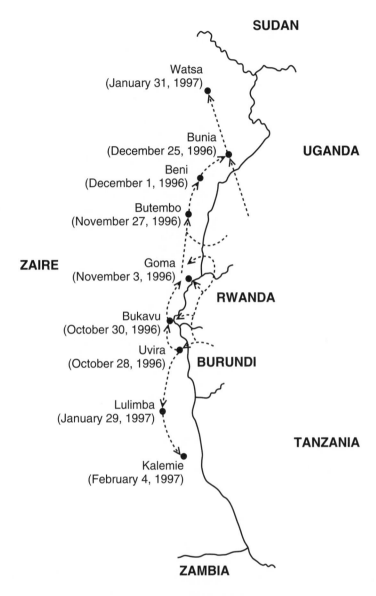

SUDAN

Watsa
(January 31, 1997)

Bunia
(December 25, 1996)

UGANDA

Beni
(December 1, 1996)

Butembo
(November 27, 1996)

ZAIRE

Goma
(November 3, 1996)

RWANDA

Bukavu
(October 30, 1996)

Uvira
(October 28, 1996)

BURUNDI

Lulimba
(January 29, 1997)

TANZANIA

Kalemie
(February 4, 1997)

ZAMBIA

------➤ Itinerary of the AFDL and its allies.
The dates indicate the capture by the "rebellion"
of the locations on the map.

Figure 1.2. First Phase of the War (Fall 1996)

--------> Itinerary of AFDL rebel units on their
march to Kinshasa, indicating the dates
on which key localities were captured.

Figure 1.3. Second Phase of the War (Spring 1997). Itinerary of AFDL rebel
units on their march to Kinshasa, indicating the dates on which key localities
were captured.

speak only Kinyarwanda. Others, their faces severely drawn, their ribs and
shoulders protruding sharply through their flesh, held out their hands in
hope of food. Others simply wanted to touch me, almost as if this tall, well-
clothed foreigner was not an apparition. . . . Most of these refugees were
slaughtered. The killings occurred just days after my visit, and the bodies
were buried so hastily that later they seemed to call out from the grave.[16]

One of lucky ones to leave Tingi-Tingi before the slaughter was Marie
Beatrice Umutesi, whose wrenching memoir recounts her encounter
with the dead and the dying:

The third day after leaving Tingi-Tingi we began to pass the bodies of the dead and the dying. . . . My eye fell on a teenager hardly sixteen years old. Like the others she was lying at the side of the road, her large eyes open. . . . A cloud of flies swarmed around her. Ants and other forest insects crawled around her mouth, nose, eyes and ears. They began to devour her before she had taken her last breath. The death rattle that sometimes escaped her lips showed that she was not yet dead. . . . I stood in a daze in front of this sixteen year old girl, lying in agony by the side of the road in the middle of the equatorial forest more than five hundred kilometers from home. . . . I was overwhelmed by revulsion. What crime had all these victims committed to deserve such a death?[17]

Another survivor, Maurice Niwese, was witness to the carnage perpetrated by the Rwandan army at Kasese, home to an estimated 60,000 to 100,000 refugees. On April 22, 1997, units of the RPA surrounded the camp and proceeded to position their machine guns in front of the refugees. This is how he describes what he saw:

There were soldiers everywhere. Pitilessly they opened fire. People died by the hundreds. Blood flowed everywhere. . . . I hit the ground. Next to me a relative, a friend, a neighbor fell. Suddenly any one still alive, including the wounded, fled into the forest. I followed them. . . . The killings lasted three days. The second and third day were spent on search-and-destroy operations in the forest, and in finishing off the wounded. Anyone caught was immediately killed. Women were taken away. A female survivor told me that they were savagely raped. Then they were killed. Soldiers would insert their guns into their sexual organs and pull the trigger.[18]

Kasese is only one of the many killing grounds illustrative of the appalling cruelties committed by the Rwandan army. Another is Mbandaka, a thousand kilometers west of Kisangani, where, according to Stephen Smith, on May 16, 1997, the day before Kinshasa fell to Kabila's AFDL, "800 Hutu refugees were machine-gunned in broad daylight." They are, he adds, "part of the 200,000 Hutu killed by the Rwandan troops during Kabila's march to power."[19] In his chilling narrative of "the carnage in Mbandaka," Théophile Ruhorahoza describes the "mad scramble" provoked by the arrival of Rwandan troops, causing the refugees to seek refuge wherever they could, some in homes and hotels, others in the buildings of the Office National des Transports (Onatra), only to be rounded up and gunned down by Rwandan troops or tied together in groups of four or five and thrown into the Congo River.[20]

How emergency aid was used by rebel troops to lure refugees out of their hiding places and kill them is graphically described by William Shawcross: "There was another way the rebels used aid agencies: as bait. The agencies would find refugees, encourage them to emerge from the jungle—for food or repatriation—and then the rebels would either drive the foreign officials out or make conditions so unsafe that they left. They then killed the refugees."[21]

Figure 1.4. The Massacre of the Rwandan Refugees

If today the scenes of horror conveyed by the few who survived the ordeal are largely consigned to oblivion, much of the credit for this goes to the frantic efforts made by the Kagame government, with the assistance of the U.S. Embassy, to conceal the truth.

The Numbers Game: The Art of Concealing the Truth

Reliable statistics on refugee populations are notoriously difficult to come by, irrespective of setting and circumstances. In addition to the technical problems involved in data collection, more often than not the political context invites radically different assessments. Nowhere is this truer than in the case at hand. To quote from a senior UNHCR official, "Events in eastern Zaïre in 1996 seemed to demonstrate that the geopolitical interests of the U.S. and its allies can still impinge very directly upon the question of refugee numbers."[22]

The root of the controversy surrounding the question of refugee numbers in eastern Zaïre revolved around radically different estimates of how many returned to Rwanda after the attacks on the camps, and the identity of those who remained behind. Kagame's position was straightforward: virtually all civilian refugees had returned to Rwanda; only the génocidaires, consisting of interahamwe and ex-FAR, refused to come home, fearing retribution. This was also the view of the U.S. Embassy in Kigali.

Unequivocally nailing U.S. colors to Kagame's murderous enterprise, Rick Orth, the U.S. military attaché, fully endorsed Rwandan propaganda, rejecting the claims of several impartial observers, including Refugees International (RI) and Oxfam, that between 500,000 and 700,000 remained in eastern Zaïre, where they were hunted down by AFDL and RPA units. At a press conference in Kigali on November 23, 1996, Orth dismissed such allegations, adding that "satellite photos had located only one significant cluster of Rwandans in eastern Zaïre," which furthermore "consisted not of bona fide refugees, but of soldiers and militia members who had been responsible for the 1994 genocide."[23] Categorically refuting the argument, Emergencies Director Nicholas Stockton of Oxfam stated that the aerial photos shown at an Oxfam meeting on November 20 "confirmed in considerable detail, the existence of over 500,000 people, distributed in three major and numerous minor agglomerations." These, along with a number of Zairian IDPs, had "in effect been airbrushed from history."[24] The implication of the U.S. stance is nowhere more clearly stated than by Johan Pottier, who wrote, "The claim by the U.S. military that practically all refugees had returned to Rwanda gave the AFDL/RPA its license to kill in eastern Zaïre: those who remained were *génocidaires* on the loose."[25]

Orth's misrepresentations cast strong retrospective doubts on U.S. Ambassador Robert Gribbin's contention that, although Kagame and his "RPF luminaries [*sic*] proved to be masters of spin," and "spin was well ingrained in Rwandan political behavior, . . . I [Ambassador Gribbin] tried to be careful to ensure that we in the Embassy did not get caught in the propaganda machine." Astonishingly, Gribbin candidly adds, "I did not mind the spin; I knew it for what it was, and I knew that in some respects Rwanda needed the spin in order to wash out the hatred, to promote unity, and to lay the foundation for a better future." His memoir, *In the Aftermath of Genocide: The U.S. Role in Rwanda*, while occasionally enlivened by comic touches, as in his use of the term "Mumulenge" as the singular of Banyamulenge,[26] makes abundantly clear the tendentiousness of his stance throughout the refugee crisis.

The controversy over refugee numbers must be seen in light of the proposal sponsored by the Organization of African Unity for a multinational intervention force (MNF), which, had it been implemented, would have made it impossible for Kagame to deal with the refugee problem on his own terms. Intended to serve a humanitarian purpose, the project was adopted in principle by the UN Security Council, while the State Department declined to commit itself "in the absence of a coherent plan." While several African countries indicated their willingness to commit troops, Canada offered to assume the command of the MNF, but only if the separation of civilians and armed combatants, and the latter's disarmament, were not part of its mandate—a move immediately seen by Rwanda as likely to increase the risks posed to its security. Canada's position, however, was contrary to that of the UNHCR, the European Union, and several NGOs, all sharing the view that separation was one of the main objectives of any kind of intervention. It soon became clear, however, that neither the United States nor Canada really intended to support the MNF.

On the very same day that the RPA/AFDL attacked the Mugunga camp the UN Security Council adopted Resolution 1080 allowing for the deployment of the MNF under Chapter VII of the UN Charter. At this point the Rwandan propaganda machine moved into high gear. The Rwandan Ambassador to the UN claimed the MNF was no longer needed, a position echoed the following day by Kabila. Meanwhile, as if to underscore Kagame's irritation over the issue, some thirty Canadian military personnel were prevented from leaving Kigali airport while another hundred were blocked in Nairobi pending authorization to land in Kigali. On November 19, the Rwandan Foreign Minister reiterated that there was no need for the MNF and, in any event, under no circumstances would Rwanda's territory be used for such an intervention. The next day Kagame declared that most refugees had come home, cynically indifferent to the claim made by the World Food Program that 700,000 of them remained unaccounted for.

With considerable help from his American friends, Kagame had won the diplomatic battle. The MNF plan was finally shelved on November 20, when the Canadian prime minister stated that military intervention was no longer needed. On December 15, the UN Security Council formally abandoned the planned intervention. The humanitarian crisis, however, was far from over.

Obstructing the UN

Through much of January and February 1997 alarming reports of human rights violations against refugees reached the UNHCR and RI. Virtually unknown until then, the names of Lubutu, Shabunda, Tingi-Tingi, Kalima, and Punia became associated with horrendous reports of savage violence. On March 6, faced with mounting evidence of abuse, UN High Commissioner for Human Rights José Ayala-Lasso instructed Special Rapporteur Roberto Garretón to conduct a preliminary inquiry. Between March 25 and 29, Garretón identified four mass graves in North Kivu. In addition, in his report he gave the location of some forty probable sites where killings by AFDL/RPA occurred. On April 15, Garretón received further instructions from the UN Human Rights Commission to head a three-member commission to look into allegations of "grave and massive violations of human rights, especially the right to life."[27]

Despite assurances from Kabila that he would not interfere with the mission, he later reneged—most probably under pressure from Rwanda —arguing that Garretón's reporting was "not impartial." Though denied access to Kivu, the commission was able to collect enough evidence to come up with devastating accusations against the AFDL/RPA. In the report of July 2, besides accusing the rebel army of consistently preventing humanitarian assistance from reaching the refugees, it identified some 134 sites of alleged massacres, and went on to note that the victims were for the most part "neither *interahamwe* combatants nor soldiers of the former FAR. They were women, children, the wounded, the sick, the dying, and the elderly, and the attacks seem to have had no precise military objective. Often the massacres were carried out after militia members and former FAR soldiers had begun to retreat."[28]

The new UN mission sent in August ran into the same stonewalling on the part of Kabila. After the team remained blocked in Kinshasa for weeks, on October 1 UN Secretary General Kofi Annan decided to recall them "for consultations." When the team was eventually redeployed on December 11, new difficulties emerged, ranging from travel restrictions and "spontaneous" demonstrations of local inhabitants orchestrated by the government to intimidation of witnesses and physical threats against team members. On February 13 the team's number-two man, Zimbabwean Andrew Chigovera, resigned, stating that he had "great difficulty in believing that an environment favorable to an independent and impartial inquiry existed in the DRC." In a *note verbale* presented to the Congolese government on February 26, 1998, the UN team said it was "extremely preoccupied" by the way it had been treated. This, in turn, prompted Kabila to accuse the UN team members of interfering in Congo's internal affairs.

In its report submitted to the Security Council on June 29, 1998, the UN team concluded that the RPA had committed large-scale war crimes and crimes against humanity. It went on to suggest that genocide should not be ruled out, but the issue required further investigation. In the report's convoluted phrasing, "the systematic massacre of those [Hutu refugees] remaining in Zaïre was an abhorrent crime against humanity, but the underlying rationale for the decision is material to whether these killings constituted genocide, that is, a decision to eliminate, in part, the Hutu ethnic group."[29] Predictably, the Congolese and Rwandan missions to the UN promptly rejected the report's allegations.

On July 13, the UN Security Council issued a pro forma condemnation of the massacres, other atrocities, and violations of international humanitarian law, including crimes against humanity, and asked the Congolese and Rwandan governments to carry out inquiries and punish the guilty. By demanding a report by October 15 on the steps taken to that effect, the council kept its options open, as it envisaged, if need be, taking the "additional measures" necessary to bring the culprits to justice. Without saying so explicitly, it thus left the possibility of taking the leaders responsible for the genocides before an international tribunal. The matter never returned to the council's agenda.

Preemption, Ethnic Cleansing, and Genocide

As the foregoing makes plain, there are serious reasons to call into doubt the position of the Rwandan government in the aftermath of the tragedy. Nonetheless, a key question is whether Hutu extremists were not directly responsible for bringing onto themselves and their kinsmen the death and sufferings they endured at the hands of the AFDL/RPA. If so, the destruction of the camps, and their tragic consequences notwithstanding, must be seen as a case of legitimate preemption dictated by the security imperative, a point frequently emphasized by outside observers.

Seen from this perspective, Rwanda is by no means a unique case. History abounds in examples of preemption as a means of warding off threats arising from power vacuums. One example from the early history of the American republic is the 1818 invasion of Spanish Florida by General Andrew Jackson purportedly retaliating for repeated cross-border raids by Creeks, Seminoles, and escaped slaves, some with the active encouragement of the British. According to John Lewis Gaddis, during the ensuing controversy, "[John Quincy] Adams alone came to Jackson's defense, persuading the rest of [President] Monroe's cabinet that the United States ought not to apologize for what had happened but rather take advantage of it by claiming the right to act preemptively in such situations." Gaddis adds, "The modern term 'failed state' did not appear in Adams's note, but he surely had that idea in mind when he insisted that power vacuums were dangerous and that the United States should therefore fill them."[30] The parallel between Spanish Florida and Zaïre as failed states is even more compelling if one recalls Jackson's next move, the forceful removal of tens of thousands of Seminole Indians from their homeland—a move that today could only be described as ethnic cleansing.

As a prelude to the carnage about to happen in eastern Congo, ethnic cleansing is indeed the most appropriate label to characterize the forced displacement of refugees fleeing the destruction of their camps. "Population cleansing," according to one definition, "is a planned, deliberate removal from a certain territory of an undesirable population distinguished by one or more characteristics such as ethnicity, religion, race, class or sexual preference."[31] Though some would argue that the return of roughly half a million refugees to Rwanda was voluntary—despite considerable evidence to the contrary—what happened to those who were forced to flee the campsites fits into most definitions of ethnic cleansing, including Jacques Sémelin's, when he writes that it consists of "removing the undesirable elements [of a given population] by deporting them and allowing them to die *en route* if need be." He goes on to observe that "the process can take on an even more radical form when individuals are killed without even having the chance to flee, or when they are slaughtered once they have been deported. The notion of a 'territory to be purified' in this case becomes secondary in relation to the aim of totally exterminating a group."[32]

This is where, in its ultimate phase, ethnic cleansing mutates into genocide. The violence that often accompanies ethnic cleansing covers a wide spectrum, up to and including premeditated mass killing. What emerges from survivors' narratives and accounts of foreign observers present at Tingi-Tingi, Lubutu, and Mbandaka and other killing grounds is an image of systematic and indiscriminate murder of men, women, and children. To lump together civilian victims under the rubric of génocidaires is to add insult to injury.

Just how many Hutu génocidaires (as distinct from civilians) were killed along with the innocent in the course of search-and-destroy operations is impossible to say. That some were caught in the net is beyond doubt. Equally clear, however, is that the vast majority of the victims were innocent civilians. It is easy to see why many if not most of the interahamwe and ex-FAR were able to escape the dragnet: quite aside from the fact that their youth and vigor enabled them to run faster than their pursuers, having weapons to use in their defense was their primary means of survival.

The enduring menace posed to Congolese society by the génocidaires and their newly recruited allies—now known as the Forces Démocratiques pour la Libération du Rwanda (FDLR)—is a commentary on the egregious failure of Kagame's policies in eastern Congo. Fifteen years after the destruction of the refugee camps, the interahamwe are showing a resilience, indeed a renewed strength, that few would have anticipated. As recent events have demonstrated, their capacity to resist the combined onslaught of the Rwandan and Congolese armies—codenamed Umoja Wetu (Our Unity)—speaks volumes for their ability to survive against the heaviest odds. Although the FDLR today differs in many important ways from its early incarnations, it remains tethered to its past through its shared memory of the subsequent carnage, often referred to as a "counter-genocide," the 1996–1997 slaughter forms a crucially important element of its ideological arsenal.[33]

With the benefit of hindsight one cannot fail to detect a touch of sinister irony in the spectacle of Kabila *fils* reenacting his father's alliance with Rwanda against their common enemy, albeit with few hints of greater success. Karl Marx famously said that history repeats itself, first as a tragedy, then as a farce. Just how tragic or how farcical this latest attempt to bring to heel the génocidaires remains to be seen.

Chapter 2

Burundi 1972
Genocide Denied, Revised, and Remembered

René Lemarchand

Contrary to widespread opinion, independent Africa's first recorded genocide did not happen in Rwanda in 1994, but twenty-two years earlier in Burundi. With the exception of a small group of Africanists, the "events" of 1972 are practically forgotten. If remembered at all, they enter the public's consciousness as yet another bloody episode in an endless series of massacres. They are seldom recognized for what they really are: one of the most gruesome genocides experienced by an African state. The bloodbath, occurring in response to a localized rural revolt—abetted by a handful of Hutu intellectuals operating in neighboring Tanzania—took the lives of anywhere from 200,000 to 300,000, the vast majority of Hutu origins.

"Extraordinary in its impact and intensity" is how the Carnegie Endowment for International Peace described the carnage: "Through the spring and summer of 1972, in the obscure Central African state of Burundi, there took place the systematic killing of as many as a quarter million people. Even among the awesome calamities of the last decade, the tragedy in Burundi was extraordinary in impact and intensity. Though exact numbers can never be known, most eyewitnesses agree that over a four-month period, men, women and children were savagely murdered at the rate of more than a thousand a day. It was, wrote United Nations observers, a staggering disaster."[1]

That a tragedy of that scale should have virtually sunk into oblivion raises disturbing questions: what accounts for the silence of the international community in the face of a mass murder that went on for months and wiped out tens of thousands of lives in every province, district, and urban community? Why did it take thirty-two years for two recognized authorities to put pen to paper and produce the most richly documented, though highly biased, chronicle of the Burundi tragedy? Why is it that so little has been said of the historic threads that link the Burundi genocide to its Rwandan counterpart?[2]

Amazingly, the most forceful expression of outrage in the United States did not come from the State Department but from President Richard Nixon. In response to a rather bland, noncommittal memo from Henry Kissinger, briefly stating the scale of the killings, and noting that neither the USSR nor the People's Republic of China was involved, thus posing no threat to U.S. interests, Nixon flew into a rage. His handwritten reaction, scribbled on the memo, captures his sense of anger in the face of what he referred to as Foggy Bottom's callous attitude and recourse to "double standards":

> This is one of the most cynical, callous reactions of a great government to a terrible human tragedy I have seen. When the Paks try to put down a rebellion in East Pakistan, the world screams. When Indians kill a few thousand Paks, no one cares. Biafra stirs us because of Catholics, the Israeli Olympics because of Jews; the North Vietnamese bombings because of Communist leanings in our establishment. But when 100,000 (one third of the people of a black country) are murdered, we say nothing, because we must not make blacks look bad (except, of course, when Catholic blacks are killed). I do not buy this double standard. Tell the weak sisters in the Africa Bureau of State to give a recommendation as to how we can at least show moral outrage. And let's begin by calling our Ambassador immediately for consultation. Under no circumstances will I appoint a new Ambassador to present credentials to these butchers.[3]

Whatever else can be said of Nixon's outburst, it provides a jarring note to the seeming indifference of the American public and policymakers at the time; more important, through Kissinger's "callously" realist memo, it brings into focus one of the principal reasons why the Burundi drama received so little public attention: however regrettable, the slaughter posed no direct or indirect threat to the U.S. national interest.

Other factors came into play to keep the genocide out of the limelight. That it happened at a time when public attention to human rights violations had yet to reach anything approaching today's salience is certainly a key reason why the international community remained comparatively unmoved. Not until the 1980s and 1990s would a transnational concern for human rights and humanitarianism begin to emerge. Furthermore, every effort was made by the Burundi authorities to deny journalists access to the country, and those few who were given an entry visa were duly accompanied by a government official.

Aside from a handful of scholars, Burundi in the early 1970s was, for all intents and purposes, an unknown entity on the map of Africa. The image it evoked was that of an exceedingly arcane form of factional politics, rendered hardly more intelligible by the fact that its population, like that of Rwanda, consisted of three communities, Tutsi, Hutu, and Twa, the first accounting for some 14 percent of a population estimated at five million, the second 85 percent, and the Twa 1 percent. Most puzzling was the fact that in spite of claiming much the same ethnic map as Rwanda, its trajectory since independence (1962) followed a radically different course. Unlike Rwanda, where a Hutu-led revolution led to the overthrow of the centuries-old monarchy and the advent of a Hutu-dominated republic, Burundi remained under the Tutsi rule, with Hutu participation in the government reduced to a marginal proportion. All of which adds up to a complicated social history, where significant political events, including those of a genocidal magnitude, appear to defy simple explanations.

The Anatomy of Mass Murder

Seen through the lens of Helen Fein's classic typology, the Burundi bloodbath can best be understood as a "retributive genocide,"[4] occurring in reaction to the perceived threat posed to the Tutsi-dominated regime of President Michel Micombero by a Hutu-led insurrection. Described by an eyewitness as a "peasant *jacquerie*,"[5] the rebellion caused untold casualties among Tutsi civilians before unleashing a devastating response from the government. Granting that there are no simple explanations for the carnage, the sequence of events leading to it is reasonably well established.

The triggering factor behind the killings was the outbreak of a local uprising in the lakeside town of Rumonge, to the south of Bujumbura, on April 29, 1972.[6] In a matter of hours terror was unleashed by roving bands of Hutu against Tutsi civilians. They were joined in many instances by Congolese migrants, mostly of Bembe origins, originating from eastern Congo. Countless atrocities were reported by eyewitnesses. In the town of Bururi all civilian and military authorities were killed. After taking control of the armories in Rumonge and Nyanza-Lac the insurgents proceeded to kill every Tutsi in sight, along with a number of Hutu who refused to join them. A short-lived "Martyazo Republic" was proclaimed in Vyanda in early May, in the southern province of Bururi, an experiment quickly brought to an end by government troops sent out to crush the rebellion.

How many were involved is hard to tell. Contrary to the deliberately inflated figure of 25,000 cited by the government, the insurgents could not have numbered more than a few thousand at the most. A French pilot, who flew helicopter missions on behalf of the Burundi army, put their number at 1,000, "including the majority of committed or con-scripted Hutu, (Congolese) Mulelistes in the middle, and the organizers at the top." Evocative of the late Pierre Mulele, the rural organizer of the Kwilu rebellion of 1964–65, the term "Muleliste" in this context refers to the remnants of Gaston Soumialot's rebel army from eastern Congo. Just as in the mid-1960s many of Soumialot's warriors had recourse to drugs and magic to claim invulnerability to bullets, similar rituals and whistle-blowing commands were observed during the rebel-lion. Recourse to hemp and "superstition" has been noted by several commentators, hence, as one report puts it, "their mystical excitation which led them to believe they would be invulnerable to bullets."[7] Just how many Mulelistes joined the insurgency remains unclear. Much the same uncertainty surrounds the number of persons killed by the rebels; although estimates differ widely, according to usually well-informed mis-sionary sources the casualties ranged between 800 and 1,200, a far cry from the 50,000 claimed by the government in the white paper issued in June 1972.[8]

However brutal the repression, what followed surpassed anything that had been anticipated. It can only be described as an appalling blood-bath. On April 30, while counterattacks were launched against the insur-gents, elements of the armed forces began to coordinate their efforts to exterminate all Hutu suspected of having taken part in the rebellion. The men in charge of military operations were all high-ranking officers: chief of staff Thomas Ndabemeye, most prominently, along with Albert Shibura, André Yanda, and Joseph Rwuri, all with close personal ties with President Micombero. As much as the threat posed to the regime, their ethno-regional ties served as a powerful source of solidarity. All were of Hima origins, a Tutsi subgroup, whose immediate enemies in the months preceding the bloodbath were drawn from another Tutsi minority group, the Tutsi-Banyaruguru. Another source of cohesion stemmed from the fact they stood as the most influential representatives of what became known as the Bururi "lobby." The significance of this phenomenon cannot be overestimated: they all had roots in Bururi province, and many indeed came from the same locality (Matana). More often than not such ties tended to cut across formal institutions, pene-trating deeply into the ruling party, Parti de l'Union et du Progrès

National (Uprona) and its ancillary organizations. The central figure behind the killing machine, however, was the Minister of Foreign Affairs, Artémon Simbananiye. After his promotion to the rank of itinerant ambassador with plenipotentiary powers, on May 12, he was given a virtually free hand to organize the killings in the capital city and provinces. In this task he received considerable assistance from the notoriously violent party youth wing, the Jeunesses Révolutionnaires Rwagasore (JRR), which played a crucial role in identifying and searching out the victims.

What began as an extremely brutal repression, centered on the principal areas touched by the rebellion—that is, Nyanza-Lac, Rumonge, and Bururi—quickly morphed into a systematic, nationwide slaughter of Hutu civilians, with purges affecting every sector of the civil society. The carnage went on unabated until August. By then almost every educated Hutu was dead or in exile. The deliberate targeting of educated Hutu elements is a point on which most observers agree. As Jeremy Greenland reported, "the government radio broadcasts encouraged the population to 'hunt down the python in the grass,' an order readily interpreted by Tutsi in the interior as license to exterminate all educated Hutu, down to the level of secondary, and, in some cases, even primary schoolchildren. Army units commandeered merchants' trucks and mission vehicles, and drove up to schools removing whole batches of children at a time. Tutsi pupils prepared lists of their Hutu classmates to make identification by officials more straightforward."[9] In Bujumbura, Gitega, and Ngozi, all administrative personnel of Hutu origins—not only local civil servants but chauffeurs, clerks, and semi-skilled workers—were rounded up, taken to the nearest jail, and either shot or beaten to death with rifle butts and clubs. In Bujumbura alone, an estimated 4,000 Hutu identified as educated or semi-educated, including university and secondary-school students, were loaded up on trucks and taken to their graves.

If the exact number of deaths is anyone's guess—estimates range from 100,000 to 300,000—there can be no doubt about the murder of the single-most prestigious victim: late on the evening of April 29, shortly after his return from six years of exile, ex-king Ntare was assassinated in his royal residence in Gitega. This was not an act of random vengeance. Whether the order to kill Ntare came from Shibura, as is sometimes claimed, or Simbabaniye or Micombero, all three shared a pathological fear of a monarchical plot, including the possibility of the king acting as the rallying point for a widening peasant insurrection.

The regicide gives us a clue as to the perpetrators' strategic objectives. To see the bloodbath as a disastrous overreaction to the Hutu uprising is of little help to uncover the perpetrators' underlying motives; the aim, ultimately, was to eliminate all future threats to the republican regime and at the same time reinforce its legitimacy in the eyes of the Tutsi population, including its Tutsi rivals (i.e., the Banyaruguru). While the assassination of king Ntare meant the elimination of the only remaining symbol of monarchical legitimacy, the purge of all Hutu elements from the army, the police, and the gendarmerie resulted in the transformation of the instruments of force into a Tutsi-Hima monopoly. Accusations of sub-ethnic favoritism carried little weight, however, in the face of the magnitude of the Hutu threat, consistently presented as a monstrous genocidal plot; in such dire circumstances, the image of a government committed to the protection of all Barundi against domestic and external foes seemed entirely credible. By shifting the onus of guilt to the Hutu insurgents, now viewed as the only génocidaires, the government could reasonably pose as the savior of the nation.

Denial and Silence

Critical to the restoration of state legitimacy was the targeting of the rebels as the enemies of the nation. This was accomplished through an *inverted* discourse where the insurgents are portrayed as having committed a monstrous act of genocide directed against the Tutsi as a group. The point comes across again and again in interviews with, and statements from, Burundi embassy officials, but nowhere more clearly than in the white paper issued by the government on June 26: "the sheer number of victims (nearly 50,000), the scale of the means deployed, the plans, maps and documents seized, convincingly demonstrate that the aggressors did not simply aim at the overthrow of the republican institutions but carefully planned the systematic elimination of an entire ethnic group: the Tutsi. . . . This is why the Burundi authorities felt obligated to inflict a severe punishment on those responsible for this genocide."[10]

In a press conference on June 7, the Burundi ambassador in Brussels echoed the same "blaming-the-victims" theme: "Besides the considerable scale of the rebels' attacks, one must underscore its barbaric and genocidal character. . . . It must be stressed that if one can speak of a genocide to describe the attacks of the rebels, one can hardly apply this term . . . to the behavior of the Tutsi towards the Hutu."[11] The implication is straightforward: the only genocide worth mentioning is the genocide committed by the Hutu rebels; in putting down the rebellion, however "severely," the state prevented the insurgents from taking an even bigger toll.

The inability or unwillingness of the international community to see through the humbug of official media is little short of astonishing. To take the full measure of Western myopia one can do no better than quote from the extraordinarily guarded tone, verging on a tacit approval of the killings, of the letter of the diplomatic corps delivered to President Micombero on May 30, at the request of the papal nuncio:

> As true friends of Burundi we have followed with anguish and concern the events of the last few weeks. We are thus comforted by your appointment of groups of wise men to pacify the country, and by the orders that you have given to repress the arbitrary actions of individuals and groups, of private vengeance and excesses of authority. With all our heart we hope that your laudable initiatives (sic!) will have the cooperation of all. We assure your Excellency that the governments and organizations that we have the honor to represent to you will do everything to assist those who have suffered and those who suffer still, at the same time support your efforts to promote the peace, unity and progress of Burundi and all its inhabitants.[12]

By then the "excesses of authority" of the Micombero government had sent well over 100,000 Hutu to their graves. At least as many would join them in the subsequent months.

Hardly more edifying was the response of UN Secretary General Kurt Waldheim to the carnage. Following the visit of UN Special Mission to Burundi from June 22–28, headed by Isoufou Djermakoye, Under Secretary General and Special Advisor on African Affairs, Waldheim expressed his "fervent hope that peace, harmony, and stability can be brought about successfully and speedily, and that Burundi will thereby achieve the goals of social progress, better standards of life and other ideals and principles set forth in the Charter of the UN."[13] The cynicism behind such pious hopes is a devastating commentary on the role of the UN during the genocide. In Burundi in 1972, as in Rwanda in 1994, the United Nations sat on its hands as hundreds of thousands of Africans were being slaughtered.

But perhaps the most surreal of all international responses came from the Organization of African Unity (OAU)—now African Union (AU)—on May 22, 1972, during the visit to Bujumbura of its Secretary General, Diallo Telli. "The OAU," said Telli, "being essentially an organization based on solidarity, my presence here in Bujumbura signifies the total solidarity of the Secretariat with the President of Burundi, and with the government and the fraternal people of Burundi."[14] It is an ironic commentary on Telli's expression of solidarity with the chief organizer of the butchery that he himself was later murdered by Guinean President Sékou Touré. Then, too, the OAU appeared in "total solidarity" with Telli's murderer.

Nixon's outburst over the State Department's "cynical and callous" reaction to the killings did little to bring about a change of course in U.S. policies. The previously cited report of the Carnegie Endowment for International Peace described the official stance of the United States on Burundi as a combination of "indifference, inertia, and irresponsibility." One official quoted in the same report aptly summed up the prevailing mood in the State Department: "If we'd involve ourselves in this we'd be creamed by every country in Africa for butting into an African state's internal affairs. We don't have an interest in Burundi that justified taking that kind of flak."[15] The remarkably detailed cables sent to Washington by the Deputy Chief of Mission in Bujumbura, Michael Hoyt, failed to elicit as much as a minimal expression of concern from the Secretary of State. In the words of Roger Morris, "on May 25, 1972, (U.S. Ambassador) Thomas Melady routinely left the country for a new assignment. He departed with a decoration from the Burundi government, he and his home office in Foggy Bottom maintaining total silence about the horror."[16] Perceptions of Burundi as an "autistic and suspicious society,"[17] to quote from a 1972 State Department policy paper, seemed entirely consistent with the kind of benign neglect displayed by U.S. policy makers in the face of irrefutable evidence of genocide.

Myth-Making and Revisionism

"Different interests tell untruths differently," writes Paul Richards[18]—a statement that succinctly captures the rival perceptions and mythologies spawned by perpetrators and victims. Seen against the obduracy of the Burundi authorities in assigning genocidal responsibility to the victims, the narratives told by Hutu survivors strike one as another example of how truth is denied, deformed, or manipulated. They come in different forms and apply to different phases of the drama, but one of the most widespread refers to the "Simbananiye plan," a plot aimed at achieving parity of numbers between Hutu and Tutsi. Out of the interviews conducted by Liisa Malki in the refugee camp of Mishamo in Tanzania the following scenario emerges:

> A major cause of the massacre was unanimously seen as an attempt by the Tutsi to "equalize the population" on a statistical scale. Every man in Mishamo can recite the statistical configuration of Burundi: The Tutsi are 14 percent, the Hutu 85 percent and the Twa 1 percent. The Tutsi, it was asserted, tried to change these numbers by killing as many Hutu as possible. This, it was said, had been "the Tutsi's secret goal for a long time." The goal was to "make Hutu 50 percent and Tutsi 50 percent also." . . . It was said that by equalizing the population, the Tutsi would be better able to say that Burundi was a democracy.[19]

To view the carnage as part of a master plan aimed at physically eliminating well over 3 million Hutu for the sake of parity does not withstand rational examination. Nonetheless, to expect a cool, dispassionate reasoning from a Hutu refugee community thoroughly traumatized by mass slaughter is itself somewhat irrational.

But if "mythico-histories," to use Liisa Malkki's phrase, are a recurrent feature of the refugee's narratives, many of whom barely survived the assaults on their lives, no such excuse can be invoked by those Western journalists whose reporting fully matches the fantasies of Malkki's interviewees, except that their aim is not to overdraw but to downplay the gravity of the killings. What is one to make, for example, of the extraordinary statement by Philippe Decraene, a seasoned journalist, in the highly respected *Le Monde Diplomatique* of July 1978, to the effect that what happened in 1972 was a far cry from the bloodbath reported in some of the media—it all amounted, he said, to "bloody scuffles between Hutu and Tutsi," resulting in "tens of victims." The mind boggles!

Revisionism belongs to an altogether different genre. The aim here is less to articulate "mythico-histories" in the sense in which Malkki uses the term as to sift out the data in order to impose a different analytic frame on the phenomena examined. Although the result may smack of myth-making, the revisionist discourse has the surface appearance of serious scholarship. One example of this is the thesis set forth by the Hutu historian Augustin Nsanze to the effect that the genocide was deliberately engineered by the Micombero government to create a pretext for the annihilation of the Hutu. To quote: "By refusing to deal with the rebellion long before it broke out, while the government had all the information about it. . . . President Micombero and his close aides intended to suppress all the opponents from all sides, real or potential, so as to ensure that the Hima of Bururi would reign forever on the (Hutu) people. . . . Thus instead of stopping the rebellion, he gave it purpose and direction."[20] Although the Nsanze thesis has struck a responsive chord among Hutu intellectuals, the supportive evidence is nowhere to be found.

Entirely different in the scope of its questioning is the brand of revisionism offered by Jean-Pierre Chrétien and Jean-François Dupaquier in their recently published book, *Burundi 1972: Au bord des génocides* (2007). The use of the plural suggests that we are dealing here with something approaching the "double genocide" thesis set forth by President François Mitterrand to describe the Rwanda holocaust; and yet on the strength of the title the unsuspecting reader is led to believe that neither genocide actually happened—Burundi found itself "on the cusp" or "at the edge" (*au bord*) of genocides without experiencing their full agony.

The authors' stance, in short, is one of normative equidistance between the two near-genocides.

Their book offers the richest source of documentation available anywhere, including countless interviews with scores of respondents, Hutu and Tutsi, including political actors, who, in one capacity or another, were witness to the killings. No one doing serious work on the 1972 crisis can afford to ignore the wealth of information presented between its covers. Unfortunately the richness of the data is inversely proportional to the care with which it is handled.

Thirty-two years after the fact one would have expected a minimum of circumspection concerning the reliability of the stories told by local informants, especially those coming from persons closely associated with the Micombero regime. Consider the case of Emile Mworoha, who served as General Secretary of the infamous Jeunesses Révolutionnaires Rwagasore (JRR) during the killings and is now a professor of history at the University of Burundi. Though frequently cited as an authoritative source to bolster the authors' argument (his name appears seventeen times in the index), nowhere is there as much as a hint that, as the top civil servant in charge of the JRR, Mworoha must have played a central role in orchestrating the killings of civilians. Nor is there any intimation that it might have been in Mworoha's interest to adjust his testimonies to the circumstances of the interview.

Just as questionable is the handling of the documentary evidence assembled by the authors. To treat as solid proof of genocidal intent the text of an anti-Tutsi tract cited in a government white paper notorious for its lies and countless inaccuracies is simply not acceptable.[21] This selective sifting of the evidence is fully consistent with the reputation of the senior author, whose pro-Tutsi biases are well known. In the absence of the most elementary critical scrutiny of the information cited in their book it is difficult to accept the authors' contention that the Hutu rebellion contained within itself the seeds of a genocide.

The tendentiousness of their argument is nowhere more evident than in the section of the book titled "Hypothesis of a global plan for the elimination of the Tutsi" (*Hypothèse d'un plan global d'élimination des Tutsi*), which, in addition to relying heavily on the thoroughly misleading government white paper, is almost entirely based on anecdotal evidence, much of it irrelevant to their intended demonstration. Of the many interviews cited in support of their thesis, the vast majority were conducted from 1999 to 2002 with Hutu respondents, at a time when lingering ethnic enmities dictated considerable prudence in stating one's opinions. Again, to see in the anti-Tutsi tracts attributed to Hutu insurgents irrefutable proof of genocidal intent raises more questions than the authors are willing to answer, including the reliability of the sources from which they are extracted.[22]

In making their case for "the peasant revolt as potential genocide" they draw heavily from Evariste Ngayimpenda's outrageously revisionist thesis, *Histoire du conflit politico-ethnique burundais* (2004), in which the killing of Tutsi by Hutu insurgents qualifies as genocide, and the subsequent genocide of Hutu as repression. In making his case the author projects back in time many of the characteristics of the 1994 Rwanda genocide, suggesting that in Burundi as in Rwanda the killings of Tutsi civilians were the work of Hutu génocidaires bent upon exterminating those they described as the "long-nosed Tutsi dogs."[23] From this massive tome (629 pages) emerges an image of the rebellion not as a "sudden outbreak out of the blue"—what the author calls "une bourrasque dans un ciel serein"—but as a long-planned annihilation of all Tutsi, propelled by a racist ideology, and involving a variety of internal and external accomplices, notably ex-king Ntare, seen as the instrument the rebels hoped to manipulate to advance their genocidal project.

Though resisting the temptation to follow Ngayimpenda's logical conclusion—the only genocide was the genocide of Tutsi—Chrétien and Dupaquier end up admitting, belatedly, what the title of their book denies, that is, that what others call a repression can best be described as a genocide. Yet the absence of any serious discussion of the concept of genocide—except to dismiss off-handedly Helen Fein's notion of "retributive genocide," despite its very obvious relevance to the case at hand—makes the authors' case for an "equidistance" of near-genocides all the more problematic. No less puzzling is why they should have waited until the concluding chapter to alert the reader to their self-correcting after-thought: the "bureaucratic aspect (sic!) of the organization of (the repression)," we are told, is what prompted us "to qualify as genocide what we were observing in 1972 from near and far."[24]

The controversies surrounding the events of 1972 are not simply of academic interest: how they are perceived, obfuscated, or manipulated are central issues in any attempt to understand how contemporary actors confront their past.

Remembering 1972: The Persistence of Hutu Radicalism

Narratives of loss and suffering among Hutu survivors are deeply rooted in their collective memory. Unlike historical memory, as Maurice Halbwachs reminds us, collective memory is in essence group memory; it projects an image of the group "seen from within," defined by shared

experiences connected in time through changes in intergroup relations.[25] The phenomenon, though distinct, has a lot in common with
what Liisa Malkki calls "mythico-history." What is involved here, specifically, is "not only a description of the past, nor even merely an evalu-
ation of the past, but a subversive recasting and reinterpretation of it in
fundamentally moral terms."[26]

No other party has come closer to institutionalizing this propensity to
subvert and mythologize the past than the Parti pour la Libération du
Peuple Hutu (Palipehutu), later to be identified with Agathon Rwasa's
Parti pour la Libération du Peuple Hutu-Forces Nationales de Libération (Palipehutu-FNL), better known today as FNL.[27] Launched in 1980
in a refugee camp in Mishamo (Tanzania), the Palipehutu was the brain-
child of the late Rémy Gahutu. Until his death in Dar es Salaam in 1996,
Gahutu stood as the most articulate proponent of Hutu radicalism. His
views are enshrined in what later became the party's manifesto, aptly
titled *Persecution of the Hutu of Burundi* (1979?). In it Gahutu presents a
view of history in which the Hutu, described as a Bantu people, are said
to have been dominated and enslaved by the Tutsi—a group "of Nilotic
stock, originally one of the Hamitic peoples of North Africa and Soma-
lia" whose "warlike spirit impelled them to subjugate and enslave the
ethnic Bantu majority that had been living in the region for centuries."[28]
This alleged ancestral enmity between Hutu and Tutsi, rooted in the
warlike dispositions of the invading Tutsi, runs like a red skein through
Gahutu's narrative. Under such circumstances the Hutu have no other
choice than to "reinforce their unity—a Kirundi proverb puts the message succinctly, *imitsi ikora ikoranye*, which means 'muscles are strong
only when they work together,'" and for this to happen "the Hutu are
invited to join together in a single political organization to strengthen
their unity and consolidate their force."[29]

A year later the Palipehutu came into being, only to be faced with a
host of problems, some arising from bitter internecine feuds, others
from the competition it faced from more moderate Hutu parties, that
is, the Front Démocratique du Burundi (Frodebu) at the time of the
fateful 1993 elections, and more recently the ruling Conseil National
pour la Défense de la Démocratie-Forces pour la Defense de la Démocratie (CNDD-FDD). While the party leadership went through major
convulsions, its anti-Tutsi fanaticism remained a constant. It is significant that its most ardent supporters are survivors of the 1972 bloodbath.
Illustrative of their uncompromising anti-Tutsi stance are the comments
of the party's spokesman, Pasteur Habimana, in an interview with this
writer in 2003: "I've been holed up in the forest since 1973; I am fifty
years old. The truth must be told about the many Hutu killed by the
Tutsi. Burundi's problem is that we are told lies! (*Le problème du Burundi*

c'est le mensonge!) The members of parliament represent no one. . . . How can we agree on a fifty-fifty sharing of power with the Tutai when they represent 15 percent of the population? . . . In 1972 I saw my brothers being killed. I was twenty years old. *I remember everything.*"

Rooted in the legacy of 1972, this irreducible core of ethnic hatred comes out with striking clarity in the statement issued by the party's chairman, Agathon Rwasa, thirty years after the event: "A major stake in the Great Lakes conflicts is traceable to the presence in this region of a group of people who feel that they are superior to others, they think they are super-men, determined to impose forever their hegemony on others by the sword and the machete if necessary." Behind this urge to dominate, we are told, lies "the dream of a Hima/Nilotic empire in Central and Eastern Africa which they intend to bring about through a variety of projects, the most deadly of all being the Simbananiye plan and the Hima-inspired Kivu colonization plan."[30] While reiterating many of the themes set forth by Gahutu, Rwasa gave a new twist to his diatribe by drawing heavily from biblical references: his text is indeed studded with citations from the Book of Jeremiah, along with Genesis, the Gospel according to St. John, and St. Paul's Epistle to the Romans, as if to underscore its divine inspiration. This transference of the sacred into the profane helps explain the fanaticism of Rwasa as a true believer, including his determination to use violence in the name of a saintly crusade.

By then the FNL had emerged as a well-entrenched armed militia bent upon wresting power from the Tutsi minority; its principal basis of support was in the vicinity of Bujumbura, among the poor and the unemployed, as well as among children. Through much of 2002 and 2003 the FNL launched multiple assaults on the capital city, most of the time carried out by teenage boys going into battle chanting religious hymns. Over the years thousands of innocent civilians perished under its blows. Its most hideous crime occurred in August 2004 when hundreds of ethnic Tutsi refugees, fleeing the revenge killings of "native" Congolese in North and South Kivu, were massacred in Gatumba, a few miles from the capital. Nor were Hutu dissenters spared the wrath of their leader. Among the members of his entourage seen as potential rivals and reported to have been killed by Rwasa in 2002, were the following: Antoine Ntirabampa, at one time vice president of the Palipehutu; Gervais Ntagisigaye, deputy secretary general; André Bigirimana, member of the party's Political Bureau; Alexandre Niyonzima, a close friend of this writer and one of the twenty-one signatories of the letter of protest sent to President Pierre Buyoya in 1988, following the army's brutal repression in the wake of rioting in the communes of Ntega and Marangara,[31] to which must be added the names of Niyonzima's brother,

Hyacinthe Nibigira, and Rémy Gahutu's wife, Immaculée. In a country whose history is soaked in blood it is hard to think of more brutal defenders of the Hutu cause.

Rwasa's blood-stained itinerary is a stark reminder of the psychic toll exacted by mass murder on both murderers and survivors. Decades after the act the monstrous wounds fester. If Burundi's history is any guide, one can hardly underestimate the continuing potential for violence inscribed in a group memory that has been alternatively thwarted and manipulated, impeded by the state and mythologized by its enemies.

To the extent that it remains a force to be reckoned with, the FNL, though badly splintered, is still captive of its past, or, better still, of its own distorted representations of the past. Its unswerving dedication to violence as the only way to come to terms with the problem of Tutsi dominance ruled out its participation in the 2005 multiparty elections. Nor did the coming to power of a Hutu president, Pierre Nkurunziza, and a solid Hutu majority in the CNDD-FDD–dominated government prove much of an inducement for the party to accommodate its demands to the new distribution of power. This said, its decision to participate in the 2010 communal elections marked a turning point in the party's history: contrary to the expectations of most observers, the FNL emerged from the contest as the biggest winner next to the ruling CNDD-FDD, with 14.15 percent of the vote; even more surprising, in the Bujumbura communes it won more than half the popular vote. What happened next is illustrative of just how inept an opposition movement can be in calculating its chances of making a difference in a context of democratic competition. Wrongly accusing the government of "massive fraud," the FNL, along with eleven other opposition parties—now forming the Alliance Démocratique Pour le Changement, better known as ADC-*Ikibiri*—declared its intention to withdraw from other races, thus leaving the ruling CNDD-FDD in virtual control of the government and parliament. Whether—and in what form—the FNL may at some future date reenter the political arena is anybody's guess. At the time of this writing Rwasa's whereabouts are a mystery; all we know is that he has left the country, Bible in hand, to seek solace and inspiration across the border.

Like all other human tragedies reviewed in this book the case of Burundi is unique. Yet it also shares with them a tangled legacy of oblivion and mystification. How to cut through this obfuscation and restore to the events of 1972 their true dimensions is one of the many challenges facing the country as it tries to come to terms with its past. For all the efforts made to silence their voices the ghosts of 1972 will continue to haunt the living for as long as impunity remains the rule.

Chapter 3

"Every Herero Will Be Shot"
Genocide, Concentration Camps, and Slave Labor in German South-West Africa

Dominik J. Schaller

As a point of entry into the first genocide of the twentieth century, it is appropriate to evoke Raphael Lemkin's memory, if only to remind ourselves that his reputation goes well beyond his ceaseless efforts to outlaw genocide. He is also remembered as an ambitious historian of mass violence and a pioneer of genocide studies.[1] The extermination of the Herero figured prominently in his projected global history of genocide, along with other cases of colonial mass murder.[2] It is worth noting that among his unpublished papers are two manuscripts on German rule in Africa, dealing primarily with the colonial war in South-West Africa (present-day Namibia) from 1904 to 1908.

Genocide Denounced, Forgotten, and Remembered

Lemkin had no doubt that the German warfare against the Herero and Nama in Namibia met his definition of genocide. There was little question in his mind that German aims and policies in Southern Africa were unambiguously genocidal: "The Germans did not colonize Africa with the intention of ruling the country justly, living in peace with the true owners of the land and developing its resources for the mutual advantage of both races. Their idea was to settle some of the surplus German population in Africa and to turn it into a German white empire. Bismarck said, 'A German who can put off his Fatherland like an old coat is no longer a German for me,' and it was undoubtedly this idea which encouraged the policy of deliberate extermination."[3]

Lemkin's view was quite common mid-century at the time he was writing his history of genocide, which unfortunately he never completed. Since the end of World War I, Germany's unprecedented brutality and unscrupulousness in its African colonies had been the object of strident criticisms, primarily in British reports. The bloody suppression of indigenous resistance in South-West Africa, resulting in the deaths of about 60,000 Herero and 10,000 Nama, was seen as a prime example of the Germans' inability to rule and develop overseas territories for the benefit of indigenous societies.

The best known and most influential of all these British pamphlets was the "Report on the Natives of South-West Africa and Their Treatment by Germany," by Major Thomas Leslie O'Reilly, published in 1918, which Lemkin used as a major source. After the conquest of Namibia by South African troops under British command in World War I, O'Reilly was given a free hand to collect all relevant information about German atrocities against the natives. O'Reilly's report focused chiefly on the German's 1904–8 colonial war against the Herero and Nama and was based on statements by fifty African witnesses. Of course British efforts to shed light on massacres committed a decade earlier was not entirely motivated by selfless humanitarian reasons; what the British wanted above all else was to come up with a credible case for adding Namibia to their colonial holdings. At any rate, irrespective of British motives, the O'Reilly report remains a most valuable source for the study of the tragic events of 1904–8, not least because of the first-hand accounts by surviving Herero and Nama.[4]

Unsurprisingly, in the days of the Weimar Republic, when colonial revisionism emerged as a major theme among German historians, many dismissed British criticisms of Germany's war as *Kolonialschuldlüge* (colonial guilt lie), itself part of the so-called *Kriegsschuldlüge* (war guilt lie). The accusation was not completely baseless. Although some British newspapers had condemned Germany's method of warfare in South-West Africa at the time, there was no official protest from the British government. British colonial authorities were hoping that the Germans would suppress the Africans' resistance as soon as possible, lest a prolonged war in Namibia destabilize the neighboring Cape Colony and British Bechuanaland. That the British exploited the fate of the Herero and Nama in order to discredit Germany's claims to retain its colonies is reasonably clear. This conclusion is further supported by the fact that South African and British authorities in Namibia ordered the destruction of O'Reilly's "Report on the Natives of South-West Africa" in 1926, when they realized that the existence of this publication might seriously compromise the prospects for cooperation with local German settlers. Copies of the report were systematically removed from public libraries in Namibia and South Africa and destroyed. What is more, existing copies in other parts of the British Empire were transferred to the Foreign Office in London and were not allowed to be issued without special permission.[5] Once British control over Namibia was secured, the story of how tens of thousands of Africans died under German rule was officially consigned to oblivion.

This episode is characteristic of the contrasting ways in which German colonial rule is remembered. After 1945, the fate of the Herero was eclipsed by the horrors of World War II. As recently as the 1960s many Germans did not even realize that their country had once conquered considerable parts of Africa. Only a handful of experts and historians were interested in the subject. Not untypically, some historians from the German Democratic Republic (GDR) saw in the horrors of German imperialism tangible proof of the imperial-fascist foundation of the capitalist German Federal Republic (GFR); predictably, most of the blame for the genocide in South-West Africa was laid upon German commercial enterprises. Ideological biases notwithstanding, these studies were by no means bereft of all empirical validity and as such contributed to a better understanding of the roots of mass murder.[6]

At the end of the Cold War and Namibia's independence from South Africa in 1990, the colonial experiment in South-West Africa and its genocidal outcome attracted increased awareness in large part because of what historian Elazar Barkan has termed "a new international morality." Barkan has observed that victims of historical injustices turn more and more to restitution in order to compensate for past sufferings.[7] Inspired by the success of the Holocaust restitution movement in the late 1990s, representatives of the Herero filed a lawsuit against the government of the GFR and three German corporations (among them Deutsche Bank) with the U.S. Federal Court in September 2001. It was the first time an ethnic group demanded reparation for colonial policies that fit the legal definition of genocide.[8] In an effort to overcome legal and political obstacles, the plaintiffs tried to attract public sympathy by showing the parallel between the genocide against their forefathers and the Nazi genocide against the Jews: "Foreshadowing with chilling precision the irredeemable horror of the European Holocaust only decades later, the defendants [the three German companies] and Imperial Germany formed a German commercial enterprise which cold-bloodedly employed explicitly-sanctioned extermination, the destruction of tribal culture and social organization, concentration camps, forced labor, medical experimentation and the exploitation of women and children in order to advance their common financial interests."[9]

The name of Eugen Fischer, the notorious German anthropologist and eugenicist who paved the way for the Nazi racial experiments, was invoked in support of their case: "German geneticist Eugene [*sic*] Fischer commenced his racial medical experiments in the concentration camps in South West Africa. He used the Herero and mulattos—the offspring of the German settlers and Herero women—as guinea pigs. Fischer tortured Herero men and women to explore his horrific theories about race. A book he wrote about his findings, *The Principle of Human Heredity and Race Hygiene*, was a favorite of Adolf Hitler. Fischer later became chancellor of the University of Berlin, where he taught medicine to Nazi physicians, including Josef Mengele."[10]

Although the connecting links between the two genocides are somewhat overdrawn, there can be little doubt about the historical continuities from colonial mass violence to the Nazis' struggle for *Lebensraum* (living space).[11] This issue is at the heart of the debate about the Holocaust's possible colonial origins and thus helps explain the growing scholarly interest in the German colonial war in Namibia. Meanwhile, many genocide scholars would not hesitate to describe the mass killing of the Herero and Nama as the first genocide of the twentieth century or as the "first German genocide."[12]

The Hereros' demand for historical justice and financial restitution, along with the growing public awareness of the dismal record of colonial rule in Namibia, has brought considerable pressure upon German authorities to come to terms with Germany's imperial past. In August 2004 the German minister of economic cooperation and development, Heidemarie Wieczorek-Zeul, visited Namibia and attended a commemoration ceremony on the occasion of the centenary of the battle at Waterberg, where the Herero suffered a decisive defeat. Wieczorek-Zeul used the opportunity to apologize officially for the German atrocities in Namibia: "A century ago, the oppressors—blinded by colonialist fervor—became agents of violence, discrimination, racism and annihilation in Germany's name. The atrocities committed at that time would today be termed genocide—and nowadays a General von Trotha would be prosecuted and convicted. We Germans accept our historical and moral responsibility and the guilt incurred by Germans at that time. And so, in the words of the Lord's Prayer that we share, I ask you to forgive us our trespasses."[13]

Guilt may have been acknowledged, but Wieczorek-Zeul's speech did not offer as much as a hint of an eventual financial restitution. Kuaima Riruako, paramount chief of the Herero, saw in this "oversight" a disturbing carryover of racist attitudes among German politicians. While

Germany was ready to compensate the Jews for the Holocaust, the Herero were left out because of their skin color, Riruako argued bitterly.[14] German politicians are of course prompt to dismiss this accusation, pointing to the fact that Namibia is one of the major recipients of German development funds. According to their view, separate payments to the Herero would promote "tribalism" and thus damage political stability in Namibia. The Namibian government, dominated by representatives of the Ovambo—Namibia's largest ethnic group and one that was largely spared the atrocities visited on the Herero—shares this view and refuses to support the Hereros' claim.[15] In Namibia, opposing views of the past thus hold profoundly divisive implications. While Herero and Nama insist that they were the main victims of German imperialists, the government rejects their exclusive claim to victimhood and portrays the Ovambo-led fight against South African apartheid as the symbol of the ultimate anticolonial resistance.

The Herero tragedy dates back more than one hundred years, but it still casts a cloud over the present and helps shape both German and Namibian identities, which is reason enough to explore these historical events in some detail. This chapter tries to shed light on the German conquest of South-West Africa and the socioeconomic and political circumstances leading to the outbreak of war. Special attention will be paid here to the radicalization of German warfare, as well as the attitudes and motivations of perpetrators. Finally, an attempt is made to describe how Africans tried to cope with the genocidal fallout.

German Imperialism and the Conquest of South-West Africa

On April 24. 1884, Bismarck declared that the South-West African estates of Adolf Lüderitz—a tobacconist from Bremen—would be placed under the protection of the German Empire. The chancellor's announcement of a "protectorate" over a territory of 580,000 square kilometers marked the birth of German colonial expansion. In July 1884 Togo and Cameroon and in February 1885 Carl Peters's possessions in East Africa became German protectorates as well. At the 1884–85 Berlin Conference, the German acquisition of colonies was internationally confirmed.

Although Germany entered the imperial scramble for colonies relatively late in the game, as an ingredient of a Pan-German identity the colonial idea had been aired for some time among the German public. For many supporters of the national and liberal movements only a unified nation-state could muster the resources needed to conquer overseas markets and secure strategically important spheres of interest.

Influential representatives of the German colonial movement were heavily influenced by Social Darwinism and viewed the possession of colonies as a necessary condition for successfully competing with the leading imperialist powers. In the 1880s, Germans in general saw in the acquisition of colonies a logical continuation of the empire's establishment. Thus they welcomed the emergence of Wilhelm II's imperialist approach. It has recently been argued that this specific self-image has to be understood as one of the reasons for the eruption of excessive violence in Germany's African colonies. Colonial officials, settlers, and indeed the majority of the population viewed indigenous unrest or opposition as a danger not only to the colonial order, but to national German identity.[16]

German rule in Namibia began under rather modest auspices. In May 1885, three government officials arrived in the region. Their aim was to sign "protection treaties" with the chiefs of the indigenous peoples. Representatives of the German Rhenish Mission (Rheinische Missionsgesellschaft) who had been in the region for decades acted as mediators. Thus, the start of Namibia's conquest by Germany followed the pattern set elsewhere by colonial entrepreneurs. Already before the advent of the German colonizers Namibia's indigenous societies had long been connected economically and culturally to the frontier society of the Cape Colony. European ideas, values, and technologies (like the rifle) were well known to them.

The political situation in precolonial Namibia can best be described as a "raid and tribute economy." It was not inevitably organized along ethnic lines; changing trans-ethnic alliances were not uncommon: Nama and Herero "commandos" often went together on cattle raids. In the second half of the nineteenth century, however, the Herero successfully overcame the military and political hegemony of Orlam-Nama groups and became themselves the major power in Central Namibia. This occurrence caused a remarkable social and economic transformation among the Herero. Like many African pastoralist peoples, Herero society was originally characterized by a fair degree of social and political decentralization, but as they began to consolidate their position in Central Namibia a slow but persistent process of centralization set in. In time they managed to build up huge cattle herds and soon became to be known as *the* outstanding cattle-breeders in South-West Africa.[17] Nama groups in southern Namibia relied likewise on cattle and enjoyed strong economic ties with farmers in the Cape Colony. Northern Namibia was inhabited by the Ovambo, who lived in different centralized and highly stratified kingdoms. It is estimated that the territory the Germans eventually claimed as their colony was inhabited by 80,000 Herero, 20,000 Nama, and up to 450,000 Ovambo.

Namibia's social complexity posed a major challenge to the first German colonial officials. In North America and Australia, European settlers seized native lands by claiming that indigenous hunter-gatherer societies could not make reasonable economic use of it. Much of the land, it was said, was unoccupied and thus belonged to no one. In South-West Africa, however, the argument of *res nullius* failed completely: the Africans were practicing intensive animal husbandry that depended on grasslands. Another major obstacle was the German government's reluctance to provide the colonial administration on the ground with necessary financial and personnel resources. For all the public enthusiasm for colonial expansion, Bismarck strenuously resisted pressure to spend huge sums for the colonial project, preferring to rely on concession companies to promote economic development. These hopes turned out to be unrealistic. Of all the factors that rendered the German conquest of South-West Africa so tenuous and violent not the least were the acute shortages of administrative and infrastructural resources.

German colonial occupation of Namibia did not unfold according to a structured, elaborate plan. Rather, much of it evolved by improvisation: In order to save expenses, only a small handful of civil servants were entrusted with administrative responsibilities. Though instructed to use peaceful means to achieve colonial control, they enjoyed considerable administrative latitude. Most of these early administrators, however, were ruthless adventurers, ready to trade the monotonous routine of an army posting at home for the promise of an exciting life in an unexplored exotic land. They looked to military prowess as a path to national glory. Many had previously served in Leopold II's "Congo Free State," where they took part in the countless atrocities committed against the indigenous population. It is thus no surprise that this first batch of colonial officials often acted irresponsibly and ran into violent conflicts with the Africans. Since they were no match for the well-armed and more numerous Herero and Nama, they were soon in danger of losing their jobs. The government in Berlin knew a defeat of European troops at the hands of Africans would attract attention worldwide and expose Germany's weakness as a colonial power. In order to avoid such a disgrace, the government felt it had no choice but to send in reinforcements.

Curt von François's career was not atypical. He was sent to South-West Africa in 1889 after the first official German administration under Reichskommissar Heinrich Göring (Hermann Göring's father) had been expelled by the Herero. Von François unleashed war against both the Herero and the Nama and tried to compensate for his lack of sufficient military capability by resorting to the cruelest method of warfare. His soldiers committed several massacres against noncombatants. Nama

Chief Hendrik Witbooi denounced von François's deliberate strategy of violence against civilians in a letter to the Rehobother chief, Hermanus van Wyk:

> Captain [von François] attacked us early in the morning while we were unsuspectingly asleep, and although I took my men out, we were unable to beat them back; and the Captain entered the camp and sacked it in so brutal a manner as I would never have thought a member of a White civilized nation capable of—a nation which knows the rules and ways of war. But this man robbed me, and killed little children at their mother's breast, and older children, and women, and men. Corpses of people who had been shot he burned inside our grass huts, burning their bodies to ash. Sadly and terrifyingly Captain [von François] went to work, in a shameful operation.[18]

This is a rare testimony. Written documents by indigenous chiefs about the colonial encounter are not easy to come by. Moreover, this letter is most significant in that it reveals how deeply the indigenous societies in South-West Africa had already been influenced by Western thinking. By stating that von François broke the rules of civilized nations, Witbooi portrayed himself as a member of a "civilized people" and thus gave the lie to the Germans' assertion that their colony was inhabited by "savages."

Whereas von François was the epitome of genocidal tendencies, his successor, Theodor Leutwein, who remained in office until 1904, was less so. During this time as governor and commander, Leutwein managed to strengthen and extend German power in South-West Africa by less violent means. Nevertheless, there can be no doubt that the new governor's overall intentions carried genocidal implications. In his memoirs, Leutwein admitted that his policy had aimed at the dissolution of the Africans' societies, the abolition of the political institutions of chiefdoms in particular, in order to establish a white settler colony in Namibia.[19] Leutwein agreed with prominent colonial politicians and propagandists that the Africans' lands ought to be seized and their societies shattered and transformed into a proletarian or helot class. Paul Rohrbach, an influential public intellectual in the time of the Empire and the Weimar Republic, made quite clear what position in colonial society the Africans ought to hold:

> Only by forcing them to let go of their barbarous dispositions by becoming a class of servants for the whites can the natives claim the right to exist. . . . The idea that the Bantus would have the right to live and die according to their own fashion is absurd. It is true for peoples as well as for individuals that their existence is only justified if they contribute to the general development towards progress. There is no proof that national independence,

national property and political organization among the tribes of South-West Africa would be an advantage for the evolution of humankind in general or the German people in particular.[20]

It is obvious that German colonial officials and politicians like Leutwein and Rohrbach favored a policy of cultural genocide or ethnocide. Only recently have historians acknowledged the genocidal continuities from Leutwein's rule in Namibia to Lothar von Trotha's war of extermination and the subsequent incarceration of the remaining Herero and Nama in concentration camps.[21]

This gruesome outcome had yet to come into view in the 1880s and the early 1890s. The Herero and Nama were militarily and economically still stronger than the small German settler community, which in 1896 consisted of only about 2,000 people. Leutwein was well aware that he depended on alliances with indigenous chiefs and that German power could only be secured through a system of indirect rule. Samuel Maharero, whose claim to the position of Herero paramount chief was disputed, seemed to be the ideal collaborator.[22] Due to Maharero's help and Leutwein's policy of divide and rule, the Germans managed to gain more and more power in the late 1890s. Although the German governor avoided costly military encounters with strong and influential chiefs, in the end he had no other option than to intervene in the Africans' political and economic affairs. The first victim of Leutwein's increased power was a Nama group. The Khauas Nama, whose economy depended on cattle raids, were an obstacle to the Germans' intention of establishing *Landfriede* (public peace) and securing a monopoly on coercion. After Leutwein's troops defeated them in 1895, the Khauas ceased to exist as a political and cultural group. The surviving Khauas were deported to Windhoek, where they were used as forced laborers by German authorities, the first example of German colonizers resorting to an effective policy of genocide.[23]

In the end it was a natural disaster that shifted the balance of power to the colonizer's advantage. The rinderpest, a virulent cattle disease, reached South-West Africa in 1897. The Herero lost almost 90 percent of their cattle, whereas European settlers managed to have their animals vaccinated. This far-reaching catastrophe was followed by a severe malaria epidemic. It hit the Herero particularly hard because they now suffered from a lack of milk, which had been their staple food. According to the German missionary Jakob Irle, 10,000 Herero died in 1898 from malaria.[24] Herero society faced a deep economic and cultural crisis. Until then the Herero had refused to sell land to Europeans, but now their only hope of survival was through the sale of their ancestral lands to settlers and land companies. Some Herero chiefs did not hesitate to sell their peoples' land at very low prices, which in turn generated serious internal tension and contributed to a sharp decline in their legitimacy. Many Herero were forced into European wage labor, a development that led to a new hierarchy of power between Africans and Europeans and resulted in increasingly brutal behavior of the latter toward the former. German farmers displayed racist arrogance and mistreated their new African workers on a regular basis.

Meanwhile, a dynamic European frontier society was emerging. Whereas the Africans were more and more marginalized and suffered from a crisis of collective self-esteem, the German community prospered. In 1904, Namibia's European population was estimated at 5,000. Moreover, the construction of a railway from coastal Swakopmund to Windhoek promised further economic growth and gave reason to anticipate in the foreseeable future the complete conquest of Namibia's land along with the final subjugation of the Africans. Although the outbreak of the war against the Herero in January 1904 seemed to seriously threaten the German colonial project, the conflict turned out to be the decisive event that provided the colonizers with the necessary means to establish almost totalitarian rule over the Africans.

Genocidal Warfare

On October 2, 1904, after the Herero had suffered a crushing defeat, von Trotha, the military commander of German South-West Africa, issued a proclamation to the Africans that came to be known as the infamous genocide order (or *Schiessbefehl* in German): "I, the great General of the German troops, send this letter to the Herero people. The Herero are no longer German subjects. . . . The Herero people must leave the country. If the nation doesn't do this I will force them with the *Groot Rohr* [cannon]. Within the German borders, every Herero, with or without gun, with or without cattle, will be shot. I will no longer except women and children, I will drive them back to their people or I will let them be shot at."[25]

In an addendum meant only for members of his *Schutztruppe*, the German commander gave the following instructions: "Shooting at women and children has to be understood as shooting above their heads, which will make them run away. I assume categorically that this order will result in taking no more male prisoners, but will not degenerate into atrocities against women and children. The latter will run away if one shoots at them a couple of times. The troops will remain conscious of the good reputation of the German soldier."[26]

Von Trotha's words were nothing if not deceitful. His addition to the *Schiessbefehl* did not mean he wanted to spare Herero women and children. Rather, he planned to drive them back into the waterless Omaheke Desert where they faced death from starvation and exhaustion. In a letter to the chief of the German general staff, von Trotha explained this measure and left no doubt about its genocidal intention: "To accept women and children who are for the most part sick poses a great risk to the force, and to feed them is out of the question. For this reason, I deem it wiser for the entire nation to perish than to infect our soldiers into the bargain and to make inroads into our water and food supplies."[27]

The 1904 campaign against the Herero was not the first colonial war resulting in the massacres of women and children. The Spanish-American War in Cuba (1895–98), the United States–Spanish conflict in the Philippines that started in 1899, and the international suppression of the so-called Boxer movement in China (1900–1901) are but a few examples. Excessive violence against civilians was thus a characteristic of colonial wars. Nonetheless, never before had the commander of a European colonial army displayed such a degree of extremism and declared the complete extermination of a people as the final aim of war. But why did the war in South-West Africa degenerate into wholesale genocide? And what were the reasons for the outbreak of hostilities in January 1904?

For a long time German settlers had been waiting for the elimination of the Africans as autonomous actors and their complete subjugation. But they also realized that the colony's military infrastructure was still inadequate for a decisive fight with the Herero or Nama. In such circumstances a major African uprising could bring the economic and political development in the colony to a standstill and at the same time pose a major threat to their lives. The likelihood of a Herero rebellion became an obsession among European settlers. It was exactly this paranoid fear in combination with an accumulation of misunderstandings that triggered the war on January 12 in the Central Namibian town of Okahandja. A gathering of important Herero chiefs in this town made the German officer Zürn believe the Herero were planning a war against the colonizers. Zürn's fears were fed by the fact that Governor Leutwein and the majority of the colonial troops were in the south of the colony to wage war against the Bondelswarts, a small Nama group that had not been ready to accept German claims of power. Zürn's panicked reactions, in turn, caused the Herero to believe the Germans wanted to kill Samuel Maharero. This was enough for them to take up their arms. Although the Herero were deeply concerned about the German increase of power and afraid of losing their lands, there is no evidence that Samuel Maharero or other chiefs had planned a war against the colonizers. The hostilities broke out more or less spontaneously and took both Herero and Germans by surprise.

In the first months of the war, about 8,000 Herero warriors (of whom 4,000 were armed with rifles) were facing 2,000 German soldiers and reservists. The Africans took the initiative; they plundered farms, killed more than 100 settlers, felled telegraph poles, and besieged small towns. German reactions were rather helpless at the beginning, but reinforcements from the metropole and the reorganization of the colonial troops, now equipped with new weapons like machine guns and modern cannons, would soon turn the tide. Meanwhile, the Herero gathered with their families and herds in the Waterberg region. Their motives are still not clear, but it is probable that they were hoping to negotiate peace with Governor Leutwein. By now, however, a negotiated solution was no longer an option. German politicians and the settlers' influential lobby in Berlin made Leutwein responsible for both the human and material losses and the humiliating military setbacks the Germans had suffered in the first period of the war. Although Leutwein remained in office as governor, real power was now in the hands of von Trotha, the new supreme commander.

Von Trotha had clear ideas about how to end the war. To quote from his diary, "My initial plan for the operation, which I always adhered to, was to encircle the masses of Hereros at Waterberg and annihilate these masses in one fell swoop."[28] After the arrival of reinforcements, von Trotha attacked the Herero at Hamakari (Waterberg) on August 11, 1904. The Germans' obvious military superiority and von Trotha's determination to annihilate the enemy led to total slaughter. Captain Victor Franke described the execution of civilians laconically in his diary: "In the camp, a Herero woman and her child are shot. The first needed two shots, the latter one."[29] Although the Herero were militarily defeated and von Trotha informed Wilhelm II about his "glorious" victory, the battle at Hamakari was a failure. The great majority of the Herero managed to escape from the battle of encirclement and annihilation and fled to the neighboring Omaheke Desert. The paths to British Bechuanaland followed traditional trade roads. However, even though the Herero knew these routes and the most important watering places, the amount of water available was hardly enough to ensure the survival of the many refugees. In order to finish off the Herero, von Trotha ordered his men to cordon off the Omaheke and to kill the refugees. Major Ludwig von Estorff, the officer in charge of the chase, described what he saw:

I followed their spoor and found numerous wells which presented a terrifying sight. Cattle which had died of thirst lay scattered around wells. These cattle had reached the wells but there had not been enough time to water them. The Herero fled ahead of us into the Sandveld. Again and again this terrible scene kept repeating itself. With feverish energy the men had worked at opening the wells, but the water became ever sparser, and wells ever more rare. They fled from one well to the next and lost virtually all their cattle and a large number of their people. The people shrank into small remnants that continually fell into our hands. . . . It was a policy that was equally gruesome as senseless, to hammer the people so much, we could have still saved many of them and their rich herds, if we had pardoned and taken them up again, they had been punished enough. I suggested this to von Trotha but he wanted their total extermination.[30]

Historians generally argue that driving the Herero into the desert and letting them die of thirst had been planned well in advance by von Trotha.[31] However, it was the failure of his original plan to exterminate the Herero at Hamakari that made him resort to the systematic persecution of the Herero in the Omaheke and the proclamation of the genocide order.

The war in South-West Africa did not end with the defeat of the Herero. Since the Nama chief, Hendrik Witbooi, had actively supported the military campaign against the Herero, the Germans were completely surprised when he initiated hostilities against them in October 1904. What exactly motivated the Nama remains unclear. Colonial officials suspected that a preacher of the so-called Ethiopian movement must have inspired the Witbooi to rise against German rule. It is more probable that the Namas' aggressive behavior stemmed from their fear of being next in line after the extermination of the Herero. The German war against the Nama lasted three years and differed significantly from their fight against the Herero. Witbooi and his men avoided open battles and launched systematic attacks against German patrols and military posts. This kind of guerilla warfare and the harsh climate and the inaccessible terrain in southern Namibia posed considerable problems for the colonialists. Furthermore, von Trotha was under immense political pressure to pacify the colony as soon as possible. All these factors persuaded the Germans to engage in scorched-earth tactics: Villages, fields, and granaries were burned and the civilian population was deported to several concentration camps set up along the Atlantic coast.

For a sense of the disastrous consequences of Germany's colonial war in Namibia, one only needs to look at the human and financial costs: About 60,000 Herero and 10,000 Nama were killed or starved to death in concentration camps. Moreover, an estimated 2,000 German soldiers were killed in action or fell victim to disease. More than 14,000 troops were necessary to suppress the Africans' resistance. The total cost of the campaign reached the astronomical figure of 585 million Reichsmark. While opposition politicians in Germany tried to make political capital out of the crisis by denouncing the mismanagement of the war, others made no secret of their concern that Germany's international image as a respected *Kulturnation* might not survive reports of von Trotha's brutality. Critical voices wondered why South-West Africa could not have been conquered and ruled at lesser cost.

Could Genocide Have Been Avoided?

In a retrospective assessment of the war, Paul Rohrbach, an ardent critic of von Trotha, saw as a fatal mistake the decision to entrust him with military responsibilities. "It was a mistake to deprive [Governor] Leutwein of the command and to send a general to Southwest [Africa] who had gained experience in China but did not understand that it would not be the important thing to 'destroy' the natives as enemies. It would have been enough to teach them a severe lesson as punishment for the uprising. And it would have been important to preserve as many of the natives and their cattle as possible. South-West Africa with natives was of much more value for us than without."[32]

Although South-West Africa was a settler colony, nothing could be further from the colonizers' agenda than the annihilation of the indigenes. Next to arable land, African manpower was the most critical resource to promote the economic development of the colony. Clearly, the extermination of the Herero and Nama in Namibia made no economic or political sense. So why then did genocide occur?

Genocidal warfare was not inevitable. As has been empirically demonstrated, genocides are complex processes that undergo various phases of cumulative radicalization and depend on a range of situational factors. Undoubtedly, the arrival of von Trotha in South-West Africa was a decisive factor contributing to the genocidal radicalization of warfare. Governor Leutwein, his predecessor as commander of the colonial troops, wanted to persuade the Herero to surrender and with that objective in mind tried to negotiate with their chiefs. Since he still enjoyed the esteem and confidence of the Herero, he stood a fair chance to bring an end to the war. His policy, however, was swiftly rebuked by his superiors in Berlin. He was ordered to stop all negotiations until the arrival of the newly appointed supreme commander.[33]

Von Trotha was an experienced colonial soldier. He had fought against the Wahehe in Tanzania in the 1890s and took part in the suppression of the Boxer Uprising in China. His worldview can only be described as racist and Social-Darwinist. Soon after his arrival, he made clear that he did not agree with Leutwein's methods and aims. In a letter to the chief of the German general staff, he made no bones about his differences with the governor. "[Leutwein] has for a long time wanted to negotiate and he describes the nation of the Herero as necessary working material for the future use of the country. I am of a completely different opinion. I believe that the nation as such has to be annihilated."[34]

In an article published in the newspaper *Windhuker Nachrichten,* von Trotha categorically rejected Leutwein's argument that the Africans constituted a much needed labor force. "At the outset, we cannot do without the natives. But they finally have to melt away. Where the climate allows the white man to work, philanthropic views cannot banish Darwin's law 'Survival of the Fittest.'"[35]

His view of history was straightforwardly Social Darwinist. Europeans, as members of a "superior race," ought to conquer and populate the world. The corresponding extermination and disappearance of indigenous societies was inevitable. As the following excerpts from his letters to Alfred von Schlieffen reveal, he perceived his duty in South-West Africa as a historical mission consistent with the laws of nature.

> From my close knowledge of many Central-African tribes, Bantu and others, I have reached the conviction that the negro does not submit to contracts but only to raw violence. . . . This [Herero] uprising is and remains the beginning of a racial fight.[36]

> I know enough tribes in Africa. They all have the same mentality insofar as they yield only to force. It was and remains my policy to apply this force by unmitigated terrorism and even cruelty. I shall destroy the rebellious tribes by shedding rivers of blood and money. Only thus will it be possible to sow the seeds of something new that will endure.[37]

Even by the standards of the time, his fanaticism strains credulity. How was it possible that such an extremist, so utterly unconcerned about the economic future of the colony and even less worried about destroying Germany's image as a "civilized nation," had become entrusted with major military responsibilities?

In fact, neither the German chancellor, von Bülow, nor his cabinet ministers were particularly happy with the appointment of von Trotha as supreme commander. They were well aware of his extremism and contempt for civilian authorities, and entertained grave doubts about his ability to end the war quickly and at minimal cost. Nonetheless, the overriding influence of the German general staff was enough to tip the scales in favor of his nomination. The chief of the general staff, von

Schlieffen, had always been a strong supporter of von Trotha, fully sharing his racist worldview. This attitude found expression in the following letter to the chancellor: "We can only agree if he [von Trotha] wants to annihilate the whole (African) nation or expel it from the country. Cohabitation between whites and blacks will be very difficult after all that has happened and it could only work if the latter were kept in a permanent state of forced labor, thus a kind of slavery. The racial fight that has broken out can only come to an end through annihilation or entire subjugation of one side. . . . General v. Trotha's aim can therefore be approved."[38]

But the really decisive factor was the backing he received from the emperor. Wilhelm II had a weakness for adventurers and warhorses like von Trotha. Moreover, the emperor himself had always been in favor of radical military actions. This was obvious on July 27 when he gave a speech in Bremerhaven to German troops departing for China to engage the Boxers. In his infamous "Hun Speech," William II stated: "Should you encounter the enemy, he must be defeated! No quarter will be given! Prisoners will not be taken! Whoever falls into your hands is forfeited. Just as a thousand years ago the Huns under their King Attila made a name for themselves, one that even today makes them seem mighty in history and legend, may the name German be affirmed by you in such a way in China that no Chinese will ever again dare to look cross-eyed at a German."[39]

The emperor's order not to take prisoners is eerily reminiscent of von Trotha's genocide order. There are, in brief, two obvious reasons behind the appointment of an extremist as supreme commander in South-West Africa: a specific military culture favoring final solutions, and the strong political position of the army high command.[40]

As the immense costs of the war found an echo in public debate, the result was to strengthen the position of the civilian government regarding colonial policy. Von Trotha was obliged to repeal his genocide order and to entrust representatives of the Rhenish mission with the task of looking after African survivors. In November 1905, after handing his military command over to a new civilian government, von Trotha left South-West Africa. His removal, however, did not mean that genocide had come to an end.

Concentration Camps and Forced Labor

In the months following von Trotha's departure the human losses recorded in the concentration camps reached frightening proportions. By March 1907, 7,682 out of a total of 17,000 African inmates were reported to have died within a period of thirty months,[41] a rate of mortality among prisoners of almost 50 percent. These figures alone are enough to suggest a continuation of the general's policy of extermination.

The decision to round up Africans and send them to prisoners' camps is traceable to Chancellor von Bülow's instructions to "set up concentration camps [*Konzentrationslager*] for the provisional accommodation and provisioning of the remnants of the Herero people."[42] Of the several concentration camps in central and southern Namibia, those in Swakopmund and on Shark Island near Lüderitz were the most notorious.[43] The harsh, cold climate of the Atlantic coast took its toll, and so did torture, malnutrition, and lack of medical care. Heinrich Vedder, a missionary, described the horrible conditions in these camps as follows:

> [The prisoners of war] were accommodated in miserable spaces made only of sackcloth and laths and set up behind double barbed wire which enclosed the whole area of the port authority dockyard. They were forced to live 30 to 50 people to a room without distinction of age or sex. On Sundays and holidays as well as workdays, from the early morning until late in the evening, they had to work till they dropped under the cudgels of brutal overseers. Their food was worse than meagre. . . . Hundreds were driven to their deaths like cattle and like cattle they were buried. . . . The record must not be silent about the fact that such thoughtless brutality, such lewd sensuality, such harsh domination was so prevalent amongst troops and civilians that it is hardly possible to give an exaggerated description.[44]

Vedder's statement makes clear that the concentration camps served different purposes. The deaths of thousands of Africans in the camps met with almost complete indifference from those army personnel and radical settlers who were still in favor of a "final solution." Lust for vengeance is the only explanation for the sadistic treatment inflicted on Africans. Consider the following quote by the colonial official Tecklenburg: "The more the Herero people now feel physically the consequences of the uprising the less they will yearn after a repetition of the experience for generations to come. Our actual successes in battle have made only a limited impression on them. I expect that the period of suffering they are now experiencing will have a more lasting effect."[45]

A major function of the concentration camps was to provide a solution to the chronic labor shortage. They served as actual work camps offering public and private companies huge reserves of human labor. In an effort to justify the enslavement of Africans, some colonial civil servants were cynically referring to its alleged educational value. The new governor, Friedrich von Lindequist, for instance, wrote to his superiors in Berlin: "Setting the Herero to work while they are held prisoner is very salutary for them, one could even say that they are fortunate, because they learn to work before regaining complete freedom. Otherwise, as far as one can tell, they would just wander work-shy around the country and eke out a miserable life having lost all their cattle."[46]

Forced labor proved considerably less "salutary" than was suggested. The construction of the Otavi railroad, in particular, where more than 2,000 African men, women, and children were employed by Arthur Koppel AG, sent large numbers of Africans to their graves. According to Traugott Tjienda, a former Herero chief from Tsumeb, mortality among the slave laborers was about 30 percent. Flogging and sexual violence against women were ubiquitous, as he reported the following to British officials after World War I:

> I was made to work on the Otavi line which was being built. We were not paid for our work, we were regarded as prisoners. I worked for two years without pay. As our people came in from the bush they were merely skin and bones, they were so thin that one could see through their bones—they looked like broomsticks. Bad as they were, they were made to work; and whether they worked or were lazy they were repeatedly sjambokked [flogged] by the German overseers. The soldiers guarded us at night in big compounds made of thorn bushes. I was a kind of foreman over the laborers. I had 528 people, all Hereros, in my work party. Of these, 148 died while working on the line. The Herero women were compounded with the men. They were made to do manual labor as well. They did not carry the heavy rails, but they had to load and unload wagons and trucks and to work with picks and shovels. . . . When our women were prisoners on the railway work they were compelled to cohabit with soldiers and white railway laborers. The fact that a woman was married was no protection. Young girls were raped and very badly used.[47]

Although the state of war was officially terminated on March 31, 1907, the destruction of African societies went on unabated. Following the disenfranchisement of the indigenous population and the expropriation of their land, a series of "native decrees" were issued in 1907 that severely restricted the Africans' freedom of movement and forced them to carry an identity badge around their necks. The colonizers' obsession with control of the natives led to policies that smacked of totalitarian methods, including having all Africans tattooed so as to thwart laborers' attempts to run away from the farms.[48] Even though the Herero and Nama were reduced to subjugation, the Germans feared possible African uprisings. In order to contain this danger, colonial authorities in Windhoek and Berlin considered large-scale deportations of Africans to the German territories in Cameroon and even Papua New Guinea. The outbreak of World War I, however, averted the implementation of their plans.

In 1944, Willem Petrus Steenkamp, a South African politician and medical doctor, published a pamphlet titled "Are the Herero Committing Race Suicide?" His answer was that self-slaughter was dramatic evidence that the Herero had never recovered from the attempt to annihilate them: "There exists in South-West Africa a widespread belief that the declining birthrate amongst the Herero is due to a nation-wide determination to commit national or race suicide. This resolution was soon taken after the German conquest, because as a race they could not reconcile themselves to the idea of subjection to Germany and thus loss of independence. . . . Having nothing left to exist for as a nation any longer, national suicide was started by birth control of a rigorous nature and artificial abortion."[49]

Historians have tended to agree with Steenkamp's theory.[50] The Herero were portrayed as helpless victims whose fate as a group was sealed by their past. Horst Drechsler, the pioneering historian of the colonial war in Namibia, spoke of the "silence of a graveyard."[51]

Only since the late 1990s have historians paid more attention to the survival strategies of the Africans in Namibia and seriously documented the reconstruction of Herero society.[52] Although the colonizers imposed a totalitarian state system on South-West Africa's indigenous population, Africans found subtle ways to resist: They escaped from farms, stole cattle, and tried to rebuild small herds. Nor did they forget their identities or collective memory.

It was the Herero servants in the German army who worked toward the social reconstruction of their society. After Germany's defeat of 1915, these *Bambusen* established a broad social support system for Herero dispersed all over Namibia. A decisive event in the history of the Hereros' social reconstruction was the funeral of Samuel Maharero in Okahandja on August 26, 1923. The former Herero chief had managed to escape to British Bechuanaland in 1904, where he remained in exile until his death. British colonial authorities had finally allowed the transfer of Maharero's body to Namibia and its burial in his hometown. Thousands of Herero from all corners of Namibia attended this event. For the first time since the Germans' attempt to exterminate their people, the Herero demonstrated publicly that they were again aware of themselves as a self-administering community with a national identity of their own.[53]

Before their confrontation with an external enemy, the Herero did not see themselves as a nation. The collective identity of the Herero as a nation can best be understood as an "invented tradition" forged on the anvil of genocidal brutality.[54]

Every last weekend in August, the Herero gather in Okahandja to celebrate "Herero Day." They make a procession to the graves of their old chiefs and remember the murder of their ancestors by the German colonizers. In recent years, "Herero Day" has become the forum for restitution claims. Because of their iron-willed determination to survive as a community, and their persistent demand for historical justice, the immense sufferings visited upon their ancestors are still widely remembered, enshrined as it were in their collective memory.

Chapter 4

Extermination, Extinction, Genocide
British Colonialism and Tasmanian Aborigines

Shayne Breen

The island of Tasmania is separated from the south coast of Australia by the stormy waters of Bass Strait. Similar in size to Ireland, Tasmania's present shape was formed around 10,000 years ago when the last ice age ended and global sea levels rose by 130 meters and flooded the land bridge that connected the island to continental Australia. Long before the flooding, some 30,000 years earlier, Aboriginal people walked across the land bridge from southeast Australia and became the island's first people. They practiced a dynamic hunter-gatherer economy that successfully weathered dramatic climate change, major topographical transformations, and 10,000 years of isolation from all outside contact until French sailors briefly landed on the island's east coast in early 1772.[1]

The ancient Aboriginal society was catastrophically disrupted by the British invasion that began in September 1803, twenty-five years after the British invasion of continental Australia began at Botany Bay in New South Wales. The invaders included military and free colonists intent on establishing an agricultural economy, transported convicts to provide slave labor, and small numbers of sealers and whalers. At first few in number, the invaders had grown to 3,000 in 1818, 13,000 in 1824, and 23,500 by 1830, of whom 75 percent were convicts. Along with the increase in the invader population, sheep numbers increased from zero in 1803 to 54,000 in 1816 to one million by 1830. By 1830, all major Aboriginal hunting grounds had been occupied.[2]

In 1803, the Aboriginal population was around 6,000; by 1818 it was fewer than 2,000; and by 1829, only some 400 people remained. From 1832 the surviving 200 or so were transported to an open-air prison at a place called Wybalenna, on Flinder's Island in Bass Strait. In 1847, as a cost-cutting measure, the remaining forty-five survivors of Wybalenna were removed to Oyster Cove, south of Hobart, and housed in a convict station that had been abandoned because it was permanently damp and infested with vermin. The so-called last of her race, a woman named Truganini, died in Hobart in 1876.[3]

Matters of Dispute

The ways in which this rapid Aboriginal depopulation have been portrayed by historians—extermination, extinction, dispossession, and more recently genocide—have been matters of dispute since the 1830s and remain so to this day. Disputation has focused on Tasmania because the Tasmanians have long been regarded as the only Australian example of an entire race that disappeared in the wake of British colonization. Geographic isolation was a key factor in producing the focus on Tasmania. Isolation encouraged Europeans to see the Tasmanians as a separate race from Australian Aborigines. The Australians were far more numerous—estimates vary from 300,000 to one million in 1788—and were seen to have survived colonization despite their annihilation over much of the continent.[4] A less-acknowledged factor in the Tasmanian focus was the way in which Europeans equated geography and race. The invaders assumed that one race existed in Tasmania and one in Australia. Anthropologists have since shown that Aborigines did not define themselves in terms of race or national or colonial boundaries; they identified themselves as autonomous peoples in terms of local place and language. There were at least four distinct peoples in Tasmania and up to five hundred across the continent.[5]

This perceived difference between the impacts of colonization in Tasmania and continental Australia is therefore false. Many separate peoples did disappear in continental Australia, mainly in temperate regions in the continent's southern half where British occupation was concentrated. In the Australian colony of Port Phillip (now the state of Victoria), from where the first Tasmanians emigrated at least 40,000 years ago, the Aboriginal population was reduced from an estimated 10,000 in 1834, when land-hungry British colonists from Tasmania first invaded the region, to 1,907 by 1853, a decline of 80 percent in two decades. Similar catastrophic declines occurred in other temperate regions, including New South Wales, southern Queensland, the south coast of South Australia, and the southwest corner of Western Australia. Only in more remote and, for Europeans, inhospitable regions in central and northern Australia did Aboriginal societies remain relatively intact, at least until the 1930s when a national policy of forced child removal was applied across the continent.[6]

Despite these catastrophic levels of depopulation, Australian historians have avoided the term genocide. Those who have discussed Australian genocides include Tony Barta in 1987 and more recently Dirk Moses, both of whom are also historians of Germany.[7] The most prominent historian of Tasmania, Henry Reynolds, while unequivocally demonstrating the widespread destruction, has argued that genocide did not occur in Tasmania. His key reason is that genocide can only occur where there is demonstrable intent on the part of the state to exterminate. In very recent years, a few Australian historians, including Ben Kiernan and Ann Curthoys, have taken up Barta's 1987 arguments and asserted that genocide did, indeed, occur in Tasmania. The position of most historians, however, remains opposed to the finding of genocide in Australia. As a result, there are many disputed genocides in continental Australia, as well as at least four disputed genocides in Tasmania.[8]

In contrast, international writers and genocide scholars, including Raphael Lemkin, have long seen the Tasmanian extermination as a clear case of genocide. Lemkin included a chapter on Tasmania in his unpublished draft of a world history of genocide from 1492. Lemkin saw a close and recurring relation between European colonization and the genocide of hunter-gatherers. He argued that colonial genocide involved the destruction of the foundations of the collective life of hunter-gatherers and their subsequent extermination. The techniques of destruction of Aboriginal life in Tasmania identified by Lemkin included land seizures, the killing of men, the abduction of women and children, exile from homelands, and the spread of imported diseases.[9]

Lemkin's method is as significant as his conceptual insights into world history. His delineation of a global pattern of European colonization and its typically genocidal impacts on the colonized underpins present international indigenous studies. He proposed a set of categories for the analysis of colonial genocide that Australian scholar John Docker recently argued also applied to Western colonization over the past 2,500 years. Lemkin's categories are used by genocide scholars as the basis of an analytical framework that is amenable to a comparative approach; his approach enables the historian to cut through the accumulated detail that characterizes chronological history to a focus on explaining how and why events occurred and the ways in which the past has been represented. Most Australian Aboriginal histories are national or colony-based chronological histories that lack a comparative dimension. Therefore, approaches based on Lemkin's categories offer an important alternative to more conventional approaches.[10]

In the past decade the word genocide has been a focus for intense dispute in public discourse in Australia. The word achieved prominence, not in the context of colonial invasion, but with the release in 1997 of the *Bringing Them Home* report into the forced removal, in all Australian states, of Aboriginal children from their families in the period from the late 1920s until the 1970s. The removals were orchestrated by state and federal governments because the high level of population increase among Aborigines of mixed descent was "a problem" that posed a threat to the White Australia Policy. The expectation was that removal and placement with white families would result in widespread interracial marriage that would eventually breed out the black blood and so maintain the assumed purity of the white Australian race. In line with the United Nations genocide convention, the report described the forced removal of up to 100,000 children as cultural genocide and it called for a national apology for those affected by removal.[11]

The use of the term genocide by the report authors, neither of whom were trained historians, was deeply controversial. It provoked widespread condemnation of the authors and helped generate the claim by conservative politicians and thinkers, in the context of the so-called history wars, that evidence for forced removal had been fabricated. This particular episode of the history wars was exacerbated by conservative Prime Minister John Howard (1996–2007), whose government refused to make the national apology that the report recommended. It was this policy of forced removal for which the newly elected Labour prime minister Kevin Rudd apologized in early 2008, although Rudd avoided using the word genocide.[12]

Within three years of the release of the *Bringing Them Home* report, conservative intellectuals affiliated with *Quadrant* magazine and the *Australian* newspaper had widened their attack to include historians of colonial Australia. Keith Windschuttle, once a 1960s left-wing student radical, led this charge. In a well-publicized 2002 book, Windschuttle claimed that historians of colonial violence in early nineteenth-century Tasmania, especially Lyndall Ryan, had fabricated charges of genocide. Ryan, who in 1981 wrote a seminal history of Tasmanian Aborigines, did not actually argue for genocide; the word genocide suggestively appeared twice in her text, but she argued for dispossession. Like Lemkin's initial meaning of genocide, the term dispossession included mass killing, but also incorporated loss of land, the abduction of women and children, exile to offshore islands, and the disintegration of Aboriginal society that followed. Windschuttle chose Tasmania as his battleground because expatriate Australian writers Robert Hughes and Phillip Knightley and international scholars, including Lemkin and Jared Diamond, described the Tasmanian extermination as genocide.[13]

Erasure, Exposure, and Rationalization

The extermination of whole peoples in colonial settings has been a feature of Western history for at least 2,500 years. As John Docker has shown, the morality of colonization has been contested for a similar time. Typically, the affirmative view portrayed the colonizer as a racially superior and divinely chosen people with the right to colonize and exterminate; the counter view pointed to the loss of life, freedom, and culture experienced by the colonized. The ethics of colonization was an important theme for the Greek historian Herodotus in his *Histories*, written between 431 and 425 B.C.E. Texts written by Greek and Roman writers, including Plato, Thucydides, Cicero, Virgil and Tacitus, all questioned the ethics of colonization. In the sixteenth century, English promoters of colonization developed the concept of the honorable colonizer, a conceit that was subjected to rigorous interrogation by Shakespeare in his play *The Tempest*, but which remains much beloved by twenty-first-century neo-conservatives.[14]

In colonial Tasmania, or Van Diemen's Land as it was called until 1853, discussions of colonization and its impacts on Tasmanian Aborigines belong in this tradition of contestation. The affirmative view was in the majority and the dissenting view in the minority. The words *extermination*, *extirpation*, and *extinction* were commonly used to characterize Aboriginal deaths. Extermination and the less-used extirpation usually referred to certain actions, including killing and the abduction of women and girls, although extermination could also refer to an outcome: the disappearance of a whole people. The word *extinction* was more often a reference to the likely outcome if exterminating practices were not curbed by effective government action. Debates about these terms changed over time and were shaped by competing impulses. Some sought to conceal or erase exterminating practices from public memory, others sought their public exposure, while still others were content to peddle rationalizations of the killing.[15]

Several factors worked to downplay the exposure of extermination practices. From the beginning of British occupation, as Reynolds has shown, Aborigines had the protection of British law. Until the mid-1820s, the fear of prosecution played some role in silencing the killing and abduction of Aborigines. The primacy accorded to the interests of the invaders was a factor. In 1817, William Sorell (lieutenant governor, 1817–24) issued a strongly worded proclamation condemning the killing of Aborigines and threatening to send perpetrators to Sydney for trial. At that time it was evident to the British government that Aboriginal hunting grounds were eminently suitable for raising fine wool sheep. Between 1819 and 1824, when he granted some 550,000 acres of Aboriginal hunting grounds to invading pastoralists, Sorell engaged in an ongoing act of silence: his despatches in those years made no mention of Aborigines.[16]

Concerns about Britain's reputation played a significant role in distorting the official story. In 1830, the so-called Aborigines Committee, set up by Lieutenant Governor George Arthur (1824–36) and consisting of leading civilian figures in the colony, including the Anglican archdeacon William Broughton, conducted an inquiry into the causes of Aboriginal hostility toward colonists. No Aborigines were called before the inquiry. In a piece of blame-the-victim reasoning characteristic of *génocidaires*, the committee found that atrocities committed by convicts against Aborigines were a major cause of Aboriginal hostility, but it concluded that Aboriginal treachery and savagery were the primary causes of violence against them. This conclusion was reached despite the fact that three earlier governors had publicly warned colonists against their habit of wantonly killing and abducting Aborigines.[17]

In contrast to official distortion, two Hobart newspaper editors argued that the Aboriginal population had been brought to the brink of extermination by appropriation of land, invader violence against Aborigines, and official indifference to those events. In 1835, Henry Melville published a history of Van Diemen's Land in which he wrote that "thousands of lives have been lost by hostile measures." In 1836, another wrote that "They have been murdered in cold blood . . . and the Government, to its shame be recorded, in no one instance, on no single occasion, ever punished, or threatened to punish, the acknowledged murderers of the aboriginal inhabitants." Threats of punishment were made until 1824, but not thereafter. In 1852, John West, an influential historian, newspaper editor, and Congregational preacher based in Launceston, engaged in both exposure and erasure; he considered that the English government had failed to protect Aborigines, although he thought that convicts who did the killing—as did the Aborigines Committee—were to blame.[18]

From the early 1830s, the word extinction was used at the highest levels of government in both England and Van Diemen's Land to predict the likely fate of the Tasmanians. By the mid-1830s the reality of certain extinction had been widely accepted. By the early 1850s, the word had assumed an evolutionist meaning. Extinction was by then a matter of the strong prevailing over the weak with the consequence that the extinction of the weak became inevitable. John West was preeminent among those who expressed this view. West was concerned that by the late 1840s too many colonists felt some level of guilt for the fate of the Tasmanians. He moved to reassure his various flocks that the moral unease many of them felt was misplaced. West asserted in his classic rationalization of colonialism in Van Diemen's Land that wherever civilized and savage peoples met, the civilized triumphed and the savage were erased from the face of the planet. This was more or less natural law. In 1870, in contrast, James Bonwick saw modern Christian civilization as "a theory which ancient heathen philosophy would have declared inhuman and unjust," but such views were too threatening for most, at least until a century later.[19]

By the late 1870s, it was accepted as fact that with the death of the woman Truganini, the Aborigines of Tasmania had, as if by natural causes, become extinct. For the following century, Aboriginal depopulation was explained as inevitable because, it was claimed, they were the least-developed humans on the planet and lacked the evolutionary fitness to survive in the new world. The arrival in their midst of the "pure," white-complected English armed by Western standards, with more advanced technological skills and a divine mission to colonize and civilize "inferior" races, only hastened what was preordained.[20]

Pervasive acceptance of the extinction myth was reinforced by a monumental act of historical forgetting. In 1853, a year after West published his defense of colonization, the colony's name was changed from Van Diemen's Land to Tasmania. The change of name marked the granting of self-government to the colony, but was a conscious strategy of historical forgetting that signified the beginning of a new era in which the colony's brutal and unsavory past would be erased from public memory, collective guilt would be absolved, and the reputation of the British nation would remain intact.

Techniques of Extermination

The extermination of Tasmanian Aborigines involved five major techniques: the officially sanctioned seizure of the bulk of Aboriginal hunting grounds by a privileged elite of British invaders; abduction of women and children, which had a massive impact on the Aborigines' ability to reproduce themselves; murder and massacre, usually, but not always, of men; from late 1826, a War of Extermination, encouraged and sanctioned by government and involving the repeated use of massacre; and from 1829, government-orchestrated capture, exile, and incarceration of Aborigines in "establishments" located on offshore islands.

Land Seizures

The wholesale theft of Aboriginal land by the British government removed from Aborigines the core foundation of their collective life. The island was claimed for the English Crown in September 1803 and small-scale land seizures continued until 1817; until then, occupation was limited to beach-heads at Hobart in the south and Launceston in the north. In 1817, Aborigines were still in control of most of their hunting grounds and an uneasy coexistence prevailed between Aborigines and the intruders. By 1817 the suitability of the Aboriginal hunting grounds for grazing fine wool was clear to colonists. The hunting grounds were not naturally occurring grassy plains, but the result of thousands of years of application of a carefully managed burning regime. Nor were Aborigines, as many colonists preferred to believe, aimless wanderers surviving from the chase; the hunting grounds were owned by discrete Aboriginal groups and maintained so that each group was supplied with adequate sustenance.[21]

Between 1819 and 1824, at least 550,000 acres of prime Aboriginal hunting grounds, a narrow 140-mile stretch of land between Hobart and Launceston that colonists soon called the "settled districts," were given as grants to free colonists. Some 350,000 acres were granted in 1823 alone. It is no coincidence that concerted Aboriginal resistance to pastoral expansion began in late 1823. From 1826, a further 250,000 acres of the best hunting grounds in the island's northwest were given under royal charter to the Van Diemen's Land Company. Further land in the island's central north was granted in the late 1820s. The land was granted free of charge to colonists willing and able to establish pastoral enterprises. In addition to free land grants, the government provided free labor to grantees in the form of thousands of assigned convicts. Military and field police, the latter drawn mostly from the convict class, were deployed to the "settled districts" to protect grantees and their property from attacks by Aborigines. It is clear the British government intended to take the land; in so doing, the necessary conditions for the destruction of the foundations of Aboriginal life were put in place.[22]

Abduction

The abduction of women and girls played a central role in Aboriginal depopulation. From the late 1790s, sealers living and working on off-shore islands in coastal areas in the northwest, north, northeast, and southeast of the island, well away from the "settled districts," regularly mounted raiding parties for the purpose of abducting Aboriginal women and girls. In 1829, the government's "conciliator," G. A. Robinson, was told by at least three Aboriginal women that a slave trade in Aboriginal women was carried on in the Bass Strait region. Captured women were often brutally treated and used for sexual purposes, as well as for labor, as were girls.[23]

The willingness of some Aboriginal men, especially in the island's north and northeast, to abduct women from rival bands and trade them to sealers contributed to the loss of women. The ritual abduction of women for marriage had long been a practice of the first Tasmanians, and it is likely that women were used by Aboriginal men as a means of incorporating the foreigners into reciprocal arrangements with Aboriginal bands. Some women, those who raised mixed-descent children, appear to have accepted, willingly or unwillingly, their new situation. By 1830, some seventy-four women were living with sealers in the Bass Strait region.[24]

In the early years of the British occupation numerous women and girls were abducted by convict hunters who had been armed by the government and sent into the bush to hunt kangaroo in order to feed the military and convicts. The numbers are not known, but a surveyor's report from 1809 suggested at least thirty kangaroo hunters were engaged in abducting women. Some women were probably traded or lent by Aboriginal men in efforts to force the invaders into reciprocal arrangements. Free colonists were involved in the abduction of children for use as domestic labor, especially before 1820 when manual labor was scarce. Government notices issued between 1816 and 1819 outlawed the practice, to no avail. John West wrote in 1852 that "child-stealing" was not uncommon in Van Diemen's Land, and that Aboriginal mothers were often terrorized into leaving their children, whereupon the children were taken and subjected to what West called "juvenile slavery."[25]

The abduction of women and girls had a significant impact on the capacity of Aboriginal people to reproduce themselves, but quantifying that impact is difficult. Across the island, abduction appears to have been common in the first decade and it continued in line with the spread of British occupation across the island. Some measure of the impact can be gained from G. A. Robinson's journals, in which he noted that in 1830, the northeast population was seventy-two men, sixty of whom were young, and six women.[26]

Murder, Massacre, and the War of Extermination

Historians have long believed that violent Aboriginal deaths, apart from the well-known massacre at Risdon Cove in 1804, were sporadic and small scale until 1824. There is considerable doubt that this view is correct. Some have argued that as few as three deaths occurred at Risdon Cove; contemporary accounts suggest that British forces killed up to fifty people. A second, little-known massacre was perpetrated by British military at Oyster Cove on the east coast in 1815 in which twenty-two Aborigines were killed. Official reports in 1809 and 1810 make it clear that in areas close to Hobart and Launceston a "considerable" loss of Aboriginal life occurred at the hands of convict kangaroo hunters intent on abducting Aboriginal women. As mentioned earlier, three official notices issued by successive lieutenant governors, in 1813, 1817, and 1819, make it clear that settlers and others were in the habit of killing Aborigines and that, if found, perpetrators would be tried and punished.[27]

Following exhaustive research conducted since 2003, Lyndall Ryan found that in the settled districts between 1823 and 1831, some 448 Aborigines were killed, of whom 413 were killed in twenty-seven separate massacres of five or more people. Given that the estimated Aboriginal population in the settled districts in 1823 was 1,000, in excess of 40 percent of those Aborigines were killed. It is likely that these figures underestimate the extent of the killing. It is clear that more reporting occurred after 1823 than before, but in 1830 a Hobart newspaper reported that "It is said privately that up the country, instances occur where the Natives are 'shot like so many crows,' which never comes before the public." For the same period, 1823–31, 250 colonists were killed by Aborigines in at least 113 separate incidents.[28]

Most of the reported post-1823 killings occurred between 1827 and 1830. This was the direct result of policy adopted by Governor George Arthur, who arrived in the colony in 1824. Arthur at first adopted a legal approach, warning both colonists and Aborigines against violence. Two Aborigines were tried and hanged for murder, but the insurgency continued. In response, Arthur invoked instructions issued in 1825 by the Colonial Office in London to "oppose force by force and to repel such aggressions in the same manner as if they proceeded from subjects of an accredited state." On November 29, 1826, Arthur removed Aborigines from the jurisdiction of British law, reclassified them as "open enemies," and authorized magistrates to send out military detachments, assisted by armed settlers and their servants, in active pursuit of any Aborigines who committed felonies or who appeared likely to commit a felony. Determining the likelihood of an Aborigine committing a felony was left to the discretion of pursuers. Colonists saw this measure as a declaration of war against Aborigines and acted accordingly. The majority of reported killings occurred after that late 1826 proclamation.[29]

In response to Aboriginal assaults against colonists in September and October 1828, Arthur and his advisors concluded that the best way to deal with insurgent Aborigines was "To inspire them with terror." On November 1, 1828, martial law was declared in the settled districts. The effect was twofold: Aborigines were forbidden from conducting their seasonal journeys across their traditional hunting grounds, and they no longer had the protection of common law.[30]

The military was now authorized to shoot Aborigines on sight. In 1830 Arthur sought to crush the Aboriginal resistance. Martial law was extended to the whole colony. A reward of £5 per adult and £2 per child was offered for the capture of any Aborigine, injured or not. Extra mounted military were deployed to quell resistance. Arthur proposed to London that two thousand convicts be brought to Van Diemen's Land, then sent to remote parts of the colony to assist in the "capture" of Aborigines. In response to Arthur's advice Colonial Secretary George Murray insisted that any person responsible for the death of an Aborigine be prosecuted, effectively condemning Arthur's policy as facilitating murder. Arthur ignored the instruction and, as James Boyce recently noted, the relevant correspondence between Arthur and Murray was later deleted from the official printed version of Arthur's correspondence on Aboriginal policy. The odd colonist agreed with Murray's assessment; most disagreed. The differing views were aired at a public debate held to discuss the proposed military offensive called the Black Line. Former Attorney-General Joseph Gellibrand criticized what he called the "war of extermination"; according to the *Tasmanian* newspaper, Gellibrand argued that the killing of Aborigines under the present policy was "murder." Solicitor-General Alfred Stephen responded that the government had a duty to protect colonists, and "if you cannot do so without extermination then I say boldly and broadly, exterminate."[31]

Arthur's policy reflected the contradictions inherent in British policy. The land was to be taken, by military force if necessary; this was done. Aboriginal access to their their traditional lands was to be respected, they were to be treated humanely, perpetrators of crimes against them were to be brought to justice; all three instructions were routinely ignored. Murders and massacres (referred to jointly as killings) occurred in several recurring situations. Killings can be grouped into five categories: abduction killings, response killings, reprisal killings, random killings, and pursuit killings. Perpetrators came from most social groups in colonial society, including senior government officials, free colonists, field police, convicts, ex-convicts, and the military.

An unknown number of abduction killings occurred when Aboriginal men resisted the abduction of their women or children, although there is some evidence that killing of men became a routine prelude to the actual abduction. In 1819, a government notice ordering an accounting of all native children then living with colonists stated that "It is undeniable that in many former Instances, Cruelties have been perpetrated repugnant to the Humanity and disgraceful to the British Character. . . . Miscreants . . . sometimes wantonly fire and kill the Men, and at others pursue the Women for the purpose of compelling them to abandon their Children." Abduction killings in the interior were perpetrated by kangaroo hunters and stock-keepers. On the north coast abduction killings were perpetrated by sealers.[32]

Response killings occurred as an immediate response to an Aboriginal attack. Most attacks by Aborigines occurred in response to trespass, dispute over the unauthorized taking of game, or some earlier attack by colonists. Response killings occurred on a regular basis from 1804 to 1831. Many killings were of less than five people and there were numerous massacres. In the Risdon Cove massacre of May 1804, up to fifty people were killed by soldiers under the command of Lieutenant William Moore and Surgeon Jacob Mountgarrett. In 1807 or 1808, two bushrangers, Lemon and Brown, tortured and killed five Aborigines, two men and three women. In 1810, a government notice reported that bushrangers George Getley, William Russell, and others had engaged in "murders and abominable cruelties" toward the natives. In December 1825, stock-keeper James Cubit, reportedly assisted by a "half-caste" woman, killed sixteen Aborigines who had launched an attack on Cubit's hut.[33] No charges were laid against any of these men.

Reprisal killings account for a significant number of Aboriginal deaths. They took place on the night following an Aboriginal attack, or soon after, when the killers tracked and massacred their presumed adversary. The 1815 Oyster Bay massacre, mentioned earlier, was a reprisal killing. Local Aborigines destroyed 930 sheep; two witnesses, a colonist and a government official, told the Aborigines Committee (in 1830) that the following day a detachment of the 48th Regiment massacred twenty-two Aborigines. In 1827 at Western Marshes, Thomas Baker killed a man who approached him in daylight; later that night Baker and James Cubit ambushed and killed nine Aborigines sitting around a fire. At least thirteen further instances of reprisal killings occurred from 1827 to 1830.[34]

Random killings were apparently common. The proclamation issued by Governor George Davey in 1813 condemned the routine killing of Aborigines. The 1817 proclamation issued by Governor Sorell outlawed the habit of "several settlers and others . . . of maliciously and wantonly firing at, and destroying, the defenceless NATIVES or ABORIGINES of this Island." Also in 1817, visiting missionary Rowland Hassall was told there were no natives in Hobart because "We shoot them whenever we find them."[35] Robinson was told that after Aborigines killed four sealers at Eddystone in the northeast in the late 1820s in response to the theft of women, sealers shot them whereever they saw them.[36] In 1830, a convict stock-keeper named Brady living near Campbell Town admitted to an official that he had killed sixteen Aborigines.[37]

Pursuit killings were often massacres that occurred mostly between 1826 and 1830. Aborigines were pursued without immediate provocation for the sole purpose of being killed. Pursuit killings were perpetrated under orders by official parties of troops and colonists, by groups of colonists who took matters into their own hands, and by groups of men who hunted and killed Aborigines for sport. In 1826 at Pittwater, fourteen Aborigines were ambushed at night and killed by District Constable Alexander Laing and four soldiers from the 40th Regiment.[38] An area called Western Marshes, in the north of the island, was notorious for pursuit killings. A government surveyor told Arthur's Aborigines Committee that "Captain Ritchie's men, to the westward of Norfolk Plains, used to hunt them on horseback, and shoot them from their horses." A stock-keeper called Punch told Robinson "that Knight, the stockkeeper who was afterwards killed by the natives near Simpson's Plains, deserved it; it was a judgment upon him, as he used to kill the natives for sport." Others who engaged in pursuit massacres at Western Marshes included stock-keepers called Lyons and Murray, and soldiers from the 40th Regiment.[39]

In the Van Diemen's Land Company lands in the island's northwest, Richard Frederick and four workers ambushed and killed twelve Aborigines in January 1828. The following month stock-keepers Charles Chamberlain, John Weavis, William Gunshannon, and Richard Nicholson ambushed a group of Aboriginal men and women mutton-birding, shot dead thirty, then threw their bodies over a cliff. Company manager Edward Curr told his superiors none were killed in the earlier incident and three in the second. In 1828, at Elizabeth River in central Tasmania, on the orders of magistrate James Simpson, seventy Aborigines were killed by a party of stock-keepers, soldiers, and field police in response to the death of one stock-keeper. In 1828 at Tooms Lake, a party of the 40th Regiment was led into the bush by John Danvers and William Holmes and slaughtered eighteen Aborigines. In 1829, an official party led by John Batman, later the "founder" of the city of Melbourne, killed fifteen Aborigines. Captain Donaldson, when hunting Aborigines in the northeast in 1831 with a dozen armed men, "told his soldiers . . . not to spare man, woman or child; not to parley with them. He was vexed at them killing two of his soldiers." According to John West, these official hunting parties killed many more Aborigines than they took alive.[40]

Capture, Exile, and Incarceration

In 1829, worried that total extermination would irretrievably stain the British reputation, the government adopted what was called a policy of conciliation and protection. The policies were devised as a result of a dialog between Arthur, his so-called Aborigines Committee, and G. A. Robinson, and were implemented by Robinson. The evidence suggests that the term conciliation was a euphemism for capture, and the term protection for incarceration. In the circumstances in which they were hatched—as a mopping up operation at the tail-end of the War of Extermination—the underlying aim of the policies was the removal or eradication of surviving Aborigines from all of mainland Tasmania and their confinement or incarceration in "establishments" on offshore islands.

In early 1829, some thirty Aborigines captured in the settled districts were forcibly removed to Bruny Island, south of Hobart. By the end of that year, two-thirds of the forty or so Aborigines taken to the establishment were dead. Robinson claimed they died from the cold, a claim lacking credibility given their ability to survive as hunter-gatherers. Confinement in an artificial environment with inadequate shelter, a high-salt diet, a poor water supply, the separation of children from parents, and a program of reeducation into Christian civilization was a radical departure from the balanced diet, fresh water, and the cultural autonomy characteristic of the hunter-gatherer lifestyle. Confinement also brought them into daily contact with Robinson's convict workers, whalers, and other colonists then living on Bruny Island, thereby exposing Aborigines to common respiratory diseases to which they had limited immunity. Some deaths were of apparently healthy people who died within days of the death of a spouse.[41]

The intent of the so-called Black Line, which consisted of 2,200 white colonists, including military, police, free colonists, and convicts, was to clear Aborigines out of the "settled districts" by herding them onto Tasman Peninsula, in the island's southeast, from where they would be sent into exile on offshore islands. An expensive exercise undertaken in October and November 1830, when there were less than 300 surviving Aborigines on the island, the line captured an old man and a boy. It was regarded by many colonists as a farce. Ostensibly a failure as a military exercise, it did succeed in persuading most Aborigines to avoid the "settled districts."[42] The aims of the Black Line were to forcibly remove Aborigines from the island and secure the widespread seizure of Aboriginal land; therefore, it was a central instrument in the Tasmanian genocide. In time, the line and its apparent failure became the central incident of the wider conflict. This had the effect of erasing from public memory, especially in the twentieth century, the brutal realities of the extermination.[43]

In early 1831, Arthur and his advisors dropped the policy of conciliation in favor of capture and removal. Most of the remaining Aborigines were removed to Wybalenna, Robinson's "establishment" on Flinder's Island. In mid-1833, twenty five west coast Aborigines who posed no threat to colonists were rounded up and imprisoned temporarily on Sarah Island at the notoriously brutal Macquarie Harbor penal station. They were denied food and medical care because they were not officially prisoners, and were brutalized and urinated on by convicts. Most died there, again from respiratory diseases.[44]

For Aborigines, exile to Flinder's Island was an unmitigated disaster. After a brief period of relative comfort, Robinson's arrival as commandant in 1835 was met with a decade of death. Efforts to transform the Wybalenna inmates into Christian peasants failed miserably, as did efforts to erase all traces of Aboriginal culture and identity. As it had done on Bruny Island, a diet high in salt weakened the peoples' immunity to disease. They were forced to live in vermin-ridden huts they would have quickly abandoned as hunter-gatherers. Fresh water and food were scarce. Medical care was inadequate.[45]

A total of nearly two hundred Aborigines died in these "establishments." Officially most died from common respiratory disease, but several observers believed that deeper causes were at work. In early 1831, after the disaster of Bruny Island, but well before any other removals or incarcerations, Chief Justice John Pedder prophetically warned Arthur that a policy of exile to offshore islands would cause the Aborigines to pine away and die once they realized the hopelessness of their situation.[46] Major Thomas Ryan, who arrived in the colony in 1835 and was army commandant at Launceston, visited Wybalenna in 1836. Noting the artificial environment, absence of traditional foods, damp and poorly ventilated huts, impure water, and inadequate provisions, Ryan warned that if the government did not act to redress the situation, "the race of Tasmania, like the last of the Mohicans, will pine away and be extinct in a quarter of a century."[47] There were, in other words, influential people who indicated that disease was but a symptom of displacement, collective grief, criminal neglect, and a deeper process of extermination by exile, but their counsel was ignored.

In 1847, the forty-five survivors of Wybalenna were transferred to a vermin-infested, abandoned army camp at Oyster Cove, south of Hobart. Two years later up to eight children were removed to the Queen's Orphan School at Hobart, where at least four of them died. The Orphan School was a carceral institution, the primary purpose of which was to prepare the children of convicts for trades or service. For the few Aboriginal children who were sent there, an additional aim was to expunge their Aboriginal identity. By 1876, all but one of those removed from Wybalenna, a woman named Fanny Cochrane Smith, were dead.[48]

Possible Alternatives

The extermination of Tasmanian Aborigines was never inevitable in the evolutionary sense that John West claimed in 1852. The idea of inevitable extinction was an evolutionary fantasy that served to rationalize the rapid disappearance of the Aborigines. Far from being inevitable, there is significant evidence of mutually co-operative relations between Aborigines and colonists. This was especially so, but not limited to, the period before 1817. Certainly much violence was perpetrated against Aborigines, especially abductions and killings, but Aboriginal willingness to forge reciprocal relations with colonists was a key factor in the uneasy coexistence with free colonists in Hobart and the "settled districts' and with whalers, sealers, convict hunters, and bushrangers in other areas. The opportunity for the British to reciprocate always existed, but successive governors before 1817 lacked the will or vision despite their apparent concern.[49]

In 1817, when the suitability of Aboriginal hunting grounds for sheep raising became clear, there were courses of action open to the government that might have prevented the violence that ensued. No attempt was made to negotiate meaningful payment for Aboriginal land, as the British government had instructed. No attempt was made to negotiate a treaty or even a less formal arrangement whereby Aborigines might agree to share the land. As the extent of the carnage became obvious, several colonists publicly lamented the failure to strike a treaty with Aboriginal leaders, and Arthur admitted in 1833 that a treaty might have avoided the war of extermination.[50]

When violence escalated in 1824–25, Arthur could have chosen to prosecute alleged perpetrators of violence against Aborigines. From the mid-1820s, the colony was a police state. It had a supreme court, military, and field police. The law was used against Aborigines in 1825–26, but no charges were brought against colonists. Rather than pursue a legal approach to preventing violence against Aborigines, Arthur effectively chose to give colonists immunity from prosecution. Why did Arthur do this? Historians have pointed to the difficulty of policing far-flung outposts and to the fact that Aborigines, since they could not swear on the Bible, were prevented from giving evidence in court. No doubt these factors played some part, as did Arthur's attitude toward Aborigines. It was well known in the colony that atrocities committed against Aborigines was the key cause of their attacks on colonists. Arthur's early despatches, however, stressed outrages by Aborigines rather than injuries done to them. From 1828, he characterized them as "bloodthirsty barbarians" engaged in the destruction of settlers' lives and property. The rights and lives of the island's original owners were no longer a concern.[51]

The other most obvious alternative was voluntary abandonment of the colonizing enterprise. Such a course was never seriously considered. Involuntary abandonment became an option for some colonists in the later 1820s, although the aim of expressing that possibility was to pressure the government to take stronger action—which is what Arthur did—against Aboriginal resistors. In late 1830, at the height of the Black Line, a very senior government official, G. W. T. Boyes, wrote in a private letter that there were three alternatives open to the government: imprisonment of Aborigines away from the settled districts; their extermination; or abandonment of the colony. The first had failed, which left a choice between extermination and abandonment, "and with that object in view," wrote Boyes, in reference to the Black Line, "the most vigorous and extensive measures have been taken that the resources of the colony could be put into operation."[52]

Consequences: Aboriginal Survivors, Colonial Unease, Social-Darwinist Mythmakers

The short-term consequences of the Tasmanian genocide can be succinctly stated. By the early 1830s, the Aboriginal society and culture that was present on the island in 1803 had all but disappeared. In the process, a tiny elite of wealthy British invaders took possession of Aboriginal lands. Aboriginal survivors were incarcerated on offshore islands where most died in despair. The genocide resonated through subsequent decades and it continues to resonate in present-day Tasmanian society. The shape and character of that resonance has been complex and has changed over time, but three long-term consequences are apparent: the emergence of a mixed-descent Aboriginal Islander population with a long history of political activism; a deep-seated ambiguity within the wider Tasmanian society about the fate of the original Tasmanians; and an ongoing dispute among historians about the causes and naming of the Aboriginal depopulation between 1803 and the 1870s.

Many people in the northern hemisphere believe that Tasmanian Aborigines are extinct. This belief, based on the view that collective identities are entirely biological and have no cultural or historical elements, is false. The abduction of Aboriginal women and girls by European sealers, and the insistence of those women on transmitting Aboriginal culture and identity to their descendants, resulted in the emergence of a mixed-descent Aboriginal Islander population based on the Furneaux Islands in the eastern Bass Strait. The Islander community has a long history of political activism aimed at securing some kind of reparation, most often the return of land, for the impact of colonialism on their ancestors and themselves. In response to these claims, the Tasmanian government incarcerated the Aboriginal Islander community on a reserve on Cape Barren Island (1881–1951), where they were denigrated as "half-castes," their common-law rights suspended, their claims to land ignored, and their Aboriginal identity denied. When the reserve was closed in 1951, many Aboriginal Islanders returned to mainland Tasmania. There are now more Tasmanian Aborigines than when the British invaded in 1803.[53]

The colonial genocide perpetrated against Aborigines produced within the colonial society a deep and enduring ambiguity about the fate of the original Aborigines and the role of colonists in generating that fate. This ambiguity consisted of a deep-seated moral unease about what had occurred and a culture of denial that was expressed in numerous ways, but most obviously in the myth of inevitable extinction. The extinction myth rejected the alternative colonial narrative of a morally compromised extermination in favor of a counternarrative of evolutionary unfitness: the myth held that Aborigines were not exterminated, but had died out because they lacked the evolutionary fitness to compete with the more advanced British race. Claims to Aboriginal identity made by Aboriginal Islanders and their descendants were a direct challenge to the myth's ascendancy. This challenge was met by one of the more insidious expressions of the culture of denial: drawing on the theories of Social-Darwinist ideologues who decreed that cultural identity was a question of race and blood quantum, the state instituted a form of cultural genocide that decreed that mixed Aboriginal survivors were half-castes, or a hybrid people with no history, no culture, and no future apart from total assimilation into mainstream Tasmanian society and culture.[54]

Moral unease about the Aboriginal past was evident from the 1820s. Despite notable efforts to erase it by Arthur's Aborigines Committee in 1830 and John West in 1852, the unease persisted. Historians James Bonwick in the late nineteenth century and Clive Turnbull in the 1940s gave the unease public expression, as did the publication of Robinson's journals in the 1960s and 1970s. Others confided to their journals. In 1977, Bronwyn Desailly completed an important but unpublished thesis called

The Mechanics of Genocide, but it was not until the early 1980s, with the birth of the modern Tasmanian Aboriginal political movement and the publication of histories by Lyndall Ryan and Henry Reynolds, that a wider willingness to confront the unease took root. The outcome was a series of divisive public debates that culminated in the official recognition of modern Aboriginal identity, the return of stolen human remains, the transfer of a series of significant places to Aboriginal community ownership, and an apology (in 1997) and financial compensation (2006) for the forced removal in the twentieth century of Aboriginal children from their families.[55]

Given these developments, and the emergence of genocide scholarship in Europe, it was perhaps only a matter of time before the myth of extinction would be portrayed as the reality of genocide. On February 28, 1999, the then–Tasmanian premier Jim Bacon officially passed ownership of Wybalenna to the Aboriginal community. At the official ceremony Bacon acknowledged that Tasmanian Aborigines were both victims and survivors of genocide. With a background in 1970s student radicalism associated with the American war in Vietnam and radical trade-unionism in the 1980s, Bacon was particularly amenable to the use of the term genocide. Curiously, the official use of the term generated no controversy. Its use was inspired not by Australian historians, however, but by Aboriginal activists with access to Bacon.[56]

Conclusions

For Raphael Lemkin, colonial genocide was a historical process that involved the destruction by an invader of the foundations of life and the subsequent extermination of the colonized. The codification by the United Nations of genocide as a twentieth-century crime provided the legal means whereby the perpetrators of the Nazi genocide could be brought to justice. There is a clear distinction here between a colonial genocide as Lemkin defined it and the crime of genocide as later defined by the United Nations. Codification does not mean that colonial genocides did not occur, or that colonial genocides should be called something else.[57]

A colonial genocide refers to both process and outcome: the indisputable fact is that Tasmanian Aborigines all but disappeared as a direct result of colonial occupation by the British. They disappeared as the result of an accretion of actions, some of which were clearly crimes, including the abduction of their women and children, the killing of Aboriginal men by colonists, convicts, and the military, and a war of extermination sanctioned by the colonial governor but which Colonial

Secretary Sir George Murray and a small number of colonists regarded as organized murder. In a more general sense, the Tasmanians disappeared as a result of the invasion of their country, the seizure of their hunting grounds, and the capture and exile of survivors. Invasion, land seizures, and exile may or may not be crimes, but they were key instruments in the near-total disappearance of the Tasmanians.

It seems trite to say this, but historians are not lawyers:, they do not operate in courts of law. It is not the role of historians to prove or disprove guilt according to the legal definition of a crime. Historians commonly infer motive and intent from what was said and what was done, or not done. The intent to take Aboriginal land is beyond dispute. The intent to protect colonists and their property from Aboriginal resistors is beyond dispute. It is one thing for governors to issue proclamations decrying the destruction of Aborigines, and entirely another another to fail to take adequate measures to protect Aborigines, or fail to prosecute offenders, or to continue granting large swathes of Aboriginal hunting grounds to the rising tide of land-hungry colonists, or to sanction the use of force against resisting Aborigines.

The insistence that unambiguous intent to exterminate must exist for genocide to occur rests on a narrow legalistic definition of genocide. It also fails to take into account the fact that at the time of the colonization of Aboriginal Tasmania, the exterminatory impact of colonization was well known in official and intellectual circles in Britain. Western writers from the time of Herodotus had criticized the morality of colonization because of the impact on the colonized. There can be little doubt the British government intended to take Aboriginal land fully aware of the likely outcome.[58]

If a government knows that the likely outcome of a particular action will be catastrophic for those affected by the action, yet goes ahead and performs that action, is that government responsible for the outcome? Where does that scenario leave the question of intent? Is it enough to say that the governors did their best, but circumstances conspired against them? Is it enough to assert that the removal of the foundations of life and the extermination of Tasmanian Aborigines was not a colonial genocide, but an unfortunate consequence of the march of history? As long as a narrow legal framework is preferred, the Tasmanian genocide will remain in dispute and the haunting it generated will persist.

Chapter 5

Tibet
A Neo-Colonial Genocide

Claude Levenson

In the aftermath of the unexpected eruptions of 2008, Tibet burst upon the world stage like never before. Once viewed as a remote land of exotica, evocative of the mythical Shangri-la, this ancient Buddhist kingdom is now widely perceived as the exemplary victim of Chinese oppression. It enters our consciousness in a variety of ways, through the media as well as through public demonstrations of sympathy for the plight of its people. Long-time human rights activists have even joined hands with Hollywood stars and film crews to give increasing visibility to the Tibetans' call for resistance, symbolized by the aura of the Dalai Lama, a figure of courage and serenity who attracts and fascinates tens of thousands beyond his Buddhist devotees.

And yet, for all this welter of media attention, the story of Tibet's brutal encounter with Chinese imperialism is largely ignored. Our aim here is to shed light on this tragic chapter in the history of Chinese-Tibetan relations, and place it in the perspective of the conceptual issues raised in this book. In the current lexicon of human rights violations, what labels can one affix to this human drama? What are the roots of the Tibetan revolt? What does it tell us about Communist China's stance in dealing with the rights of minorities? And above all, are Tibet and Tibetans a "minority," or just a people with its own history, territory, past, and—why not—future? But before turning to these questions, let us take a closer look at recent events and try to place them in proper historical perspective.

China's reaction to the protests gives us a sense of the extreme tension prevailing in Lhasa, the capital, and beyond. The whole of Tibet, that is, the so-called Tibetan Autonomous Region (TAR), as well as the historical provinces of Kham and the Amdo on the southern borders of Gansu, Sichuan, and Qinghai, was again closed to foreigners for some months in 2009, notwithstanding official claims that calm reigned in the "Roof of the World." In the wake of the sudden protests of 2008, and as a warning, seventy-six "agitators against public order," which included nine Buddhist monks from Samye, the oldest Tibetan monastery, were given stiff prison sentences. As a gesture of magnanimity, just before Losar, the Tibetan New Year, a few pitiful-looking prisoners were released for fear they might die in custody. Tibetans in rural zones were forced to "participate" in the New Year festivities under threat of being punished if refusing to do so. Adding insult to injury, March 28 was formally declared a holiday to remember "the day of the liberation of the serfs." Meanwhile a heavy military presence could be noticed around such monasteries as Labrang in Amdo, the Jokhang in Lhasa, and others. Close to one thousand "preventive arrests" were made, accompanied by warnings and threats. To describe this situation as merely an area "under control," as claimed by Chinese propaganda, is a singularly inappropriate understatement.

Half a century after the historic 1959 Lhasa uprising, marked by the shelling of the Dalai Lamas's Summer palace and his flight to India, the Tibetans made dramatically clear their resistance to Chinese invasion and colonization. Estimates of the 1959 death toll vary between two thousand and ten thousand. As many as four thousand were taken prisoner. Faced with unrelenting repression during much of 1960, tens of thousands sought refuge in India and Nepal. Meanwhile Chinese penetration went hand in hand with sustained efforts at acculturation, aimed at a radical transformation of Tibetan society.

What happened in the wake of the Chinese invasion of 1950 can only be described as a systematic attempt to thoroughly sinicize a society whose language, religion, and political organization were, and continue to be, strikingly different from their hegemonic neighbor's. The peak of China's assimilationist thrust occurred shortly before the Cultural Revolution, in 1964, when the Panchen Lama (the most senior hierarch after the Dalai Lama in their Gelug-pa school) was labeled "an enemy of the people, of the Party, and of Socialism," and then imprisoned, only to be released in 1978. The thoroughgoing cultural assault mounted in the name of the revolution is aptly captured by the Panchen Lama when he recalled: "Before democratic reform, there were more than 2,500 large, medium, and small monasteries in Tibet. After democratic reform, only 70-odd monasteries were kept in existence by the government. This was a reduction of more than 97 percent. . . . In the whole of Tibet in the past there was a total of about 110,000 monks and nuns. . . . After democratic reform was completed, the number of monks and nuns living in the monasteries was about 7,000 people, which is a reduction of 93 percent." Some pages later, he states, "Once a nationality's language, costume, customs, and other important characteristics have disappeared, then the nationality itself has disappeared, too. That is to say, it has turned into another nationality."[1]

In his study published in 2010, Warren W. Smith, Jr., notes,

> Chinese depictions of the events of March 1959 are similarly distorted for propaganda purposes. Contrary to China's claims, the Tibetan revolt was not a 'revolt of serf owners' who were against reforms. In Central Tibet, the reform program had been postponed by Mao in 1957; therefore, the serf owners had no reason to revolt at that particular time. . . . Tibetans of all classes were in open revolt at that time, but against China, the revolt having begun in 1956 in eastern Tibetan areas outside the future TAR due to the imposition of democratic reforms, which for most Tibetans was their first experience of manifest Chinese control over their lives. The revolt spread to Central Tibet in late 1958 and early 1959 and culminated in an open rejection of Chinese rule by the citizens of Lhasa beginning on 10 March.[2]

The Tibetan Paradox

Viewed in historical perspective, there is a profound anomaly in the timing of the Chinese colonial thrust into Tibet. Under the post–World War II pressures of East-West rivalries, just as colonial empires were disintegrating and granting independence to new states, Tibet was about to be subjected to a foreign yoke, as if to give the lie to a relentless global historic trend. The yoke in this case proved exceptionally burdensome, accompanied by such far-reaching transformations of Tibetan culture and traditions as to evoke the vision of a genocidal enterprise.

So many received ideas, phantasms, and lost illusions seem to be floating above the "Roof of the World," not to mention sheer ignorance, that it seems somewhat incongruous or ill-advised to place Tibet under the rubric of twentieth-century genocides. Only recently have commentators begun to take the full measure of the drama unfolding in the heights of the Himalayas, so remote from our day-to-day concerns, so carefully sheltered from the prying eyes of foreign observers. It is important, therefore, to give further attention to some of the fundamental events and circumstances at the root of the present crisis.

Without going back to the meandering complexities of their historic relationship, let us recognize at the outset that China and Tibet have their own interpretations of the same historical facts—and these are totally at odds with each other. Suffice it to note that amid the wide-ranging international upheavals that followed World War II, the invasion of Tibet by Communist China went almost unnoticed. Soon after staking out his territorial claims to Tibet, Mao Zedong planned his next move, dispatching tens of thousands of "volunteers" to the Korean theater. In view of the magnitude of international interests at stake in the Korean War, it is hardly surprising that the Tibetans ended up being the victims of this wider confrontation. Although Tibet's religious and temporal leader, the youthful fourteenth Dalai Lama, felt he had no other choice but to turn to the UN to help him restore his kingdom's sovereignty, his appeals, predictably, went unheeded.

Thus, even though the total death toll, and it was considerable, is impossible to assess, the net result of the Chinese invasion has been the forced annexation of a country whose status according to conventional international norms was that of an independent state. Described by the new rulers in Beijing as a "feudal, barbarian theocracy peacefully liberated from imperialist influences," Tibet nevertheless claimed international boundaries, vague though they were in some places, that had been defined by way of a treaty with the British Crown when it still held sway over its Indian Empire.

The Tibetans have a language of their own, from the Tibeto-Burmese language family and hence different from Chinese, as well as their own alphabet, not ideograms. They identify themselves with a centuries-old ancestral culture in a well-delimited territory with little in common with China's, and take pride in the historical legacy of an efficient civil service capable of levying taxes and administering far-flung provinces, their regional specificities and rivalries notwithstanding, and a functioning transportation and communications grid to meet the needs of the state. Last, but not least, they could boast of a valiant though poorly equipped national army, a flag recognized by the community of nations, a national anthem, a national calendar, and a national currency (in use until 1959), all of which are part of the conventional criteria for assessing a state's claims to independent nationhood.

The argument receives additional support from a recently declassified Canadian source dating back to November 1950. In it Canada's Department of Foreign Affairs registered the legal opinion of one of its experts as follows: "On the basis of facts brought to our attention, Chinese suzerainty is nothing but a mere legal fiction. In the course of the last 40 years Tibet has controlled its own domestic and foreign affairs. In light of this situation I am of the opinion that from the standpoint of international law Tibet qualifies to be recognized as an independent State." [3] At about the same time Canada's High Commissioner to India noted: "If Tibet really belonged to China there would be no need to send in an army to conquer it. Dispatching an army is sufficient proof that we are not dealing here with a domestic issue."[4]

Invasion and Colonization

Though vastly superior in military capacity, the Chinese People's Army (CPA) was put to a strenuous test before finally claiming an inglorious victory. As well as the courageous resistance of Tibetan troops, perhaps the biggest challenge faced by the Chinese stemmed from the daunting obstacles of the Himalayan environment. Effective occupation of Tibet was a long, drawn-out process, involving a slow but methodical introduction of an imported administrative grid and a partial dismemberment of its territory: the eastern frontier territories of Greater Tibet, areas formerly known as Kham and Amdo, were forcefully integrated into neighboring Chinese provinces and given Chinese names as if to blur in one fell swoop the boundaries of history and memory. It is worth noting in this regard that it is precisely in such supposedly well-integrated regions that the wave of widespread protests arose in March/April 2008, to the utmost surprise of Chinese authorities.

The first stage in this process of Chinese imperial expansion was a slow transfer of adversaries real or so-labeled, to reeducation and labor camps, the so-called *laogai*, followed by the appropriation of lands previously owned by Tibetans, including monasteries and large and small land holdings, and the creation of collective farms paving the way for the settlement of traditionally nomadic populations. These are crucial elements behind the 1959 anti-Chinese popular uprising that signaled the beginning of a major Tibetan exodus in the wake of the Dalai Lama's flight to exile. What happened next is an all too familiar tale of woe, beginning with the destructive aberrations of the Cultural Revolution (1966–76) after the creation of the so-called TAR, the development of a frenetic urbanization under the guise of modernization, accompanied by the mass migration of Han populations toward the Tibetan high plateau, a phenomenon encouraged by the so-called "Western Development Program" launched at the turn of the twenty-first century and consecrated by the inauguration on June 1, 2006, of the first railroad connection between Beijing and Lhasa. Extensions of the rail network to other Tibetan cities and eventually Nepal and India are anticipated. The net result of all this has been a dramatic reversal of demographic distribution, with the Chinese settlers becoming a majority and the Tibetans a minority in their own land.

A most revealing event happened in 1959, the real meaning and significance of which went almost unnoticed at the time. This was the Lhasa Revolt, clearly aimed at the Chinese occupiers, which was quelled in a pool of blood. A year after the Hungarian uprising and ten years before its even more violent replay in Prague, both of which were symptomatic of the rising tide of resentment against Soviet-imposed regimes, much the same phenomenon occurred in the Tibetan capital. The aim was to protect the Dalai Lama, because Tibetans were afraid with good reason of an invitation they interpreted as a kidnapping in disguise. They also sought to expand the scope of resistance against the ruthless imposition of Chinese rule in the eastern regions of Kham and Ando.

Brutally suppressed, the Lhasa revolt led to the flight to exile of the Dalai Lama, soon followed by the unprecedented exodus of some 100,000 Tibetans. Most of them settled in India, but others also found refuge in Nepal, Bhutan, Western Europe (mainly Switzerland and UK), and more recently in the United States and Canada, as well as Australia and New Zealand. The total number of Tibetan exiles is estimated at 180,000, but the majority are not recognized as bona fide refugees and are therefore facing countless administrative complications. If the presence of a large number of Tibetans in India is a source of friction with Beijing, and more recently between Nepal and China, one might add that the Chinese invasion of Tibet lies at the root of the as-yet-unresolved border conflict between India and China. One may note parenthetically that by 1962 the tracing of the Sino-Indian border was already a major subject of discord; it was the central issue behind the brief armed confrontation between the two, and this at a time when Washington and Moscow were edging closer to the potential abyss of the Cuban missile crisis. Could this be the reason why this short-lived though bloody conflict barely attracted the attention of the international community, who thus failed to grasp the symbolic significance or understanding of the Tibetan tragedy?

It was shortly after the 1959 flight to exile of the Dalai Lama that the International Commission of Jurists (ICJ)[5] concluded its investigations and for the first time used the term "genocide" in connection with Tibet. Based on historical fact and the testimonies of refugees interviewed in transit camps, in two major reports published in 1959 and 1960, the ICJ reached the conclusion that the Chinese government had failed to meet its obligations under the terms of the "Seventeen Points Agreement," also known as the "peaceful liberation of Tibet accord." More specifically, it drew attention to the systematic violations of the human rights and liberties of the people of Tibet, including massacres, ethnic cleansings, and other criminal transgressions likely to cause their extinction as a national and religious community. One may wonder, parenthetically, why such an accord was necessary if, as the Chinese claim, Tibet had for centuries been an integral part of China. Be that as it may, by way of counterargument to the ICJ position some might question the relevance of the G-word in this context on the grounds that it carries specific connotations, including that of intentionality, that may appear to be missing from the case at hand.

Such considerations must seem distressingly academic to the victim group, assuming they ever reached their ears. Indeed, they may soon become irrelevant when one reflects on the rate at which the Chinese are pushing the assimilation of Tibet and appropriating its culture and its resources in the name of modernization. Nonetheless, some facts die hard. As a result of the social dislocations brought about by the military occupation of the 1950s, Tibet experienced its first famine in history. From 1950 to 1959, out of a total population of six million, more than one million Tibetans perished in one way or another in the wake of the Chinese invasion. Some 6,000 monasteries, oratories, and other religious buildings were destroyed during the so-called Cultural Revolution. Entire libraries were ransacked, looted, wiped off the face of the earth, along with ancient manuscripts and other irreplaceable items. Priceless works of art were torn to pieces, lost forever. Potentially adaptable age-old institutions were sent to the dustbin of history and replaced by imported ones based on the dominant metropolitan model. In brief, in addition to causing untold deaths among Tibetans, the Chinese occupation led to the extinction of an entire way of life revolving around ancestral village communities and their religious symbols.

In most cases when one opens such ticklish dossiers, counting the victims is wishful thinking. Figures are contradictory, difficult to check. Who was present on the killing grounds to count the dead? Murderers rarely bother to keep count of their victims. And there is the predictable alibi, in such cases, that perpetrators were merely obeying orders from above. With perhaps a single exception, at first the heads of Auschwitz meticulously tattooed the date of arrival of the victims on their arms and registered their date of death. By the end of 1942, the magnitude of the task made them give up this grisly bookkeeping. And, later, before the final debacle, they tried to hide their crimes by setting fire to the gas chambers. As for what some refer to as "the numbers game," at what level of bloodshed do killings turn into a massacre, mass murder, crimes against humanity, or genocide? Exact figures are nowhere to be found, only educated guesses, and even these are subject to controversy.

As in many other cases in this book, estimates of the number of Tibetan victims is a matter of guesswork. According to Tibetan authorities in exile, more than one million died after the 1959 Chinese invasion. Early resistance and guerilla actions cost the lives of 423,000;

350,000 died from famine or exhaustion; 73,200 in prisons and forced labor camps; almost 100,000 under torture; more than 150,000 were executed; and there were some 9,000 suicides. These estimates, based on individual testimonies, have been made available by the Information Bureau of the Tibetan (IBT) Administration in Exile at the beginning of the 1980s. The first IBT report in 1959 was based on research and interviews of the first wave of refugees, and did not hesitate to denounce ill-treatment in prisons, parodies of judgment, summary executions, and sterilization and forced abortions for women, as well as segregation against Tibetans that has been likened to apartheid.

Measures aiming to lower the Tibetan birthrate have been docu-mented over the years, especially since 1980. Campaigns of mass sterili-zation, regularly carried out by mobile medical teams even in the villages, have never ceased; as for abortions, according to witnesses, they are performed by lethal injection until the very last months of preg-nancy. Uncooperative women may be heavily fined or sometimes jailed. After extensive field research and on the strength of many interviews with Tibetans, Blake Kerr, a medical doctor and author of *Sky Burial*,[6] concluded, "I do not know if China is committing genocide in Tibet, but I am convinced that China's politics of family planning and the colo-nization of Tibet is having a genocidal effect on Tibetans."

Some sixty years after the military invasion, it is worth recalling some of the less well known stages in the process of annexation. After the people's revolt in Lhasa in 1959, the official message was no longer about a "peaceful liberation of Tibet from foreign imperialist influ-ence," but of the "liberation of millions of slaves from the bondage of theocratic feudalism." A short respite and a hope of timid liberalization loomed on the horizon with the May 1990 visit to Tibet of Hu Yao Bang, then-secretary of the Chinese Communist Party. Amazed by the poverty, misery, and tense relations between Tibetans and Chinese he found on the spot, the communist leader exclaimed, "This is pure colonialism!" going so far as to apologize to the Tibetans. The remedial measures proved ephemeral. After Deng Xiao-Ping took over in the 1980s, the mass transfer of Han and Hui (Chinese Muslim) populations to Tibet began in earnest, a harbinger of more to come.

At the time, the Dalai Lama stated that "a Chinese version of the final solution is rampant in Tibet," but his words were not heard. At the end of the 1980s, recurring troubles and a brutal crackdown provided the context for the rise to eminence of Hu Jintao, nicknamed the "Butcher of Lhasa" because of the brutality of his repressive policy. Reassigned to Beijing in 1989, Hu was superseded by Chen Kuei Yuan, who did not hesitate to publicly declare his aim to "wipe out Tibetan identity" through an accelerated policy of sinicization. From now on Tibetans were expected to "develop a Chinese identity." With this goal in mind, religion became a favorite target of power. Besides "systematic reeducation campaigns" in the monasteries, Buddhism was now officially declared "seditious" and openly identified with "separatism."

Since then this trend, camouflaged as modernization and the opening of Tibet to the outside world, has only accelerated, adding to the frustrations of the Tibetans. This is all the more ironic when one considers that the white paper published in 2004 by the Information Bureau of the State Council of the People's Republic of China states that, by law, "the Tibetan people enjoy an equal right to take part in the administration of State affairs as well as the right to govern themselves on affairs concerning their own region and ethnic group." The paper came to the unsurprising conclusion that "without the prosperity and the development of Tibet, the complete modernization of China and the great regeneration of the Chinese people cannot be attained." That Tibetans were not convinced became dramatically clear with the outburst of popular protests of March/April 2008. When asked to comment on these events at a press conference held in Dharamsala on March 26, 2008, the Dalai Lama went straight to the core issue: "Whether or not the Chinese government admits it, there is a Tibetan problem. An age-old cultural heritage faces a serious danger. Intentional or not, a form of cultural genocide is taking place in Tibet."

Within Tibet, colonization is pursued relentlessly, with an iron fist. The so-called Tibetan Autonomous Region, as well as the Tibetan districts and counties now incorporated into neighboring Chinese provinces, remains out of bounds, or under strict official control that rules out all possibilities of independent inquiry. Even the UN High Commissioner for Human Rights was refused a request for entry after the 2008 uprisings, and the handful of journalists who managed to get in were closely monitored or, for a few, just happened to slip through the net. Meanwhile population transfers continue, along with the systematic exploitation of natural resources (water, minerals, forests) with utter disdain for both the environment and the repercussions that brutal changes will have on the life of nomads now forced to become settlers. The same is true for those peasants who have no choice but to abandon their meager landholdings to look for jobs in the slums mushrooming around the mines and construction sites, grim testimonies of a relentless push to expand the economy. In a new essay published in March 2009,[7] Zhu Rui writes, "the Chinese government has not only destroyed thousands of centuries-old Buddhist monasteries and interfered in their practices, it is now causing rampant destruction to Tibet's fragile eco-system, thereby endangering the very fiber of the Tibetan people's traditional and cultural way of life. China's irresponsible actions in Tibet are silently but quickly eroding the Tibetan people's rich cultural values."

The destruction of an already precarious environmental balance is gathering momentum through urbanization policies favoring the new Han and Hui settlers, to the detriment of the Tibetans. Meanwhile the multiplication of roads, dams, and airports, as well as the extension of railroads, helps consolidate the hold of the regime on the whole region. Unsurprisingly, Chinese authorities are utterly indifferent to the stipulations of the Geneva agreements that forbid such practices in an occupied country; their unshakable belief is that Tibet has always been, and remains to this day, an integral part of China. This forced modernization is accompanied by a constant repression of traditional religious practices; the same applies to expressions of discontent, including peaceful demonstrations. The overriding objective is a through and through sinicization by every possible means.

Thus, in 2008, the local authorities of Kardze, a Tibetan district of Sichuan, proposed a modification of the rules of family planning enforced for the Tibetan populations, reducing the number of children allowed from three to two for nomads, and from two to one for city dwellers. After mass sterilizations and abortions in the 1980s and 1990s, these rules are to be extended to the official TAR as well as the Tibetan enclaves of Gansu and Qinghai. Disregard for the new rules will be met by huge fines and prison terms. Particularly worth noting in the context of this discussion is Article 2 of the UN Genocide Convention that includes among acts of genocide "imposing measures intended to prevent births within the group" along with "forcibly transferring children of the group to another group." The same provisions were later incorporated in the statutes of the International Criminal Courts (ICC) for ex-Yugoslavia and Rwanda. Why should the case of Tibet be an exception?

The International Community: Ignorance or Indifference?

A combination of unfortunate circumstances contributed to Tibet's tragic fate in the middle of the twentieth century. To the military invasion that took by surprise a cloistered community too confident in the power of its spiritual protection must be added the inability or unwillingness of the international community to adopt and implement post–World War II issues of self-determination and democracy. Then, mention must be made of the dithering of the Indian government, all too absorbed by the prospect of imminent partition from Pakistan, the recovery of its national sovereignty, and the siren song of non-alignment and brotherly friendship with China, all these encouraged by an idealistic Indian prime minister, Jawaharlal Nehru. Last but not least was the inability of the West to properly grasp the significance of the crisis unfolding on China's doorstep.

Additional obstacles were raised in the following years, for example, the barrier imposed by Beijing's "Bamboo Curtain," the fascination exerted on many European intellectuals by the Maoist experience, and, with few notable exceptions, the lack of interest on the part of American scholars and policy wonks in distant horizons. Not until 1989, when the Dalai Lama was awarded the Nobel Peace Prize—in the wake of repeated protests in Lhasa from March 1987 through 1989, culminating with the tragic events in Tiananmen Square in June 1989—did it finally dawn on an inattentive public that a "Tibetan question" even existed. Although the Dalai Lama today enjoys unprecedented popularity in the West, notwithstanding evident qualms among some government leaders, he is more often than not received as a spiritual leader, which relegates to the sidelines his political role as the legitimate representative of his people. The political dimensions of his role were brought into sharp focus during the wave of popular protests across Tibet in 2008. All too often, however, concern in the West over commercial and economic interests has taken precedence over adherence to ethics and morality, human rights, and basic liberties. It is with reason that some have denounced as blatant hypocrisy the stance of those leaders who, while vaunting democracy, bow and scrape to the authoritarian and greedy regime of an increasingly powerful and vocal China.

Washington's attitude perfectly illustrates the two-faced policy of democratic nations, which in private often recognize the righteousness and legitimacy of the Tibetan cause, but shrink from translating their sympathies into concrete official commitments, lest these compromise their economic and financial interests with China. In 1995, a resolution of the U.S. Congress did recognize Tibet as "a sovereign nation under illegal occupation as regards international law, its legitimate representatives being the Dalai Lama and the Tibetan government in exile." Issued in 2001 and becoming law in September 2002, the Tibetan Policy Act created the post of Coordinator of Tibetan Affairs. Following the tradition of offering Tibet cold comfort, the U.S. Congress awarded the Dalai Lama its Gold Medal in 2007. President Obama's decision to postpone his meeting with the Tibetan leader in fall 2009, before his maiden trip to Beijing, was interpreted by the Chinese leadership not as a goodwill gesture, but as a sign of weakness, and the subsequent reception of the Dalai Lama at the White House some weeks later left a mostly sour taste in the mouths of most commentators. Of course, a White House spokes-man reiterated the U.S. commitment to "protect and save Tibetan cul-ture," but how to do that remains problematic considering that the Tibetan people are living under martial law that dares not say its name, and that most of the "Free World" leaders set far greater store in the current financial crisis than in their own principles and commitments.

What next? Although the Dalai Lama on various occasions has been received with full honors in Strasbourg and Brussels, the European Par-liament (EP) has done little more than engage in the harmless ritual of a "constructive dialog" with Beijing. Once all is said and done, the implementation of the few resolutions adopted by the EP depends on the political will of member states that do not care to irritate the thin-skinned Chinese. Thus, a 2000 resolution, seeking European recogni-tion within three years of the Tibetan government in exile as the sole representative of the Tibetan people should no authentic dialog start between the Chinese government and the leadership in exile, still waits in the wings. While there have been some attempts to engage in inter-mittent discussions, especially before the Beijing Olympics, the manifest absence of political will on the part of the Chinese regime to tackle the question makes it unlikely that the deadlock will be broken any time soon. Yet the events of 2008 make plain how urgent is the need for a negotiated solution, if Beijing really intends to ensure "stability in a harmonious society" for the country.[8]

There is no gainsaying the lack of a political will to promote demo-cratic principles, but this is no reason to underestimate the efforts of many associations throughout the world in support of the Tibetan cause, or to ignore the determination of the Tibetan people to make their voices heard. There is no lack of defenders of human justice willing to carry on the fight. Undeterred by the exceedingly cautious attitude of the International Court of Justice (ICJ) and the ICC, and taking into account the conclusions of three reports by the ICJ and the advice of top international jurists who looked into the case of Tibet, the Audiencia Nacional de España (Spanish Supreme Court or ANE) under the princi-ple of universal jurisdiction that it claims, took up the torch. In January 2006, the ANE decided to examine the dossier on the "Tibetan geno-cide,"[9] including documents and testimony of Spanish citizens of Tibetan origin against several high Chinese Communist officials, now retired. Further information was added to this dossier concerning con-firmed cases of torture leading to death between 1998 and 2004. The court also agreed to investigate crimes against humanity committed after the Chinese announced the entire country was off limits and Tibet was put under military rule. The case was eventually dismissed, however, after passage of a Spanish law, adopted under Chinese pressure, aimed at "preserving higher national interests," but whose national interests seems purposively obscure. Several inquiry commissions were sent out and justice seemed to follow its course in the first case despite numerous attempts to stop it by outside international institutions linked to the United Nations organization, itself subject to policy struggles between the major players and smaller nations and the interests dictated by changing alliances.

From Oblivion to Memory

As years go by, the Tibetan community in exile fights to keep alive a memory that is slowly fading in its own country. The elders, who knew Tibet before the invasion, become fewer and fewer; those who fought against the invader and for liberty are resentful of the international community's indifference or lack of understanding of their trials and sacrifices. The younger generation is adjusting to the loss of a "mythical" country and a modernization in which they want a share. For those who live through the usurpation, it is hard for them to define their future as they waver among a longing for independence, hope of an eventual return to a country liberated from foreign occupation, or, in the face of the globalization, acknowledge a new world run by cynicism and cash. They know that the Chinese vise is tightening and their ancestral culture, insidiously transformed into mere folklore, faces extinction.

Sacrificed on the altar of Western interests, Tibet agonizes under the unyielding Chinese yoke. Its inhabitants try to tread the hard path of nonviolent passive resistance, fighting inch by inch to preserve the founding values of their Buddhist civilization. Like many other people and communities that no longer have a voice in shaping their own future, the Tibetans have no choice but to bow to their oppressors. The problem is no doubt political, and this is where a solution must be found. The G-word has lost none of its pertinence in the context of calls for justice. There is a crying need to recognize genocide for what it is, and therefore insist that the voice of justice be heard in seeking redress and retribution, after which it will be up to the interested parties themselves to begin to discuss, with mutual respect for each other's feelings, restitution and compensation in order to make some sense of and reparation for the trauma, the wounds to be healed, and the strength to share the memory so that their descendants need not wonder whether fighting for cultural and national survival was worthwhile.

In his reexamination of the dynamics of mass murder, Jacques Sémelin writes: "To differentiate among mass murders may seem indecent. Yet it is important to understand and judge. Although the emotion caused by atrocities numbs the mind, . . . we need to go further." He goes on to note that "there are two forms of destruction. Destruction in order to cause submission: it is a political logic. Destruction to eradicate: it is a genocidal logic."[10] To a question posed by this writer in the course of a brief conversation in 2008, Sémelin gave a straightforward answer: "What's going on in Tibet in my opinion belongs to the second category."

Can one translate into words the unspeakable atrocities the Tibetans have undergone? In the present circumstances, at a time when the Chinese become infuriated the moment the question of Tibet is raised, who is willing to listen to Tibetans' grievances? Like many other voiceless victims of inhumane policies, the people of Tibet may have been listened to, but their voices have never been truly heard. Can such experiences be expressed and passed on? Even more, Tibetans don't call for revenge. The way they see the world does not meet our usual criteria because what they ask is primarily for justice and for respect of their inalienable right to self-determination and also for the right to live free in a society they want to build for themselves, and in accord with the interests and aspirations that they themselves have chosen. According to Robert D. Sloane,[11] "There is a principle widely recognized in the twentieth century that an illegal occupation cannot end the sovereignty of a State." One remembers the cases of Poland, rebuilt after World War II; of the Baltic States or Central Asia after the USSR's implosion; or again even East Timor after it was temporarily annexed by Indonesia.

Genocide, Ethnocide, or War Crimes?

"One wonders whether there is a more cruel way for a people to die than to be robbed of their culture, their roots, their values, thus killing their very identity." L. V. Thomas's words[12] resonate powerfully in the context of this discussion. As one who has kept a close watch on the situation on the Roof of the World over a period of years, I cannot help wondering what words to use to convey the plight of the Tibetans. Genocide, ethnocide, genocidal massacres, mass murder, crimes against humanity—all the above figure prominently in the lexicon of contemporary horrors, yet their meanings change over time, and so do the interests of those who use them. Strangely, many tend to instinctively back away from such terms because of the sense of revulsion they inspire in us, and because of the haziness inherent in such elusive down notions.

Since we are the prisoners of language to both communicate and to comprehend, let us first try to further elucidate the meaning of one crucial word, genocide. This is a relatively new word, coined by Raphael

Lemkin,[13] an American jurist of Polish descent, to put a name to what Churchill had called "a crime without a name," that is, the wartime massacres perpetrated by Nazi Germany, which is, in the words of the Lemkin-inspired 1948 UN Convention on Genocide, "The systematic extermination, in whole or in part, of a national, ethnic, or religious human group." The planned destruction of a culturally defined human community is indeed the touchstone of genocide. Unfortunately, it appears to be the essence of Chinese policy in Tibet.

Chapter 6

The Anfal Campaign Against the Kurds
Chemical Weapons in the Service of Mass Murder

Choman Hardi

> I will kill them all with chemical weapons! Who is going to say anything? The international community? Fuck them!—the international community and those who listen to them. . . . I will not attack them with chemicals just one day, but I will continue to attack them with chemicals for fifteen days. . . . Then you will see that all the vehicles of Allah himself will not suffice to carry them all.
> —Ali Hassan Al-Majid (dubbed Ali Kimiyawi or "Chemical Ali")

This is how the architect of Anfal, the notorious "Chemical Ali," in a speech to the directors of the Ba'ath Party headquarters of the northern governorates in 1987, foretold the mass extermination soon to be visited upon the Kurds in northern Iraq.[1]

Arcane as it may seem to readers unfamiliar with the case at hand, for most Kurds within and outside Iraq the term "Anfal" is evocative of one of the worst human rights violations ever committed by Saddam. The word itself, meaning "spoils" in Arabic, is borrowed from the eighth *sura* of the Quran. It describes the revelation made to the prophet in the wake of his first jihad against nonbelievers: "He that defies God and His apostle shall be sternly punished by God. We said to them 'Taste this. The scourge of the Fire awaits unbelievers.'"[2]

In this context it refers to a scourge unleashed by Saddam through a series of eight military offensives during the last year of the Iraq-Iran war, which lasted from September 1980 to August 1988. The slaughter of civilians went on for two weeks after the signature of the peace treaty. The resulting extensive dislocation of the rural society was the price paid by the Kurds for Saddam's decision to use all means, including chemical weapons, to bring Iraq's borders with Iran and Turkey and the nearby areas under his unfettered control.

This border region, home to thousands of farming communities, is where Kurdish resistance to Saddam's dictatorship was most active. It is no coincidence that this region became the principal target of his vicious repression. Anfal brought utter devastation to the area—buildings were razed to the ground, water sources concreted over, animals killed, farm machinery and personal belongings looted.

Although reliable statistics are difficult to find, it is estimated that some 2,600 villages were destroyed[3] and between 50,000 and 100,000 civilians ended up in mass graves.[4] Many more civilians died as a result of the shelling and gas attacks, from the inhuman conditions in the prison camps, and during their flight to Iran and Turkey. The majority of the men were summarily executed within days of their capture. Countless women and children were also executed while others, including the elderly, were released during the general amnesty in September 1988. They were forcibly relocated to housing complexes on the main highways and were left to fend for themselves without any means of support.

Anfal has become a synonym for Kurdish victimhood in Iraq. It stands as the emblematic reminder of the countless atrocities they suffered at the hands of the Iraqi dictator. Anfal is also the ever-present legitimizing symbol for formulating demands for political independence. In Iraqi Kurdistan, the term is now being used as a verb. Those who disappeared are said to have been "Anfalized." The term has entered common usage and is now applied to many other instances of mass disappearance.[5]

Why Anfal Has Nearly Fallen into Oblivion

Rare are those students of genocide, outside Kurdistan, who remember Anfal for what it is—a case of mass murder by chemical weapons and mass executions committed at the peak of the Iran-Iraq war. In part this is because it is overshadowed in public attention by the dramatic events that followed in the wake of the 2003 invasion of Iraq, in part because it is all too often seen as a minor sideshow in the larger drama of the Iran-Iraq war.

This misperception is directly related to the efforts made by the U.S. government at the time to keep Anfal under wraps. The Reagan administration bears a major responsibility for downplaying the annihilation of the Kurds. This position was taken not for want of information about the extent of the tragedy, but because the United States, politically, economically, and militarily, was Saddam's closest ally in his war against Iran. No other figure in the Middle East seemed more threatening to U.S. interests than Ayatollah Khomeini, the embodiment of radical Islam and tireless critic of American policies. Viewed through the prism of realpolitik it made sense, therefore, for U.S. policy-makers to refrain from voicing criticisms of their Iraqi client, even if it meant looking the other way when confronted with irrefutable evidence of his crimes.

"Official knowledge, official silence," Samantha Power's terse phrasing captures the essence of the U.S. government's stance on Anfal.[6] Silencing the truth eventually led to denial, and denial to near oblivion. The Reagan administration's effort to thwart passage of the Senate's "Prevention of Genocide Act" was tantamount to denying the conclusion reached by Peter Galbraith in his 1988 report to the Senate Foreign Relations Committee. Galbraith states: "We knew of the systematic destruction of Kurdish villages, the targeting of cultural institutions and orchards, chemical weapons attacks against the Kurds, killings (both from chemical weapons and by execution), and refugee flows to Turkey in what appeared to be an act of genocide."[7] As Hiltermann notes, "the word 'genocide' acted as a red flag," and that "apparent stretching of the available information," he adds, "undermined support for the bill and provided ammunition for its detractors."[8] While the full extent of genocidal killings became available only after 1991, it was not until 1995 that the U.S. State Department finally recognized that these crimes could only be described as genocide.[9] By then, however, the Iran-Iraq war had lost much of its salience in public memory, and Anfal much of its resonance.

Furthermore, the war served the interests of the powerful farm lobby in the United States, a fact that helps explain the reluctance of the House of Representatives to support Galbraith's courageous initiative. "U.S. farmers," writes Samantha Power, "annually exported about 1 million tons of wheat to Iraq, as well as 25 percent of the overall U.S. rice output." She reports that at one point a staffer representing Senator John Breaux of Louisiana appeared before Galbraith "in tears and accused him of committing genocide against Louisiana rice growers"![10] This, along with the stakes held by U.S. and foreign companies in post-war reconstruction projects, estimated at $50,000 million, are a crucial element behind the silence of the international community.[11] Indeed, even before the end of the war Western firms were heavily involved in trade with Baghdad. According to one report, more than eighty German companies were involved in supplying Iraq with materials essential to its chemical and biological weapons program.[12] The U.S. supply came second with more than twenty companies providing non-nuclear build-ing parts, a fact all the more significant when one considers that some U.S. government officials held key positions in such companies. This could well be the reason why, after the Dujail trial, Saddam was swiftly executed for killing 148 Shiite civilians in 1982, well before the Anfal trials had come to an end.

Adding to the conspiracy of silence, few states in the West were willing to jeopardize their relationship with those Arab and Islamic countries that were supportive of, or in sympathy with, Iraq. According to Joost Hiltermann, during the early 1990s not a single state showed a willing-ness to use the UN as a tool to initiate legal proceedings against Sad-dam.[13] The assumption was that the dictator had been rendered harmless by the imposition of sanctions. Further attempts to bring geno-cide charges against him were generally seen as counterproductive.

Significant as they are, these are not the only factors behind the fail-ure of the U.S. media to give full exposure to the horrors of Anfal. For-eign journalists were systematically barred from travel to Kurdistan at the time the killings occurred. It was only after 1991 that they were allowed to visit the region. Finally, it is worth remembering that the circumstances leading to the bloodbath were inherently complicated, having to do as much with internal Kurdish politics as with the relations of Kurdistan to Iraq and its neighbor to the east. Making sense of the internal dynamics of Kurdish politics in relation to the Iran-Iraq war is by no means a simple exercise.

Harbingers of Disaster

This said, a number of gruesome events did receive considerable media attention before Anfal's atrocities emerged in full light. But these were rarely seen for what they were: warnings of potentially worse atrocities. The first major attack that attracted the world's attention to Anfal was the gassing of Halabja on March 16, 1988, a crime that Christopher Hitchens says "was for the Kurds what the Warsaw ghetto is to the Jews, or Guernica to the Basques, or Wounded Knee to the Sioux."[14]

Samantha Power calls it "a Kurdish Hiroshima."[15] She compares the scenes of death and devastation revealed in the wake of the attacks on Halabja to a "modern version of Pompeii," with the victims "frozen in time . . . some slumped a few yards behind a baby carriage, caught per-manently holding the hand of a loved one or shielding a child from the poisoned air, or calmly collapsed behind a car steering wheel." Not all victims died instantly; she writes, "some of those who had inhaled the chemicals continued to stumble around town, blinded by the gas, giggling uncontrollably, or, because their nerves were malfunctioning, buckling at the knees."[16]

Although this attack was launched during the first Anfal offensive (February 23–March 19) it was not part of the Anfal operation. Halabja was a town with a population of about 80,000 and it was not part of the region that the Iraqi government had declared "prohibited for security reasons." It was gassed in retaliation for its occupation by Kurdish fighters, assisted by Iranian soldiers, two days earlier. If Halabja did not go unnoticed in the media, it was because it was accessible to foreign journalists, being only fifteen miles from the Iranian border. Proximity to Iran also meant that Iranian television crews were able to film victims. These images were repeatedly shown by Iranian news media in their coverage of the war.

The second major crime was the final Anfal attack, from August 25 to September 6, 1988, which took place after the ceasefire of August 20 between Iraq and Iran. More than thirty villages were gassed during this attack, leading to a mass exodus of Kurds to Turkey. Unlike Iran, which was only too keen to expose Saddam's atrocities, Turkey acted as a complicit bystander. On September 3, the British government spoke of "grave concerns" about possible use of chemical weapons and asked Turkey for further information.[17] On September 9, 1988, the Turkish Foreign Ministry announced that it had "no evidence" that the Kurdish refugees were suffering from chemical weapons injuries.[18] Yet, following their visit to southeast Turkey in mid-September, members of the U.S. Senate Foreign Relations Committee reported "overwhelming evidence" that Iraq had used chemical weapons.[19]

On September 12, 1988, the United States, along with twelve other countries, asked the UN Secretary General to investigate the matter, but Iraq and Turkey denied access to the UN team.[20] The representative of the Turkish Foreign Ministry confirmed that Turkish medical experts had "found no trace" of chemical weapons. In this light, he argued, a UN investigation was unnecessary because it would "create a wrong impression that Turkish medical experts are inadequate to [conduct] related research."[21] Iraq, on the other hand, continuously denied these allegations and declared this to be an internal affair.

The full extent of destruction remained unclear until the March 1991 uprising in Iraqi Kurdistan. Iraq's defeat in the first Gulf War and America's encouragement of the people of Iraq to overthrow Saddam's regime triggered violent anti-regime insurrections among Shiites and Kurds. Although they would soon be crushed by Iraqi security forces, while these mass upheavals were going on, a number of local prisons and security and intelligence offices were ransacked by the insurgents. With the accord of the Patriotic Union of Kurdistan (PUK), and the assistance

of Human Rights Watch and the U.S. Senate Foreign Relations Committee, fourteen tons of Iraqi government documents were transferred to
the U.S. National Archives for "research and analysis."[22] These documents laid bare the full extent of Saddam's crimes, including the Anfal
campaign. A year later, an important first account was produced by the
Middle East branch of Human Rights Watch that was a full report of the
Iraqi state's conception, planning, and execution of genocide.[23]

Background to Anfal

The immediate reason for the slaughter is well established: it was meant
to punish the Kurds for the alliance of their resistance movement with
Iran during the war, but this just reveals a small fraction of the broader
historical forces at work in the region. Anfal was only the bloodiest episode in a movement for independence whose origins are traceable to
the incorporation of Kurdish populations into the new state of Iraq after
World War I.

The Kurds are a nation without a state; the creation of such a state
lies at the core of their political aspirations. For all the hopes raised by
the Treaty of Sèvres (1920), which briefly gave legitimacy to their
demands for statehood, the emergence of a Kurdish state remained a
distant objective. The reason for this lies in part in internal dissentions,
but even more crippling have been the geopolitical constraints on their
autonomy. "Time and again," writes Joost Hiltermann, "the Kurds have
faced the same set of questions: to accommodate or to rebel? To fight
for minority rights or for secession? To participate in Baghdad politics
or to retreat to mountain strongholds? . . . Invariably they would find
their quest for self-determination tempered by the bitter fact that, once
again, historical and geopolitical circumstances conspired to thwart
their aspirations."[24]

Armed dissidence is the leitmotiv that runs through much of the
history of the Iraqi Kurds, beginning with the Kurdish revolt of 1961.
Led by Mullah Mustafa Barzani, this revolt culminated in the 1970
accord with the new Ba'ath government, in power since 1968. The
"Autonomous Region" was to include all the areas of Iraq that a
planned census would determine as having a mainly Kurdish popula-
tion. This census, however, which would have determined the fate of
Kirkuk, was never carried out.[25] In the Algiers Treaty of 1975, when
Iraq struck a deal with Iran the Barzani revolution was crushed and a
unilateral accord was announced by the Iraqi government. The
"Autonomous Region" was to exclude the oil-rich areas of Kirkuk,
Khanaqeen, and Sinjar. The government intensified its Arabization

process in these regions. Kurdish civilians were deported to the Arab south or fled to the mountainous region and their homes were given to Arab settlers.

In 1976, the Kurdish opposition resumed its activities in the mountains. The various revolts, with considerable cost in human lives, failed to deliver independence for the Kurds in Iraq. This was partly due to the perennial struggle for power between the two leading figures of the independence movement, Jalal Talabani and Mullah Mustafa Barzani, identified respectively with the PUK and the Kurdistan Democratic Party (KDP).

The outbreak of the war with Iran, triggered by Saddam's decision to invade the predominantly Arab, oil-rich Iranian province of Khuzestan, at first did little to bridge the rift between the PUK and the KPD. How internal disputes interacted with external arenas is well described by Edgar O'Balance: "The Kurdish resistance pattern remained the same bizarre one in which Kurdish groups were fighting both as proxies and against each other. The Teheran government supported the Iraqi KDP, and perhaps also the PUK to a much lesser degree, in their struggle against the Baghdad government, while the Baghdad government was paying the Kurdistan Democratic Party of Iran [KDPI] to fight the Teheran one."[26] In this fluid environment, alliances waxed and waned depending on calculations of strategic advantage. At first Saddam tried to make concessions to the Kurds by engaging in negotiations with the PUK, whose initial stance in the Iraq-Iran conflict was neutral. The aim of Saddam was to buy time and to isolate the PUK from the rest of the Kurdish opposition movement, thereby stimulating conflict between the PUK and its rivals. Although an accord of sorts was apparently reached, its content was never made public.[27] By 1986, the negotiations had all but collapsed. Violent confrontations soon erupted between the Iraqi army and the Kurdish Revolutionary Army, also known as the *peshmarga.* Beginning in early 1987, Iraqi Kurdistan was subjected to continuous bombardment, accompanied by widespread destruction of villages and the deportation of rural inhabitants. The net result, predictably, was to hasten Talabani's decision to join hands with Iran.

In March 1987, a year after the breakdown of negotiations with the PUK, Ali Hassan Al-Majid, who came to be known as Chemical Ali, was appointed secretary general of the Northern Bureau, a position that gave him unlimited authority over the Kurdish region. Al-Majid issued a number of decrees and administrative orders designed to give the army and civil servants unfettered control over rural areas. In April 1987, less than one month after his appointment, Al-Majid ordered a poison gas attack on villages in the Balisan Valley. That attack caused major civilian causalities in Shekh Wasan, Balisan, Malakan, Totma, and other nearby villages. In the absence of outside intervention, and encouraged by the international community's silence, Chemical Ali was ready to unleash Anfal's fury.

His extreme brutality made the Kurdish parties realize that they needed to unite. Finally, in July 1987, they formed the Iraqi Kurdistan Front (IKF). With the radicalization of Iraq's military attacks, the Kurdish factions had agreed, in what turned out to be a suicidal move, to form close links with the Iranian government. While IKF's collaboration with Iran must be seen as the main reason behind Anfal, by the same token it gave the government an ideal pretext to solve the Kurdish problem once and for all.[28]

The Unfolding of Mass Murder

Anfal involved eight consecutive offensives in six geographical areas. The pattern was everywhere the same: first the gas attacks to kill and terrorize the victims; then came conventional bombings, followed by ground assaults that were launched from several fronts so as to corral the survivors through a single exit. The aim was to steer civilians toward certain collection points near main roads where they were met by the *jash* forces (Kurdish mercenaries who worked for the government) and the Iraqi army. After being transported to the temporary assembly points, they were divided into three main groups: the men and teenage boys, the women and their children, and the elderly.

The women were transferred to Dibis prison (in the Soran region) and Salamiya near Mosul (in the Badinan region). The elderly were taken to Nugra Salman on the border with Saudi Arabia. The men were stripped down to their *sharwal* (Kurdish baggy trousers) and vests. Their hands were tied and they were blindfolded, taken to mass graves, and executed. Six survivors, subsequently interviewed by Middle East Watch in 1991, told the same story: they had been brought before execution squads at night to be shot by the edge of empty pits.[29]

Abdul-Hassan Muhan Murad, one of the bulldozer drivers in charge of digging the mass graves, confirms that military convoys brought to their graves scores of bound and blindfolded men to the execution sites. In the cases Murad witnessed, eleven soldiers did the shooting. Each took out a blindfolded man and brought him to the edge of the grave and shot him, only to go back and seize another victim, until the vehicle was empty. Throughout the shooting, the bulldozer drivers and the drivers of the IFA trucks and other vehicles were told to keep their engines running to cover up the sound of screams; women and children were brought out in groups and shot indiscriminately.[30]

The first Anfal attack started with the siege of the Jaffati Valley where the headquarters of the PUK was based (see map). It took place between February 23 and March 19, 1988.[31] The valley is located in the mountainous region on the border with Iran. Until then, the harsh terrain had protected the so-called *peshmarga* militias from conventional military attacks, but the use of chemical weapons left them defenseless. The villages targeted for gas attacks were Yakhsamar, Sergelu, Bergelu, Haladin, Chokhmakh, Gwezeela, Chalawa, and the surrounding mountains. In the heat of the first Anfal attack, the PUK decided to open another front with the Iraqi government to deflect attention away from the Jaffati Valley. By mid-March, PUK forces, along with units from other Kurdish parties with support from Iranian forces, occupied Halabja. This catastrophic move led to the gassing of Halabja, in which an estimated 5,000 civilians died immediately; thousands of others have since died of cancer and other illnesses.

The *peshmarga* now realized they would not be able to hold their ground against the Iraqi army. In the midst of a harsh winter with mountain routes blocked by snow, they had to think of a way to protect civilians from destruction. Clearing a passage through the snow they escorted them to the border. Many died on the way, including eighty people who froze to death in the Kani Tu region while trying to cross into Iran.[32] Although the majority made it to safety, a few unfortunate ones were arrested in April on the border with Iran, where they had taken refuge. After hearing the rumor of an amnesty, others left Iranian refugee camps and surrendered to the Iraqi army. Predictably, they were all arrested and never heard from again.[33]

The second Anfal offensive, between March 22 and April 2, targeted the Qara Dagh region, where the villages of Jafaran, Belekjar, Sewsenan, Mesoyee, Serko, and the Qara Dagh Mountain were attacked with poison gas. Although orders came from higher up to hold the displaced villagers in special camps, the rounding up was "less systematic . . . compared to later stages of Anfal."[34] The majority of the Qara Dagh inhabitants fled north to Suleimanya and the housing complexes. Those who were arrested on the Qara Dagh-Suleimanya road were then taken to Suleimanya Emergency Forces (Tawari) where the men were separated from the women and each group trucked away to different destinations. During the April curfew, house-by-house searches were conducted in Suleimanya and outlying housing complexes. Many of the Qara Dagh inhabitants who had managed to escape were arrested and disappeared.

The *peshmarga*, accompanied by some civilians, retreated to the Germian region (the warm country) subsequently targeted by the third Anfal. This offensive took place from April 7 to 20. The vast flat plains

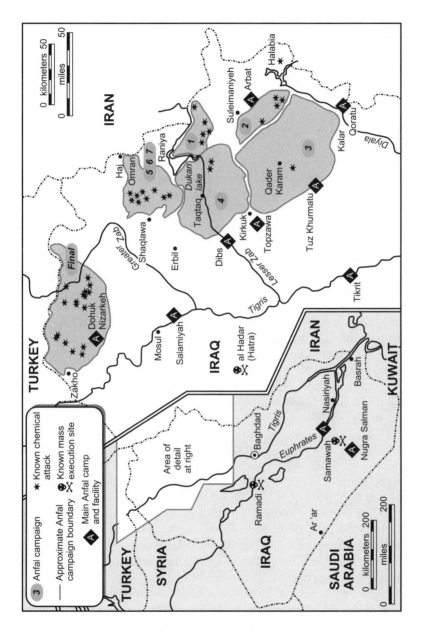

Figure 6.1. The Anfal Campaigns (February–September 1988)

of the Germian region made it impossible to hide or escape. Known as the bloodbath of Anfal, it resulted in the greatest number of women and children killed since the attacks began. Tazashar was the only village bombarded by chemical weapons, because the flatness of the region and the dense army presence ruled out extensive gassing. The army attacked from several fronts, steering civilians toward the Qader Karam Road. To lure in the people, *jash* leaders announced a false amnesty. Some of the *jash* leaders gave their word of honor that no one would be harmed. Some villagers bribed the *jash* or were helped by them and secretly sneaked into the housing complexes. Others were arrested in their own villages, their homes looted and bulldozed before their eyes. As before, they were sorted and trucked away to different destinations.

The disappearance of vast numbers of women and children on April 14 made this a date of particular significance, later chosen by the Kurdistan Regional Government as Anfal Memorial Day. The motive behind the exterminations is something of a mystery. Given that the Germian region is near the Kirkuk oil fields, and bearing in mind the Iraqi government's long-standing policy of Arabization, the most plausible explanation of the tragedy is that it was part of the government's strategy to alter the ethno-regional map to the advantage of the Arab population. On the other hand, Middle East Watch found that in the areas where resistance was fiercest, the largest number of civilians disappeared.[35] It is also possible that, as the attacks went on and the government realized that the international community was not going to intervene, its stance hardened into systematic mass execution.

As the third Anfal drew to a close, the *peshmerga* retreated to Askar and Shwan, the region that became prey to the fourth Anfal. That attack, lasting from May 3 to 8, targeted the Valley of the Lesser Zab, the region that includes Kirkuk and Koysinjaq. It started with gas attacks on Askar and Goptapa. The local populations panicked and fled. Some headed south, while others moved west and were arrested by the Iraqi Army. Some people in the north of the valley tried to escape to Koysinjaq, which later became subject to house-to-house search to capture the fugitives. The villages to the north of the Lesser Zab River suffered the most. According to Middle East Watch 1,680 families disappeared from six villages in that area.[36] After another rumor of amnesty began to circulate hundreds of men came out of hiding and surrendered. They were never to be seen again.

The fifth, sixth, and seventh Anfal targeted the valleys of Shaqlawa and Rawandiz in the Erbil district on the border with Iran. Among the many villages whose inhabitants were gassed were Ware, Seran, Balisan, Hiran, Smaquli, Malakan, Shekh Wasan, Rashki Baneshan, Kaniba, and

Nazaneen. The eighth Anfal, between August 25 and September 6, wrought havoc on the Badinan region, a KDP stronghold. Chemical attacks were launched on more than thirty villages, causing the panic-stricken populations to move en masse toward the Turkish border. On August 26, however, Iraqi troops blocked the escape route to Turkey. Those who managed to cross the main road or were closer to the border were able to escape; the rest were arrested and, in a too familiar fashion, divided into three groups.

It is estimated that 65,000 to 80,000 civilians from the Badinan region fled to Turkey during the final Anfal.[37] Initially Turkey would not allow anyone to enter. After two days, however, refugees who were being chased by the Iraqi army stormed the border and poured into the country. Those who had been captured suffered the same fate at the hands of the Iraqi army as their predecessors; the men were executed and the women sent as captives to Fort Duhok and then to Salamya, until the September amnesty, after which they were dumped in Bahirka Desert near Erbil.

By September 1988, the Iraqi government had achieved a large part of its aims. The Kurdish countryside was ravaged. All men aged fifteen to sixty had been killed or forced to flee. The Kurdish resistance movement was crushed and its remaining supporters had fled to Iran. Through the systematic use of terror, the whole of Iraqi Kurdistan had been brought under Saddam's control.

As already noted, by August 1988 Peter Galbraith was firmly convinced that what was happening in Iraq was "genocide."[38] He and the late Senator Claiborne Pell, chairman of the Senate Foreign Relations Committee, were the main force behind the Prevention of Genocide Act, which, had it been adopted by both houses of Congress, would have set drastic limitations on U.S. exports to Iraq and other forms of assistance. Meanwhile, though defanged by the House, the Prevention of Genocide Act sent a strong message to the Iraqi government. This led to the first large-scale anti-U.S. demonstrations in Baghdad and Saddam no longer used gas against the Kurds.

In any event, Saddam was seriously concerned about being indicted for genocide. Iraqi intelligence services were instructed to keep a close eye on all activities likely to bring attention to Anfal. The regime went to great lengths to monitor any mention of Anfal inside the country and abroad. Thus the real purpose of the general amnesty decreed by Saddam was to deflect possible charges of genocide by showing that Anfal was a counterinsurgency measure and that civilians were not killed, but merely deported, and this despite the fact that half the rural inhabitants—men, women, and children—had already been wiped out.

Anfal's Aftermath

Anfal had devastating long-term consequences for the region. Rural society, including community and family ties, was all but destroyed. The collective trauma suffered by survivors gradually engulfed the whole of Kurdistan. The legacy of gas attacks is not limited to long-term health problems, deep psychological trauma, and economic hardships; it also sowed the seeds of the rebirth of a nationalist movement among the Kurds.

The immediate challenge was to reintegrate the internally displaced population. Many of the villagers continued to live in refugee camps in Iran and Turkey. Some returned to Iraq after the September General Amnesty, while the majority remained in the refugee camps until the "no-fly" zone was set up in 1991. Others remained incarcerated in Iraqi prison camps. Those who survived the starvation diet, exposure to extreme heat and cold, and lack of sanitation were eventually released after the General Amnesty was declared. The returnees, as well as the released detainees, were then taken and left in relocation areas near military bases.

Rebuilding life after Anfal was a major challenge for women. They experienced a radical change of status when they became the sole bread-winners in their families. Most village women had limited education; they had worked as farmers and, while having no apparently transferable job skills, moved into working as porters, laborers, bakers, builders, and factory workers. Many Anfal mothers could not afford to send their children to school and some children had to work to help their families. Most families lived in substandard housing with minimal services like water and electricity. Bassuk and Donelan point out that poverty and bad living conditions lead to stress for individuals and societies, and eventually to the "erosion of social mores."[39] Within this context, individuals are more likely to develop physical and mental health problems, and by extension, families and communities were similarly affected.

Following the Iraqi government's withdrawal from the region in 1991, many civilians returned to their villages to rebuild their lives, but agriculture did not recover. The absence of men, lack of farm machinery, and lack of support from the Kurdistan Regional Government contributed to this situation. Later, because of children's schooling and better employment opportunities in the main cities, many decided once again to leave their villages. Not only did the infamous UN-sponsored Food for Oil program (1997–2003) fail to breathe new life into the countryside, if anything it turned out to be largely dysfunctional. The program offered wheat, rice, cooking oil, and other basic necessities to the Iraqi public in return for petroleum, but instead of encouraging food production,

Food for Oil crippled the market for local produce by importing food from abroad.

Anfal was nothing if not a violent process of destruction. The results went beyond physical injury. Encounters with violence were a major source of traumatic stress,[40] often accompanied by mental disorders, including the loss of a sense of emotional and psychological security. Post-Anfal Kurdistan was no exception to this rule. Among those who witnessed the destruction and death, many suffered profound mental disorders.

Many who survived the 1987 and 1988 gas attacks were and are suffering from delayed effects. Long-term effects of mustard gas, the internationally outlawed gas of World War I, include chronic lung disease and bronchitis, permanent impaired vision, cancer, infertility, and congenital malformations of fetuses. According to Gosden, mustard gas can affect the membranes of the nose, throat, and lungs, causing respiratory problems and chronic chest infections.[41] In a study of the prevalence of long-term health problems in the town of Halabja ten years after it was gassed, Baban et al. found that the risk of developing cancers and most other gas-related disorders in people exposed to gas attacks was "three to four times more common" when compared to unexposed populations.[42] The high rates of congenital abnormalities, sterility, and cancer were found to be comparable to those of the atomic bomb survivors in Hiroshima and Nagasaki, indicating that "chemicals used in this attack, especially mustard gas, have effects similar to those of ionizing radiation."

Anfal also led to a revival of nationalism among Iraqi Kurds. In response to the pro-Iraqi stance of many Arab leaders and their indifference to the atrocities suffered by their Kurd kinsmen, Kurds felt betrayed by the Arab world. There was a sense of disillusionment regarding the promise of Islamic brotherhood and peaceful coexistence. In the post-1991 education system, young Kurds rejected learning Arabic in school even though this has meant further isolation and inability to access Arabic language, literature, and philosophy. In January 2005, while Kurdish leaders were busy rebuilding the Iraqi government after the fall of the Ba'ath regime, 95 percent of Kurds voted for independence.[43] Currently the relations between Kurds and Arabs are fraught with danger and distrust. The deadline for the implementation of Article 140 of the Iraqi constitution, which states the right of deported Kurds and Turkomans to return to their homes in Kirkuk and Khanaqeen, passed without the article being implemented. Many Kurds are frustrated and angry that even though the Iraqi constitution was passed by popular vote, the articles that concern the rights of the Kurds had been sidelined and rejected.[44]

Anfal and the Question of Genocide

Denial has been the standard response of the Iraqi authorities to accusations leveled against them. Although Saddam and Ali Hassan Al-Majid were charged with genocide, war crimes, and crimes against humanity, the expeditious hanging of Saddam in December 2006 before the Anfal trial was concluded made it impossible to establish his full responsibility in organizing the annihilation of the Kurds. The five other defendants were charged with war crimes and crimes against humanity. Throughout the proceedings, the defense argued that the operations were a legitimate counterinsurgency measure, targeting pro-Iranian Kurdish guerrillas. Sultan Hashim Ahmed, who was commander in charge of Anfal, flatly stated that civilians were not targeted; in fact, they were "safely removed."[45] The defendants blandly denied the use of gas attacks.

During the trial, Kurdish television channels repeatedly played a tape-recorded meeting of Al-Majid with Ba'ath party officials in which he pointedly warns, "I will not attack them with chemicals just one day, but I will continue to attack them with chemicals for fifteen days."[46] After questioning the authenticity of the tape, he later explained, "If I had said such things it was merely to frighten people into submission, but we never used gas attacks."[47] Never at a loss for a lie, he further added that he had "never before heard of Nugra Slaman and Dibs camps" nor had he heard of "mass graves."[48]

By any measure, including the criteria spelled out in the UN Convention on Genocide, there is every reason to define Anfal as an act of genocide, that is, an act committed "with intent to destroy, in whole or in part, a national, ethnical, racial or religious group [such as] killing members of the group, causing serious bodily or mental harm to members of the group, deliberately inflicting on the group conditions of life calculated to bring about its physical destruction in whole or in part, imposing measures intended to prevent births within the group, forcibly transferring children of the group to another group."[49]

The targeted group in this campaign was a subgroup within the Kurdish community in Iraq. In this sense, "a part" of this ethnic group was slated for annihilation, namely the mountain dwellers. According to Faqe Abdullah of The Committee to Defend Anfal Victims' Rights, who was one of the first people to research Anfal in the early 1990s, the total number of the disappeared is around 70,000.[50] This number is consistent with the Middle East Watch estimate of 50,000 to 100,000. This, however, refers to the human losses resulting from mass executions, which account for the largest number of deaths, but does not include those who died as a result of gas attacks, starvation, and illness in the camps. Once due account is taken of the total number of human lives lost, we end up having a frighteningly large percentage of the rural population, estimated to be around 200,000 at the time of Anfal, killed. While Anfal is perhaps best described, in Helen Fein's terminology, as "retributive genocide," occurring in reaction to a perceived threat,[51] this must not obscure the fact that some of the most vicious attacks against the civilian population occurred after the belligerents signed an armistice to end the war, on August 20, 1988. Anfal's ultimate objective was not merely to mete out an exemplary punishment to Iran's strategic alley, but to eradicate the vast majority of the rural Kurds. As a culturally distinct minority specifically targeted for annihilation, the rural Kurds appear to meet all three conditions identified by Fein as presumptive victims of genocide: they were perceived as alien, they stood "outside the universe of obligation," and they were perceived as "unassimilable." Their physical elimination removed a threat while at the same time opened up new opportunities. Thus there is every reason to view Anfal as illustrative of Fein's definition of genocide as "sustained purposeful action by a perpetrator to physically destroy a collectivity directly or indirectly, through interdiction of the biological and social production of group members, sustained regardless of the surrender or lack of threat offered by the victim."[52]

Raul Hilberg's classic work on the Holocaust argues that "the machinery of destruction" is a process that starts by defining the victim group, then sapping its ability to resist the assaults of the state, and then finally destroying it.[53] Anfal offers a striking illustration of the processual dimension of genocide, beginning with the identification from the 1987 census figures of Kurdish villagers as a culturally separate group, then by subjecting them to an economic blockade, then killing the majority, and finally concentrating the remaining targeted group in resettlement camps, "not unlike the ghettoes established by the Nazis during World War II," writes Mia Bloom.[54]

What Helen Fein calls "genocide by attrition," meaning the "interdiction of biological and social reproduction of group members," is a key characteristic of the horrors associated with Anfal. In describing the deadly side effects, psychological and physical, of the gas attacks, Christine Gosden, a British geneticist, writes, "Not only do those who survived have to cope with memories of their relatives suddenly dying in their arms, they have to come to terms with their own painful diseases and those of their surviving friends and relatives." This is what she calls "the persistent genocide."[55]

The phrase is equally apposite to describe the extraordinarily brutal repression conducted against the Kurds after their 1991 uprising against Saddam that caused a massive outpouring of refugees into Turkey and Iran. "They fled in their millions to Turkey and Iran," writes Patrick

Cockburn, "leaving their dead and dying by the roadside, and their sufferings were shown on television screens around the world."[56] Impossible though it is to assess the number of victims, what is reasonably clear is that the organizers of the revolt expected the United States to provide military and logistical assistance. On February 15, 1991, President George W. Bush publicly stated, "there's another way for the bloodshed to stop, and that is for the Iraqi military and the Iraqi people to take matters into their hands, and force Saddam, the dictator, to step aside." This statement was widely interpreted among Kurds as an encouragement to take up arms against the regime, only to realize that their expectations had been in vain. Like the Shia in the south, who had shared similar hopes in rising up against the regime, the Kurds were left at the mercy of the Iraqi army; unlike the Shia, however, who suffered an estimated 300,000 killed in the six months following the uprising,[57] the Kurds were able to secure effective protection through the no-fly zone declared by the United States, now under growing public pressure to intervene.

This belated move to prevent the worst from happening has done little to exonerate the U.S. government; among the politically conscious Kurds, few would deny that they have been consistently betrayed by the United States in their efforts to resist Saddam's dictatorship. In the post-Saddam era, at a time when the political map of Iraq is being drastically redrawn, many wonder whether they can reasonably expect American support for their aspirations for an independent Kurdistan.

Chapter 7

The Assyrian Genocide
A Tale of Oblivion and Denial

Hannibal Travis

So thorough has been the cultural and physical annihilation of the Assyrian people that even the memory of their distinctiveness is at risk. They may end up being relegated to the marginal category of those onetime Arab, Kurdish, or Turkish Christians who eventually became refugees before they were assimilated into Western societies. Despite overwhelming evidence to the contrary in virtually all prominent histories of classical antiquity, from Herodotus and Strabo to Xerxes, Darius, and the Sassanian Persian sources, modern historians frequently deny the existence of an Assyrian people after 600 B.C.E. Instead, the modern Assyrians are often called Aramaeans, Chaldeans, Nestorians, Syriacs, Kurdish Christians, Turks, Arabs, Syrians, or other terms that conflate them with other groups and deny their common history. This is music to the ears of the Turkish, Arab, and Kurdish nationalist parties, including the Motherland and Justice and Development (AK) parties of Turkey, the Ba'ath and then the Islamic Call (or "Dawa") parties of Iraq, and the Kurdistan Democratic Party of the Kurdistan Regional Government of Iraq. All deny in various ways that Iraq or Turkey were home to an indigenous population whose origins are traceable to ancient times.

Many Assyrians converted from polytheism to Judaism or Christianity prior to the Arab and Turkish invasions. This conversion did little to protect them from catastrophic human losses, not to mention the cultural depredations, culminating in the late nineteenth and early twentieth centuries with large-scale pogroms and ethnic cleansing campaigns. Assyrian claims to recognition as a victim group have been consistently thwarted and denied by militant Turkish nationalists and their Arab counterparts.

Several myths help perpetuate the denial of the Assyrian tragedy. Some involve an unjustifiably narrow legal definition of genocide, in particular the notion that the term only applies to the total destruction of a given community, or the view that genocide never occurred prior to 1948, when the UN Convention on Genocide was formally adopted, or the claim that mass violence cannot be genocidal in conditions of international war, civil war, or insurgency. Reinforcing these misconceptions are a number of historical myths. Examples include the hoary notion that the Ottoman Empire was an innocent victim of the British Empire and/or the Russian Empire during World War I, or that the Ottoman Empire and its successor the Turkish Republic were tolerant, secular governments who could never have countenanced religious persecution, or that there is no objective or verifiable evidence of an official policy to endorse massacres, enslavement, rapes, or cultural devastation. This chapter seeks to explode these myths and instead lay bare the fundamental contradiction between Turkey's "negativist" position on the Assyrian genocide and its willingness to recognize genocides elsewhere involving a smaller number of victims and proportionally smaller reductions of target group populations, as in the former Yugoslavia (Bosnia and Kosovo). This profoundly ambivalent stance, sustained by a rigorous censorship, amounts to rejection of basic historical facts coupled with distortion of the international law of genocide.

Background to Genocide

The Assyrian people are indigenous to Mesopotamia and northeastern Persia, with a history that goes back more than 4,000 years. Their rich cultural heritage—from language to philosophy and politics, and from religion to technology—is traceable to the Akkadians and Sumerians, and radiated from the plain of the river Tigris in present-day Iraq into eastern Syria, southeastern Turkey, and northeastern Iran, all of which comprised ancient Assyria. In the early first millennium of the Common Era (c.e.), many of the Assyrian people converted to Christianity, as most of them had done by the Middle Ages, although large pockets of neo-pagans practicing the remnants of ancient Assyrian beliefs survived in Iraq until the present day. These neo-pagans, known as Mandaeans and Yezidis, retain references in their holy scriptures to the ancient Assyrian deities such as Shamash, Sin, Bel, Ishtar, and Tammuz.[1]

Like the Armenians, Greeks, and Slavs, the Assyrians are a non-Turkish group whose ancestral lands were incorporated into the Ottoman Empire in the sixteenth century C.E. With the help of the Kurdish tribes—upon whom they relied as paramilitary forces in order to enforce their "divide-and-rule" strategy—the Ottomans carried out wholesale massacres of Assyrian tribes, notably the Tiyari, Tkhuma, Jilu, and Baz, all of whom resisted Turkish rule. From 1843 to 1845, on the strength of the evidence from British representatives and Western missionaries, some 10,000 Assyrians were massacred, a countless number of Assyrian women and children were taken into bondage, and many Assyrian leaders, including their priests and tribal chiefs, were eliminated. Meanwhile, many Assyrians felt they had no choice but to become converts to Russian Orthodoxy, Anglicanism, or Catholicism in hopes of obtaining Russian, British, or French aid in a human-made famine. So dire was the situation that in 1864, the Assyrian patriarch appealed to the Russian Empire to intervene to save his people, who were "constantly" suffering the kidnapping of Assyrian girls and women.[2] This did not prevent Turkish and Kurdish landlords from continuing to demand "unpaid labour" and vast amounts of grain from Assyrian farmers.[3]

In 1914, about 500,000 Assyrians lived in the Ottoman Empire and Persia, based on conservative British estimates.[4] Inspired by the rise of German militarism in Europe and a racist ideology of "Turkification" in their own empire, the Ottomans and their Kurdish allies declared holy war (*jihad* in Arabic, *cihad* in Turkish) against Christianity.[5] The objective was to expand Ottoman influence east to Afghanistan and India and in the process hasten the demise of the British Empire in those areas.[6] Although motivated by Assyrian ethnic and religious differences and the potential for Assyrian independence with British or Russian help, the Ottoman massacres extended far outside the geographical scope of armed Assyrian resistance. Enver Pasha, an admirer of Prussian total war strategy and an ambitious modernizer hoping to liberate British, Italian, and Russian colonies with Muslim populations, planned a holy war stretching far beyond Assyrian lands to North Africa, Central and South Asia, and Eastern Europe.[7]

To achieve these objectives, Ottoman forces invaded Persia in August and September 1914, and began deporting thousands of Assyrians from their homes near the Ottoman-Persian border, over 8,000 of them by January 1915.[8] The Turkish army then attacked the Assyrian tribes of the Hakkari mountains, already decimated by the massacres of the 1840s, so that by July 1915 their villages had been burned down, their wealth had been plundered, and many faced starvation. The Ottoman Ministries of War and the Interior then proceeded to recruit Kurdish tribesmen, members of criminal gangs, spies, saboteurs, and professional assassins into a "Special Organization" (Teşkilat-I Mahsusa) under the command of the Third Army. By November 1914, the Ottomans had distributed the proclamation of *jihad* among the Kurdish tribes of southeastern Anatolia, upper Mesopotamia, and northeastern Persia. The Interior Ministry and Special Organization also began deporting hundreds of thousands of Armenians, Assyrians, Greeks, and even Jews and Kurds from their homes, leading to widespread death from starvation, exposure to the elements, and disease.[9]

In January 1915, the governor of Van invaded Persia and destroyed the Assyrian populations he encountered, burning all Assyrian villages and massacring the columns of refugees in flight from his forces. In February, he reported that he had made a "clean sweep" of the Assyrians of Persia and intended to do the same to the Armenians of Van. In March, the vice commander of the Russian Empire's First Caucasus Army discovered more than 700 Assyrian and Armenian massacre victims in Haftevan, Persia, and Persia's minister of foreign affairs complained to the Ottoman ambassador that in many villages inhabited by Assyrians, the population had been "mercilessly massacred" and "many villages" burned down.[10] Harry P. Packard, an American doctor, wrote from Persia that 20,000 Assyrians were dead or missing, as more than 100 villages had been destroyed, and several large massacres had occurred.[11]

The anti-Assyrian campaign reached a climax in the summer of 1915. Turks and Kurds massacred the Assyrians of Amadia in May 1915, turning in June to the killing of up to 20,000 Catholic Assyrians (Chaldeans) in the district of Seert. The Armenian and Assyrian populations of the Gawar district, Harput, Hasankeyf, and Urfa were also "wiped out" in June.[12] The district governor of Midyat disappeared in June after refusing to implement the Ottoman policy of massacring Assyrians, and his replacement mobilized the local Kurdish tribes to massacre the Assyrians there, plundering their homes.[13] In Mardin, Armenian and Assyrian Christians "suffered the same fate without differentiation as to race or denomination."[14] The German vice consul in Mosul, Walter Holstein, reported that the governor of Diyarbekir was raging like a mad dog against "the Christians of his vilayet," and had massacred 700 from Mardin "like sheep."[15] The Ottoman interior minister wrote in July that "the Armenians of the [Ottoman] province of Diyarbekir, along with other Christians, were being massacred."[16]

In July 1915, Turkish cannons broke the Assyrian resistance in the Hakkari mountains; the remaining Assyrian villages were burned down, allowing starvation and disease to eradicate all traces of an Assyrian presence. The German ambassador to the Ottoman Empire was moved to protest to the Ottoman interior minister that 2,000 "Armenians and other Christians" had recently been massacred.[17] The victims included all the Assyrians of Faysh Khabour, and all the Armenian and Assyrian men of Seert and Mardin, leaving the widows and orphans of the latter to flee on foot to Mosul, where they died daily of hunger and exposure.[18] Throughout 1915, massacres claimed up to 25,000 Assyrian lives in Midyat, along with 21,000 in Jezire, 7,000 in Nisibis, 7,000 in Urfa, 7,000 in the Qudshanis region, 6,000 in Mardin, 5,000 in Diyarbekir, 4,000 in Adana, 4,000 in Brahimie, and 3,500 in Harput.[19]

In January 1916, the Assyrian patriarch appealed to the Russian representative in the Caucasus that Turkish leaders "had determined to kill all of us," causing the Assyrians to abandon their villages and all their property, and causing many to die to disease and hunger in flight across Turkey and Persia en route to Russia.[20] In April, the German imperial chancellor received a report that the Assyrians of the eastern Ottoman Empire had been "exterminated."[21] By 1917, the U.S. vice consul in Persia reported that thousands of Assyrians had died of disease, and his wife (who was with him in Persia) had come to believe that the Persians had determined to "wipe out" the Christians.[22] After the Russian Revolution of 1917, about 65,000 Assyrian refugees were killed by Turks and Kurds in Persia or in flight to British-controlled territory in Mesopotamia.[23] Ultimately about 250,000 Assyrians died in the massacres and related famines and outbreaks of disease.[24] The number of Assyrian victims nears 500,000 once the massacres of the 1890s and the Yezidi communities subjected to massacres are included.[25]

Scholars Confront the Assyrian Genocide

Until the early 2000s, few if any of the books and articles on the Armenian genocide ever mentioned the fact that Assyrians, Greeks, and Yezidis were killed in similar ways and for similar reasons, and often in the very same communities and time periods. Since 2004, Armenian-American scholars have increasingly recognized that the exclusion of Assyrian and Greek victims from the record of Turkish atrocities is indefensible. Much of the credit for correcting this omission goes to Professors Peter Balakian and Richard Hovannisian, two of the most respected analysts of the Armenian bloodbath. Although Balakian's prize-winning book, *The Burning Tigris: The Armenian Genocide and America's Response*

(2004), barely mentions the Assyrian tragedy, he has since made references to the Assyrians in his accounts of the Armenian genocide. Professor Hovannisian has likewise included a chapter on the Assyrian
genocide in the volume of essays he edited on the Armenian genocide:
in it, Anahit Khosroeva, of the National Academy of Sciences of Armenia, argued that two-thirds of Assyrians lost their lives in a genocide from
1895 to 1922.[26]

Scholarly research on the subject has made considerable headway
since 2006. Social historian David Gaunt, while conducting research into
the Ottoman archives, found evidence that fear of a Christian revolt,
though utterly unfounded, was the main reason behind the massacre
Christian populations.[27] This author attempted a comprehensive legal
analysis in that same year.[28]

Today, the Assyrian genocide has been recognized by the European
Parliament, the International Association of Genocide Scholars (IAGS),
and the Armenian National Committee of America. Genocide scholars
Adam Jones and Thea Halo have gathered a large quantity of materials
in support of the IAGS resolution on the Assyrian genocide, which are
archived at their respective websites.[29] Samuel Totten and Steven L.
Jacobs included the Assyrian genocide in the *Dictionary of Genocide*,[30] and
the dean of genocide studies in Israel, Professor Israel W. Charny, wrote
that he was "deeply ashamed" for not including the Assyrians in the
Encyclopedia of Genocide, and planned to rectify the oversight.[31] Thus, an
academic consensus on the Assyrian genocide is building.

Denial of the Assyrian Genocide: Censorship and Money

A careful study of Turkish law since 1925 provides ample evidence for
the view that denial of the Assyrian genocide was entirely predictable
given the legally sanctioned censorship of Turkish history. In 1925, the
Law for the Maintenance of Order prohibited the expression of ideas
that conflicted with the racist, ultranationalist vision of Mustafa Kemal
"Atatürk."[32] The Kemalists established the Turkish Historical Society,
Turkish Language Society, and "People's Houses" to articulate the ideology of a monoethnic "Turkish" Anatolian population.[33] The Turkish
Penal Code of 1926 made it a crime to "insult" Turkey, "Turkishness,"
the Turkish parliament, "the moral personality of the government," or
"the military or security forces of the State." Article 312 criminalizes
inciting hostility or "resentments" against a religion, sect, or race.[34]
Under the Turkish Motherland Party, Article 8 of the Anti-Terror Law
of 1991 banned all "[w]ritten and oral propaganda and assemblies,
meetings and demonstrations with the aim of damaging the indivisible

unity of the State of the Republic of Turkey, the nation and its territories."[35] In 2000, an Assyrian priest who affirmed that Assyrians had been systematically exterminated went on trial for violating Article 312, but was ultimately acquitted of the charge.[36] This type of censorship has been universally condemned by democratic societies with a tradition of the rule of law, whether in the European Union, North America, East Asia, Latin America, or Africa.

In the United States, the Turkish government has provided funding to U.S. and British historians who are willing to attack Ottoman Christian minorities as rebellious and deserving of massacres, and to laud Ottoman officials as humane and enlightened even when they had been regarded by their Turkish contemporaries as criminals. In 1982, the Turkish dictator Ahmet Kenan Evran founded the Atatürk Supreme Council for Culture, Language, and History (Atatürk Supreme Council) as an apparatus controlled by the Turkish state, and responsible for publishing books, organizing conferences, and subsidizing foreign research in support of the myths that the Turks are the indigenous and only valid culture in Anatolia, and that other cultures are more recent intrusions that have been consistently disloyal and deserved to be liquidated. Under this "Turkish Historical Thesis," the Turkish race of white Aryan men brought culture and civilization to Greece, Anatolia, Iraq, and Egypt, rather than conquering and depopulating these areas as virtually all indigenous chronicles document and detail at length.[37] Believers in this thesis characterize every national and cultural leader who resisted one thousand years of Turkish imperialism, from Byzantine times down to the Cold War era, as a "terrorist" similar to Hezbollah in Lebanon.[38] Once a person accepts Turkish hegemony over all other peoples in the region as natural and inevitable, as the "Turkish Historical Thesis" dictates, all opposition to it becomes "terror."

In 1982, Evran's ambassador to the United States established the Institute for Turkish Studies to deliver millions of dollars of subsidies to British and American scholars who were willing to collaborate in this campaign of denying the Ottoman Christian genocides, and to build relationships with U.S. public officials and corporate executives who might become allies.[39] A series of books in prominent university presses were linked to this campaign, by such authors as Bernard Lewis and Heath Lowry of Princeton, Stanford Shaw of the University of California, Guenter Lewy of the University of Massachusetts, and Justin McCarthy of the University of Louisville.[40] The former director of Middle East Studies centers at the University of California and New York University concludes that "The Turkish government, through its investment of time and money, and through the institutionalization of its efforts, has managed to project its views in Turkey, Europe, and the United States."[41]

The central tenet of these views, that Turks rather than Armenians or Assyrians were the victims in World War I, is implausible and contradicts all available demographic evidence.

The Assyrian Genocide in Comparative Perspective

A more substantive denial tactic is to argue that the Convention on the Prevention and Punishment of the Crime of Genocide has no application to events occurring prior to its entry into force in January 1951. The Turkish government claims that the convention is not retroactive. So did the Nazi defendants at Nuremberg, unsuccessfully. Based on customary international law, the Nuremberg tribunal indicted Nazi officials for "deliberate and systematic genocide, viz., the extermination of racial and national groups, against the civilian populations of certain occupied territories in order to destroy particular races and classes of people and national, racial, or religious groups, particularly Jews, Poles, and Gypsies and others." Similarly, the drafting history of the Genocide Convention itself indicates that events prior to 1945, and not those occurring between 1945 and 1948, motivated its language and widespread adoption.[42]

The nature of law is that it is invoked after the fact, to characterize and frame a reasoned societal response to a given set of phenomena, and not, on the other hand, to predict and preempt every conceivable culpable act in the future. Nearly all of the participants in World War II established military tribunals or mobilized their civilian courts to try Nazis, Nazi collaborators, and other fascists, often for "genocide." Many of these officials were convicted under laws applying the Genocide Convention to events occurring prior to 1951.[43] The United Nations repeatedly endorsed the jurisdiction exercised by the Nuremberg tribunal over crimes committed prior to the entry into force of the Genocide Convention in 1951. Occupied Germany did not sign the treaty creating the Nuremberg tribunal, and West Germany did not join the United Nations until 1973. Thus, from the time of its invention, the crime of genocide was applied in retrospect and did not require a government's consent in order for its officials to be prosecuted.

Other defenders of the Young Turk regime argue that genocidal intent was absent during World War I and its aftermath because Armenians and Assyrians survived in major cities of the Ottoman Empire, such as Constantinople or Mosul. They point to Armenian and Assyrian insurgencies, and the decision by some Assyrians to resist massacres and deportations by Ottoman forces and allied militia, as evidence of legitimate warfare in limited geographic areas, rather than empire-wide genocide. For example, the Atatürk Supreme Council, in a volume by Salâhi

Sonyel, argues that genocide cannot have occurred in the Assyrian case because, like the Armenians, "The Assyrians had rebelled against the Turks during the Great War . . . because they wanted independence at the instigation of foreign Powers."[44] He adds: "Disaster did not befall them until they, like the Armenians, made common cause with Russians, and betrayed the Turks and their own country during World War I."[45] These arguments misunderstand the nature of genocide, which does not refer to the complete destruction of a group or a totally one-sided slaughter. As noted above the first indictment for genocide included Poles within its scope, and Poles had of course rebelled against the Third Reich, many fighting on the side of the Americans, British, and Soviets.

One need not have recourse to examples from World War II and the Holocaust to show that partial survival of a group, and its active resistance to massacres, are in no way inconsistent with the conclusion that genocide has been committed. The founder of the Genocide Convention, Raphael Lemkin, was part of a particular European minority, the Polish Jews, but he had a wide-ranging and encyclopedic view of the sweep of ethnic and religious violence across human history. In his book *Axis Rule in Occupied Europe,* in which Lemkin articulated the crime of genocide for the first time, he named several religious wars as constituting the principal examples of the crime, including the Third Punic War (149 to 146 B.C.E.), the Great Revolt or Roman-Jewish War (66 to 72 C.E.), the wars between Muslims and Christians that culminated in the Crusades (1095 to 1272 C.E.), the anti-Albigensian Crusade (1209 to 1229 C.E.), the anti-Waldensian Crusades (1487 to 1535 C.E.), and the siege of Magdeburg in the Holy Roman Empire (1631 C.E.). He also cited the massacres of Timur Leng (Tamerlane) and Genghis Khan, which were similar in many ways to the Ottoman genocide of the Assyrians, Armenians, and Pontic Greeks during World War I.[46] There were resisters who survived all of the massacres Lemkin cited as examples of genocide. Foreign powers also played a part in most of them.

Lemkin argued that genocide need not, but could, involve the immediate destruction of all individuals belonging to a national or cultural group.[47] He argued that slavery, eviction from homes, protracted hunger and exposure to the cold, destruction of cultural heritage including churches, and separation of families were more typical of genocidal campaigns.[48]

The concept of genocide became politicized during the negotiations of the Genocide Convention in the 1940s. The movement away from Lemkin's conceptual rigor was accelerated by efforts by states and statist scholars to justify or minimize the importance of various massacres of ethnic and religious minorities throughout history. Advocates for the rights of human rights and indigenous peoples, such as Lemkin, the

UN General Assembly, numerous diplomatic officials and heads of state, several domestic courts, and the two ad hoc international criminal tribunals, recognized that evidence of genocide included not simply the immediate killing of all group members, but also deportation, torture, the prevention of births within groups, and the destruction of cultural and religious sites. When politically expedient, however, several large states and statist jurists on the International Criminal Court (ICC) and International Court of Justice (ICJ) have ignored these precedents and confined the concept of genocide to an extremely small, probably useless, concept.

This attempt by the ICC and ICJ to render the Genocide Convention inapplicable to everyone except perhaps the inmates of a death camp such as Auschwitz, or perhaps a Rwandan commune in which all Tutsis without exception were massacred, is inconsistent with international law. First, the Genocide Convention itself clearly states that the destruction of a group "in part" may constitute genocide, and that the infliction of "serious bodily or mental harm" short of death in order to destroy a group may constitute the crime of genocide.[49] Second, the UN Security Council and UN General Assembly have condemned genocide in situations of civil war and ethnic cleansing where there were many survivors, including in the former Yugoslavia and Rwanda.[50] Third, the Turkish government itself has repeatedly condemned far smaller and more geographically limited massacres of Muslims as genocide, including in Cyprus in the 1970s; Bosnia and Herzegovina, Kosovo, and Chechnya in the 1990s; and the Xinjiang/East Turkestan province of the People's Republic of China in 2009.[51] Insurgent groups killing security forces, and declaring a people's right to political independence, triggered each of these "genocides."

Oblivion and Memory: Scholarship and the Assyrian Genocide

The survival of the Assyrian people as a distinct group is at risk due to assimilation into Western societies, demographic collapse, economic marginalization, and deprivation of land rights.[52] Professor Lemkin argued that genocide is typically intended to, and in fact does, damage a minority group's sense of personal security, liberty, dignity, moral cohesion, cultural heritage, economic prosperity, and physical health. He described genocide proceeding in stages, including incitement of racial or religious hatred, destruction by massacres and leveling of cultural centers, economic exploitation and cultural assimilation, and propaganda denying the claims of the victim group and rationalizing the crimes of the aggressor group.[53] The diplomats who drafted the Genocide Convention apparently agreed, and decreed that the mental and moral integrity of ethnic, national, and religious groups deserved independent protection. A proposal by the United Kingdom to require death or "grievous bodily harm" as a predicate to genocide was rejected in favor of a definition including "serious . . . mental harm."[54]

The thoroughness of the extermination of the Assyrian people goes a long way toward explaining why their tragedy and cultural heritage have been virtually forgotten. The Assyrian population of southeastern Turkey, northern Iraq, and northwestern Persia was so small in the immediate aftermath of the genocide that a region called Assyria, Mesopotamia, or Persia in ancient and medieval times came to be known almost exclusively as "Kurdistan." The Turks, Kurds, and Arabs cynically resisted Assyrian and Armenian efforts to attain statehood after World War II on the basis that these Christian populations were too small, due to all the massacres. In the 1990s and early 2000s, politicians and scholars used the term "genocide" in reference to the Middle East in a contemporaneous sense almost exclusively to refer to the Kurdish plight in Iraq. This was justifiable in that the Saddam Hussein regime targeted many Kurdish villages for destruction and killed their populations, but other, smaller populations also faced threats to their cultures. It was rarely noted that the Kurdish population in Iraq doubled from about two million in 1970 to four million in 2002. Today, there may be five to six million Kurds in Iraq, as well as up to 20 million in Turkey.

Even the term "Assyrian" fell into increasing disfavor in the twentieth century. As the Turkish and Iraqi governments associated the group with rebellion and secession, they eliminated the Assyrian category from the census, replacing it with Christian Kurds, Turks, or Arabs. In Turkey, even Assyrian personal names and town or village designations were outlawed. The Turkish and Iraqi governments claimed Assyrian land, cultural monuments, and artifacts as the property of the state.[55]

Revisionist histories of the late Ottoman Empire invert every pertinent event between 1894 and 1925 to argue that Turks were the victims, and the tyrannical Christian nationalists were the aggressors and ultimate victors. The claim is that the Ottoman Empire was the innocent victim of a European imperial strategy in western Asia, sometimes referred to as a "Great Game" between the British and Russian Empires.[56] Actually, the Ottoman Empire was the aggressor during World War I, bombarding Russian ports, invading Russian and Persian territory, and massacring and deporting entire Christian populations prior to the formal outbreak of war in November 1914.[57] But the persistence of this kind of argumentation contributes to the denial of Ottoman crimes.

As in World War II, in which countless Germans were killed in combat or raped or deported under Allied occupation,[58] Christian resistance did claim Turkish lives, and probably accounted for some massacres. But these had an insignificant impact on the Turkish and Kurdish peoples, with more than 55 million and 20 million members today, compared to fewer than 100,000 or 0.1 percent of Turkey's population that is Armenian or Assyrian. Far from simply responding in a proportionate way to intolerable provocations, the Ottoman Empire had been massacring and enslaving its indigenous populations for centuries, and indeed over the entire span of its existence. The British, French, German, Austro-Hungarian, Greek, Vatican, Russian, and Swedish diplomatic archives confirm these Ottoman policies and their disastrous effects in extensive detail. Newspaper articles and books published in the hundred years or so leading up to the Ottoman Christian genocide of 1914 to 1923 are to similar effect.

The Ottoman archives, particularly of the court-martial proceedings and indictments translated into English by Vahakn Dadrian, also clarify that the provocation thesis is false or at least inadequate.[59] Even if there had been insurgencies that threatened to dismember the Ottoman Empire, Turkey has supported many such campaigns for self-determination in Yugoslavia and elsewhere despite the UN Charter, and can hardly complain about them in 1914, prior to the United Nations attempting to prohibit the use of force in violation of international treaties or the territorial integrity of nations. In fact, most court decisions finding genocide to have been committed since 1945 recognize that partisan warfare, ethnic secessionism, and counterinsurgency operations were a factor, from the Nuremberg trials to the trials of perpetrators of genocide in Cambodia, Ethiopia, Iraq, Rwanda, and Yugoslavia.

In short, despite many valuable studies on the Armenian genocide and the events of World War I in general, the horrendous mass murder was virtually unknown to many scholars and jurists until recently. An analogy may be drawn to the process by which the well-documented and often-condemned Rwanda genocide of 1994 eclipsed the genocide of the Hutu by the Tutsi in Burundi in 1972, or to the process by which the deaths of six million Jews in the Holocaust obscured millions of Roma and Slavic deaths.

Commemoration and Compulsion: The Twenty-First-Century Politics of the Assyrian Genocide

There is cause for hope that the academic consensus on the Assyrian experience will build into a political consensus. In 1995, the Parliament of Kurdistan in Exile issued a proclamation stating that "the Ottoman administrators began a policy of annihilating the Armenians and the Assyrians," which was "carried out with the aid of some tribal Kurds who were organized into an auxiliary force," with the result that "millions of Armenians, Assyrians, and Kurds were murdered."[60] Since 2004, three governors of the State of New York have declared that "alongside their Greek and Assyrian imperial co-subjects, Armenian men, woman and children met their end in mass killings, organized death marches, starvation tactics and other brutal methods employed against civilians."[61] In a remarkable statement on May 23, 2009, Turkish Prime Minister Tayyip Erdogan admitted that past "Fascist" regimes had "ethnically cleansed" non-Turkish minorities, using a term equated by the United Nations with genocide.[62]

The main difficulty confronting scholarship on Assyrian history is the criminalization in Turkey of all speech and discourse that could be construed as anti-military or anti-"Turk." These laws are slowly giving way to European Union law and political pressure, because they are in direct conflict with the international and European law criminalizing and condemning the denial, trivialization, or celebration of genocide, crimes against humanity, and religious hatred.

An additional obstacle in representing the Assyrian genocide is the plethora of languages, cultures, religious sects, countries, and empires that must be understood in order to fully grasp it. To provide a complete account of the differences between the Assyrians and their Turkish and Kurdish rivals in the early twentieth-century struggle for survival in upper Mesopotamia and northern Persia, one would need to study the history of the Church of the East (the Assyrian church), Catholic and Anglican inroads into its adherents, the forswearing by many Assyrians of their ethnic identity in favor of such terms as "Syrian Catholic" or "Chaldean" due to Turkish and Arab persecutions over the past several centuries, the geography of the Middle East nearly 100 years ago, the distribution and populousness of cities and villages that are very obscure in global terms compared to major centers such as Warsaw or Sarajevo, and debatable questions of international law. Documentation of the Assyrian genocide exists in multiple languages, out-of-print works, unpublished manuscripts, and national archives that are difficult to access and photocopy. The archives of Turkey alone may exceed 100 million documents, and Ottoman Turkish is not widely spoken or read by modern historians or legal scholars, unlike French or German.[63] Unsurprisingly, until very recently there was no complete account of the Assyrian genocide, spanning international law, history, cultural context, and political aftereffects.

A further problem confronting the Assyrians is the systematic omission of evidence on Assyrian and Greek deaths and deportations during the Armenian genocide, by both Turkish- and Armenian-centric scholars, and by Western scholars who rest their work on Turkish or Armenian sources. This omission at times reaches the level of purposeful concealment, as when scholars who have clearly studied in detail every scrap of paper relating to the Armenian genocide pretend that these materials *never once* mention anti-Assyrian or anti-Greek massacres.

Finally, the main obstacle to recognition of the Assyrian genocide by the U.S. Congress, United Nations, or other official bodies is the demographic weakness and dispersion of the Assyrians, especially as compared to the wealth and power of the Turkish, Arab, and Kurdish governments and political parties favored by Washington. With an extremely small population of about four million Assyrians worldwide in 2003, the Assyrians currently lack the compact economic and political power of an Armenia, Bosnia, or Israel, or even of larger minorities such as the Yugoslav Albanians, southern Sudanese, Tibetans, or Chinese Uighur Muslims. Weighing very heavily on the other side of the scales is a large and growing Turkish economic and military juggernaut, at the strategic pivot between Europe and Asia. Iraq's importance goes without saying. Turkey's campaign of denial is concentrated in large and lavishly financed embassies around the world, as well as in government ministries and universities inside Turkey.[64] The Assyrians, by contrast, are steadily losing their remaining homes and institutions in Iraq, Iran, and Turkey due to religious persecution, persistent poverty, and dictatorial rule.

Chapter 8

The "Gypsy Problem"
An Invisible Genocide

Michael Stewart

Else Schmidt was nine years old in the summer of 1944 when two men
in uniform knocked at her door asking for her by name. The men had
come for her two years before, but on that occasion the man she called
"father" had brought her back from the docks in Hamburg where
Zigeuner or "Gypsies" were being rounded up. Else—though she did not
know it then—was the daughter of a "half-Gypsy" who had married a
non-Gypsy Aryan. As such, she counted in Nazi terminology as a "Z
minus," a *mischlinge* or mixed-race *Zigeuner* with "a greater proportion
of German blood." She had been fortunate to have been adopted,
before the war, into a German family but had been too young to remember anything of her birth parents and had no inkling of a family other
than the one she lived with.[1]

When the men came for the second time her adoptive father
explained to Else that she was not his biological child. "He cried when
he said this. And my mother said, through her tears, 'we are not your
real parents. You will meet your real mother at the place where you are
going now.' I was completely unprepared for all this and I just could not
understand it."[2]

Among the tens of thousands of people of Gypsy descent who were
taken away from their homes and caravans between 1933 and 1945, Else
Schmidt was almost uniquely fortunate. Her adoptive father, who before
1933 had been an active trade unionist, braved the Reich Security

Offices and, after a prolonged correspondence, secured letters of release. Five months after her deportation he traveled to Ravensbruck to reclaim her.

Upon her return, Else's parents drew a protective veil over the lost months. Whatever she had seen and experienced at Auschwitz and Ravensbruck was left unspoken. Despite their efforts, her parents could not protect her from the—perhaps unintended—consequences of school procedures.

> I was told to tell people that I had been with an aunt in the German coun-tryside. That was what I was to tell them—to get away from the bombing. I had the concentration camp number tattooed on my arm with just a plaster to hide it. And the children did not guess. . . . But not the adults, the teachers, you see. . . . In front of the classroom the teacher asked me what was under the elastoplast. I froze, froze again. Knowing, remembering . . . remembering. You see anything that made me remember made me freeze. . . . And [the teacher] obviously never realized this. And I was told not to sit down till I told what was under the plaster. I just stood there like a zombie.[3]

Else never told her parents about this. "Anything, anything relating to that wasn't touched upon. Instinctively, I knew I would freeze up again." From that day, for nearly thirty years, Else spoke with no one at all about what had happened to her aged eight and nine in the concen-tration camps. She says she was numb, "Too numb. I don't think I came out of that numbness till I was thirty-nine years of age."

Between 1939 and 1945, in every country that was brought under Nazi control, in every city, in every village, in every concentration camp, Gyp-sies, like Jews, were persecuted because of their birth. By the end of the war, two-thirds of Germany's 30,000 Gypsies, a greater proportion of Austrian, Czech, and Croatian Gypsies and tens of thousands elsewhere, were dead. Of those who remained in Germany, many had been steri-lized, others had been crippled from slave labor. Although it is still extremely difficult to put precise figures on the total number of dead, it seems that at least 130,000 Gypsies and perhaps many more were killed as a direct consequence of racial policies pursued by the German state and its various allies in Italy, Croatia, and Romania in particular.[4]

Genocidal initiatives directed at Gypsies were proposed, if not always enacted, from the first to the last days of the war. Three weeks after the outbreak of hostilities, on September 21, 1939, at a conference called by the head of the Security Police, Reinhard Heydrich, it was agreed that the 30,000 German Gypsies were to be deported to "General Govern-ment in Poland." This deportation did not in fact take place—but only for administrative reasons. Two years later, in late autumn 1941, the first transports of "racial aliens" were sent from Austria to the occupied territories: 5,000 Austrian Gypsy citizens accompanied 20,000 Jews. With more than half of these Romany deportees being children, and crammed together in a few buildings in the center of Lodz (Littmannstadt), typhus and other diseases spread with such rapidity that even the Germans became alarmed—particularly after the epidemic brought down the German ghetto commandant, Eugenius Jansen. It was in fact in response to the difficulties of managing the ghetto at Lodz that the decision was made to experiment with mass gassing at a camp in the village of Chelmno, some fifty kilometers northwest of the city. A special commando unit that had been operating in eastern Prussia, carrying out euthanasia killings among Germans, was brought over and the first Jews were killed there in December 1941. Five weeks later, in January 1942, 4,400 Gypsies were taken from the Gypsy ghetto. The liquidation of their ghetto was completed with almost no one noticing.[5]

Three months later, on the eastern front, formal instructions were given to the Wehrmacht and other fighting forces that Gypsies were to be treated "as the Jews." In this situation, the Gypsies may actually have been the worse off. Jews who were captured might be subject to selection—the Germans needed skilled slave labor. Gypsies, lacking formal education, were shot upon capture. Wherever the Germans went, Gypsies fell: in the Ukrainian forests where they had sought refuge with partisan units and on the Baltic coast, where 800 of the tiny Estonian Gypsy population of 850 were dead by 1944. In the Reich itself, in December 1942, Heinrich Himmler signed what is now known as the Auschwitz Decree as a result of which the special facility at Auschwitz, the *Zigeunerfamilienlager,* or Gypsy family camp, was brought into operation in March 1943. It housed the majority of Germany's Gypsy populations until the first days of August 1944 when the remaining inmates were gassed. Toward the end of the war, some Gypsies were given the possibility of having themselves declared "socially adjusted." If they then "consented" to sterilization they would be exempted from the oppressive and often murderous regulation of their people. Hanjörg Riechert, who researched this very practice, estimated that 2,500 German Gypsies lost the ability to reproduce thus.

In the Romanian wartime fiefdom known as Transdnistria, alongside 150,000 Jews deported from Bessarabia, at least 25,000 "nomadic" and "asocial" Romanian Roma were sent to starve to death; our best evidence suggests that possibly 40 percent of the deported Roma died there. On the Reich's southern front, in Serbia, Gypsy "hostages" were shot alongside Jews and partisans; in neighboring Croatia, the Ustasha-run camp of Jasenovac became the graveyard for somewhere between 50 and 95 percent of the Croatian and Bosnian Gypsy populations.

In brief, despite profound differences in motivation, scale, and intensity of the persecutions of Gypsies and Jews, the Romany peoples were threatened with extinction—and, had the course of the war turned otherwise, without the slightest shadow of a doubt they, like Europe's Jews, would have disappeared.

And yet the mass murder and sterilization of the Roma, Sinte, and Gypsies provides, perhaps, the locus classicus in the modern world of a genocidal catastrophe denied and cast into public oblivion. Despite the efforts of a number of historians and activists, the general European public remains almost totally unaware of the Nazi treatment of the Romany peoples and in no European country are these persecutions taught as a part of the national curriculum.[6]

In this essay I will link the particular character of the Nazi persecution of the Roma and Sinte people with the treatment this genocide received after the war and its fate in terms of historical memory. In contrast to the attempt to contain and then destroy the supposed power of European Jewry, which was a central ideological platform of the German Nazi National Socialist Workers Party (NDSAP), the persecution and then genocide of the Roma came "from the bottom up" and was at first organized at the municipal level. Indeed, despite the existence of several bodies claiming expertise in this area (and formally authorized as such by the Central Reich Police Authority, RKPA) the decisive institution in this history was not any of them, but the Kripo, the criminal police, who worked alongside the welfare offices of various towns to redefine what had been called "the Gypsy peril" (*zigeunerplage*) in biological terms. As part of a general shift from social to racial hygiene, the Roma and Sinte fell victim to the radical plan to eliminate all "*gemeinschaftsunfahig*" (asocial) persons from the "folk community." They were thus eliminated because of their alleged social deviance, not in the first place because of racial, ethnic, or religious identity markers, though their social deviance was imagined as the function of their biological (racial) heritage. This, then, was a genocide that fits neither the definition of the group concerned nor the model of a centrally planned campaign, both of which were derived from Lemkin's pioneering work and then were codified into the UN convention. And for this reason, the Gypsy catastrophe remains contested today, to the extent that "denial" and forgetting of the Romany calvary is still widespread.

Who Were the Roma, Sinte, and Zigeuner?

It was as Zigeuner that people like Else Schmidt were persecuted. But this was not how her natal family would have conceived themselves. They were speakers of Romany whose ancestors had handed down a distinctive way of life. They recognized other related Romany peoples as *sinte,* a word that here means simply "relatives." Such in-group identifications did not register with outsiders. To understand the Nazi persecutions we need, therefore, to determine what the perpetrators intended by their classifications.[7]

The question then becomes, for German state officials, who were the Zigeuner? Under this label were grouped various peripatetic or formerly peripatetic peoples irrespective of whether they spoke Romany. By the early twentieth century the use of this term was wholly pejorative, but it would be wrong to think that at all times and places the term Zigeuner was used to label social outcasts and pariahs. In early modern Germany, as across the whole of central Europe, Zigeuner had played important social, economic, and ritual roles in everyday life. But by the nineteenth century the term commonly appears with its sister term "nuisance," as in the semi-official form: *Zigeunerplage*—the Gypsy nuisance. The connotation shifted once again in the twentieth century and by the 1930s a notion of a "Gypsy race" had taken root in popular parlance. It is a commonplace of population biology and genetics today that there are in reality no such thing as races in the folk sense of the term that refers to physiognomically distinct human populations whose inner character or "essence" correlates with their outer, physical distinctiveness (which is also, it should be stressed, largely imagined). This understanding is, however, a modern achievement. In the 1930s, it was assumed that such populations as those labeled Zigeuner, with their slightly darker skin and distinctive dress and bodily manner, were clearly a distinct "race" of persons.

Zigeuner then applied to what one may best think of as a family of families or community of communities that had a history of their own, unwritten and unrecorded though it was. Many of those so labeled spoke Romany, a language that has north Indian roots, but whose true cradle lies in the Balkans. It is there that we find the largest number of Romany speakers and the greatest linguistic diversity. The pattern of dialect differentiation in the rest of Europe suggests that over the past six or seven centuries there were waves of migration of Romany speakers north-westward from the Balkan peninsula. One of those waves brought the ancestors of the German Sinte and the French *Manouches.* By 1933, according to reliable estimates, there were more than 20,000 Sinte in Germany and somewhere under 10,000 Ziguener who spoke other dialects of Romany and who had arrived in the Reich more recently.

These different groups of Gypsies were seen somewhat differently by German officialdom. In particular, families whose ancestors had long resided in German lands (and who spoke, thereby, that "western dialect" of Romany associated with the Sinte today), were seen by officialdom as "German Gypsies." The newcomers were traditionally assumed to be "*staatenlose*," without state citizenship. In time the Nazis, adopting ethnographical labels, classified them as "*Rom-Zigeuner.*" Most of these people's ancestors had come from the territories of the Austro-Hapsburg Empire, often carried names of Hungarian origin, and spoke an eastern dialect, often a so-called *Vlach* dialect.[8]

Curiously, however, when in 1943 and 1944 officials tried to distinguish "pure blood" Zigeuner from "mixed blood" to work within the categories laid down in Himmler's final decree for the regulation of the Gypsies, none of these categories mattered, for then it was the *metissage* of Romany and German blood that had to be wiped out.

Rendering Romany Victims Invisible

The story of Else Schmidt with which I introduced this chapter is, of course, the unique tale of one Hamburg girl, but it speaks to the experience of many Gypsy camp inmates. At the end of the war, when Gypsies returned from the camps, they found the price of readmission to their homes, villages, and towns was silence about their exile and the attempted destruction of their people. When they did try to speak out, their fellow citizens would often comment, "You know, we suffered, too." Often it was they, the victims, who were blamed for their own suffering due to their "criminal" or "asocial" lifestyle. While such convenient rewriting of history slipped easily into place for those who had stood by and watched or even supported their neighbors being deported, for the Gypsies, their experiences could not simply be willed out of consciousness.

After the war Else would dream of things she had seen but not fully understood at the time in the camps. At Auschwitz, she had seen piles of "white corpses," bodies that had been sprinkled with white lime, "all piled on top of each other. As a child, I just could not understand what it was. Very much later, years after my liberation, I had awful nightmares about this sight: that I am standing under the portal at the city hall in Hamburg, and the people standing next to me are saying to me I should come with them. But I say, 'No, I cannot walk on the ground, the whole floor is full of corpses.' But the other people in the dream cannot see the dead; they just walk over them with their high-heeled shoes and take absolutely no notice of the corpses."[9]

Else Schmidt had no family left to keep her in Germany. She escaped the nightmares that had welled up inside her by fleeing to England and leaving the world of her childhood behind. Most of Europe's Gypsies could not get away so easily.

In the years after World War II, many Gypsy victims of the Nazis began to campaign for proper acknowledgment of what they had been through, as well as some sort of monetary compensation for everything they had lost. In the majority of cases satisfaction was never achieved. In every case the ensuing struggle with the authorities involved the humiliating discovery that the attitudes that had sent them to the concentration camps were alive and flourishing and had found new legitimacy.[10]

The treatment of Berhardt Reinhard, a Sinto, or German Gypsy, from one of the many socially consolidated German Gypsy families with Reich citizenship and a strong sense of belonging to the German nation, is typical. After military service from 1941, discharge as a Gypsy straight into Auschwitz in early 1943, sterilization in Ravensbruck, and suffering a war wound in January 1945, when he was conscripted into a military "suicide" unit set up for common criminals and "asocials," he might have thought that he would be eligible for some sort of indemnification for his treatment.

It took over sixteen years of legal and administrative misery for him to win a state pension. Along the way, in 1957, he was examined in the clinic of a Professor Dr. Villinger and a Professor Dr. Sophie Erhardt, two people who were, you might say, particularly well qualified to understand where their patient was coming from. In November 1957, Werner Villinger had not yet been exposed as one of the higher-ranking doctors involved in the secret "T4 action," the euthanasia murders of over 100,000 people in mental hospitals between 1939 and 1941. Sophie Erhardt had also managed to avoid prosecution for her work in the Racial Hygiene and Population Research Office of the Reich, where the central work had been to determine which Gypsies were to be sterilized and which sent to Auschwitz. No surprise then that they examined this case with uncommon thoroughness; nor at their perverse conclusion: while there had been no adequate hereditary or medical reasons to justify a sterilization in the first place, now that it was done, Reinhardt was still in good health with no "morbid perturbations" or "psychoneurological impairment." So there were no grounds on which to compensate him! Others talked of him suffering "a pension neurosis," justified as follows: Were Reinhard now to receive a pension, this would only serve to tie him to his past, reminding him every month of the original trauma. Compensation could only worsen his condition. It was thus not cold-heartedness, but a "duty of care" to refuse him the money he requested.

The enduring inability of the German court system to recognize and compensate Gypsy victims of the Nazis had a number of different causes.

American and British military administrations after the war had wished publicly to recognize all victims of the Nazis and, as a moral and political gesture, to reward them with financial compensation to be taken from the coffers of the German state.[11] In so doing, however, they had made a fundamental error when they restricted the eligible victims to "racial" and "ideological" enemies of the state. In so doing they denied compensation to those who had been interned for any kind of common crime. The logic appeared flawless at the time. Why should rapists, thieves, drunks, or murderers be treated as victims of the Nazis? But for the Gypsies this reasoning was fateful. "Asociality" counted as a common delict, or misdemeanor, and thus most Gypsies whose lifestyle had been classified as "asocial" by the Nazis and had been persecuted for this reason were denied access to the compensation funds.

In this way the interim allied administration failed to acknowledge that the Nazi system of criminal justice worked in deeply discriminatory ways against members of ethnic minorities and other social outcasts. Many Gypsies had convictions for petty offenses such as begging, loitering, selling goods without a license, or even holding foreign currency and, since Nazi justifications for interning Gypsies always referred to their criminal tendencies, the Allied definition of political or racial victim implied that every Gypsy would have to go through a special procedure to establish their *individual* eligibility. Even more fundamentally, the Allies failed to understand that by 1940, if not earlier, the whole of criminal law had been poisoned and perverted by political considerations. Central to this perversion was the highly politicized notion of "preventive justice," which justified imprisonment of potential offenders before any crime had actually been committed. In this way, the treatment of even quite minor crimes could become a political matter. After the outbreak of war, the very distinction between "ordinary" and "political" crime was explicitly suppressed, as the former was seen and punished as a form of opposition to the regime.[12]

With a far too restrictive definition of victims of Nazism installed, as power and authority were handed back to the Germans, the Gypsies were ever more systematically excluded from procedures for official recognition and compensation. Punctilious and thrifty local bureaucrats, who felt charged above all to conserve their limited resources, allied themselves with the plain prejudice of others involved in cases like these. The presence at all levels of the state bureaucracy of officials who had been active partners in the Gypsies' persecution meant that claimants for compensation came up against almost exactly the same prejudices as they had under the Nazis. In several regions of postwar Germany, compensation to Gypsies was limited to those who could prove they had fixed accommodations and employment.[13]

So while few officials would have dared after 1945 to use Nazi anti-Semitic language and imagery to suggest to Jewish applicants that it was their membership in a parasitic community aiming at world domination that had given rise their persecution, Gypsy supplicants had the old accusations thrown in their faces. From the end of the 1940s, people like Reinhard were told that the measures taken against them were their own fault. It was the Gypsy character type, their "antisocial behavior," "crime," and "wandering drive" that were the root of the problem.

Further hindering the recognition of their claims, Gypsies inevitably stood at the bottom of the heap in terms of the victims' social rankings. As the full extent of the criminality of the Nazi regime was revealed for the first time in 1945, it was only natural that the sheer overwhelming scale of the Holocaust should provide the standard measure for all the other crimes of the regime. Those persecuted for their religious faith, like the Jehovah's Witnesses and some other Christian sects, were quickly recognized. The mentally ill, apparently an embarrassment to all concerned, were forgotten; homosexuals, communists, Gypsies, and other so-called "asocials" all had a hard time asserting the injustice of their persecutions.

Sophie Erhardt, the anthropologist who had been called as an expert witness in the Reinhard case and who had worked during and after the war on Gypsy specimens taken from prisoners, easily aligned her own, deeply ambivalent stance with views like these. In 1963, in the context of a debate about general compensation for all the forcibly sterilized, she wrote to the finance ministry in these terms: "What would people say if some asocial alcoholic, who from the point of view of hereditary science (*erbbiologisch*) was wrongly sterilized, should from now on be treated as the equal of all those who, as reputable citizens, were tortured for years on end in concentration camps simply because of their race, their beliefs, or their political convictions. A compensation provision for the sterilized would in many cases lead to a disavowal and ridicule of restitution among right-thinking minds [*echten Gedankens*]."[14]

This moral hierarchy was moreover built into the institutional structure of the Federal Republic. The compensation offices, for instance, used Nazi anti-Semitic ideology and practice as their point of reference for defining "political" persecution. And the Gypsies struggling for recognition found themselves trapped within this logic.

The Fog of Genocidal Planning

Between 1950 and 1985 a political, legal, and intellectual campaign was fought for the Gypsies to be included as victims of the Nazis. For Roma

and Sinte involved in this struggle, their interest, indeed their obligation, has been to assert the similarity of the Jewish and Gypsy persecutions. The most significant efforts were focused on battles within the
judicial system since these would result in material compensation claims,
but this implied that the terms of the debate over the status of the Gypsy
persecutions was set by the types of arguments that are successful in a
legal context. Given legal procedures, the most persuasive, perhaps the
only, way to win the argument was to trace the evolution of Nazi policy
to the Gypsies in dated, signed decrees and orders. It was as a result of
providing documentary evidence of a decree from December 1938,
signed by Heinrich Himmler, as head of the security apparatus and
police forces, announcing that Gypsies would henceforth be dealt with
"according to the nature of their race," that the start date for "racial
persecution" was moved up from January 1943, when Himmler's Auschwitz decree came into force.

It is essential to understand that it was the misleadingly intentionalist
model of a genocidal campaign—traceable in orders, decrees, and regulations and coordinated by political superiors—and not the ambivalent
attitudes of the officials involved in these cases (many of whom probably
held racially prejudiced views about the Gypsies) that hindered recognition of the Gypsies as victims of Nazi politics. This much became clear
in the 1980s when a new generation of lawyers, prosecutors, and judges
came to office. Many of them were ashamed by the earlier failure to
identify individual perpetrators or hold anyone accountable for the persecution and genocide of the Gypsies and were determined to use their
newfound power to try to set the historical and judicial record straight.
In a number of German cities, long-abandoned investigations into
employees of the Racial Hygiene and Population Research Offices were
reopened, but time and time again these reached a similar dead end
when the judges reasoned that since the court had not been presented
with an *order* for the extermination of all Gypsies, they could not accept
that the accused's actions had been part of a broader *plan*.[15]

Beyond these disputes over the interpretation of bureaucratic procedure, there may have been other reasons to assert that the Nazis had
not turned on the Gypsies. Policy toward the Gypsies after the seizure
of power was an extension and intensification of pre-1933 democratic
practices. This meant, first, that it was difficult to read as persecution.
The central role, before and after 1933, was taken by the criminal police
and not the secret police or the SS. Second, in contrast to the persecution of the Jews, there was often popular support for the increasingly
brutal measures taken by regime officials.

I will return to the role of the criminal police, but it is worth noting
that their involvement with the Gypsies went right back to their earliest

surveillance efforts, composing registers of legitimate tradesmen and illegitimate (Gypsies), creating card registers, and in some cases, even books of descriptions to enable rapid identifications. In the late nineteenth century the police were devoting specific resources and seeking special measures to address what they now dubbed "The Gypsy Plague" or "The Gypsy Question." From 1899, a Central Office for Countering the Gypsy Peril operated out of Munich. Its director, Alfred Dillman, published his synoptic work, *The Book of Gypsies* (1905), building on more than one hundred years of police documentation, providing aliases, regular locales, occupations, and identifying features of different "clans." From this time forward, the issuing of what were called *Wandergewerbschein*, or traveling-tradesman permits, became a central point of conflict between Gypsies and the local authorities.[16]

And when the Nazis began to racialize these issues, in particular after the publication of implementation of regulations for the Nuremberg Laws that included Gypsies in their provisions, this tradition of police surveillance fed directly into the research work of the racial "scientists," providing them with much of the genealogical material that enabled a genocide of the Gypsies, organized and structured by the persecution of particular genealogical, that is to say familial, lines to come into shape.

Steps Toward an Uncoordinated Genocide

In the official treatment of the Roma and Sinti after World War II, we see how a simplified version of the Jewish Holocaust, as the outcome of an order from the Führer, misled legal and other professionals when they came to consider the case of the Gypsies. But even were the judges and prosecutors to have operated with a richer, more complex understanding of how the Final Solution came into being, they would have had great difficulty sustaining an equation of the Jewish and Romany genocides. Let me be clear: I do not wish to belittle the treatment or fate of the Roma and Sinte. The point is rather that "the Gypsy problem" occupied a totally different place in Nazi ideology than that of "the Jewish problem." Likewise, the measures necessary to exclude a socially and economically marginal minority from German society were not the same as those required to remove a highly educated and culturally dominant elite.

I stress here some of the fundamental differences and derive these from the history of public policy toward these two minorities in the halfcentury and more preceding the Nazi takeover. For many European Jews, the institution and consolidation of the modern nation-state meant—in fits and starts, but ineluctably nonetheless—their emancipation and integration into European societies, Germany included. Jewish legal and civil equality in the German states was established during the 1860s following the great movement out of the Jewish ghettos and into the cities from the 1870s on and, above all, their integration into banking, trade, and the professions. These transformations marked the passage of Germany's Jews into full membership in the national citizenry.

For the Gypsies, the same period saw a decline in their status and the reversal of a number of "privileges" or "protections" from which they had benefited in early modern Europe. It is true that even in the eighteenth century many Gypsies had occupied radically marginal and often impoverished socioeconomic niches and had profoundly circumscribed claim on the political authorities. But in localities where they could demonstrate longstanding affiliation, they were subject to the "protection" (*Schutz*) of the *Herrschaft* and, as Thomas Fricke has brilliantly demonstrated, found a substantial degree of integration into the local social order. The end of the nineteenth and beginning of the twentieth centuries saw a set of institutional moves the effect of which was to exclude many Gypsies from the new social and political protections of the modern German state. Traditionally well integrated and tolerated as the providers of cheap labor, until the early nineteenth century the Gypsies had lived a kind of caste existence, providing specialized services to the otherwise more or less socially isolated and economically insulated communities of farmers in early modern Germany, bringing news of the outside world and purchasable tokens of modernity with them. With the rise of a mass, increasingly urbanized, consumer society, as all kinds of tradesmen, commercial travelers included, were coming under state regulation, the Gypsies found themselves caught in a whole new set of administrative procedures. In country after country local authorities sought to determine who was a legitimate "salesman" and who was merely "a Gypsy," using their wanderer's status as a cover for supposedly shadier activities. The task of distinguishing one from the other was handed on to the body that, till then, had had the most systematic dealings with the Gypsies: the police.

The Gypsies suffered in another way from the transformation of the old social structures. In the past, in each region the local *Herr* had had to provide for his "own" poor. This way was one in which he extended his *Schutz* over his subjects. Under Bismarck, this personal relationship of dependence was transformed into a nationally imposed obligation on the local authority to provide various forms of support (*Fürsorge* or, still, *Schutz*, as in *Kinderschutz*) for the locally registered needy. This in turn led to efforts to define the boundaries of responsibility, and many Gypsies found themselves excluded from such social support. As Andreas

Wimmer has argued, the first moves toward creating what was later to become the welfare state went hand in hand with restrictions on immigration (on the import of new, potentially welfare-dependent persons) and with efforts to cleanse the population of problematic "elements." Wimmer talks of a "logic of inclusion and exclusion" that is central to the specific form of "social closure" that is a national community. Clearly, with the "nationalization of the regime of mobility," those beyond the borders were pushed out of mind. But that was not the end of the matter. Since integration and exclusion were articulated around notions of national citizenship, questions of ethnic attachment and the status of persons and groups as "proper citizens" acquired novel force. And these lines were drawn within the state. With limited resources to distribute among the needy, the local state even had a pecuniary interest in such time-consuming demarcation work.[17]

Moreover, the terms in which the nationalist "compromise" on social solidarity among citizens was justified included powerful notions of social improvement. If *Kinderschutz* were to be handed out to the socially and morally dubious classes, then the authorities had to be assured that their generosity was inducing moral improvements. There was no single language in which such socio-moral reform was phrased, but in the different countries of Europe and across the political spectrum from left to right the latest fashionable ideas from biology, psychology, and sociology were brought to bear on these questions. With the rise of early genetic science, the possibility emerged, on the horizon, of population improvement by regulation of demography. Just as pasteurization had made milk safe to drink for the masses congregated in the cities, so population science offered to decontaminate the nation's demographic profile. In Germany in particular, even more than Italy, France, or the United States, notions of eugenics, "racial hygiene," and the language of "degeneration, decay, and corruption" took deep root among many intellectuals. Graphic and lurid imagery, implicating not just the clearly alien, like Gypsies, but the poor, the alcoholic, and, a brilliantly vague term, the "asocial" spread in the years before World War I, turning illness itself into a political concern. Under the Nazis, this trend led to a situation where anyone who "stood out" or "came to the attention of the authorities" (the German term *auffalig* is hard to render exactly) because of their idiosyncratic or irregular behavior, might be labeled "asocial" (*gemeinschaftunfahig*) and carted off for correction.[18]

In Germany, it was in the various regional police forces that these disparate trends came together in a particularly pernicious constellation. The Reich Police as a national institution had in fact come into being in part in response to the perceived threat posed by "rootless," "wandering," and "hard-to-identify" criminally inclined social groups, the *herrenloses Gesindel* (hordes of masterless men) and among those, the *Zigeuner* in particular. The very first "police circulars" and list of wanted persons had been created at the end of the eighteenth century to help track down families of Gypsies, and the gradual centralization of the German state and modernization of police procedures had, if anything, intensified their professional interest in this area of work.[19]

With the rise of modern policing came the first efforts at scientific criminology. Considering the overall intellectual climate, many of these inevitably were couched in more or less biological terms. It was not necessary to have signed up to the rococo agenda of Cesare Lombroso's pseudo-science of "anthropological criminology" to adopt the apparently innocent idea that "if the father is a loafer and thief, so will be the son."

So, at the end of the nineteenth century the police were being asked to determine administratively who was and was not a Gypsy, just as welfare services were deciding who was and was not a worthy recipient of public charity (with a considerable overlap in the families being labeled deviant) and leading criminologists and detectives were adopting notions drawn from the ever-expanding field of "criminal biology" to account for the phenomenon of the "incorrigible" or "habitual" criminal. After 1933, the room for police to maneuver was dramatically expanded, in particular with the adoption of the program of preventive detention (*polizeiliche Vorbeugungshaft*) introduced on November 13, 1933, by the Prussian minister of the interior. Habitual and sex criminals could now be indefinitely detained in concentration camps to prevent them from committing the crimes to which they were biologically driven. After Himmler unified the German police and security apparatus under his command in 1936, the number of persons held in such custody rose dramatically. A few hundred such were in camps at the end of 1935, but mass arrests in March 1937 and in December 1938 took the number to more than 13,000. At least 2,000 of these were "Gypsies"— incarcerated for their "asocial" and "work-shy" lifestyles.

It is important to keep in mind that these policies represented both a departure from and continuity with traditional police stances toward the Gypsies. Before 1933, Gypsies had been subject to special police measures reserved for them and those who lived like them. In 1926, the state legislature in Bavaria passed a law that aimed to drive Gypsies, travelers, and the "work shy" out of the state. Among its numerous repressive measures, one stands out: any Gypsy over the age of sixteen who could not prove regular employment could be sentenced to up to two years labor in a workhouse. This was punishment for a disposition, not an actual crime, and the sentence was renewable and as such provided a model for the kind of preventive policing that we have just discussed.[20]

Then, following the "father to son" logic, once they had detained the son, the whole family and clan should follow. Discontinuity came in the form of the Nuremberg Laws, which after November 1936 applied to Gypsies as well as Jews and therefore called into being a whole classificatory apparatus designed to determine the Gypsies' racial status. But the true impact of this racialization of the issue was not so much in introducing new conceptual and persecutory systems than in providing the genealogical records that turned the persecution into what Henriette Asséo has called a "familial genocide"[21]—a persecution carried out on and through family social structures.

The Decisive Role of the Municipal and the Local

Beyond the exclusion of Gypsies from their trading and craft niches, their exclusion from welfare and their inclusion among those social layers declared to be biologically predisposed to crime, one final ingredient was needed for the complete institutional encirclement of these populations: the ability of local conflicts to create a national tidal wave of sentiment that someone should step in and "sort things out," coupled with the way that the press could turn highly specific local conjuncture into an issue threatening national security. After 1933, few ever thought to "get rid of *the* Gypsies," but the coming to power of a regime proclaiming national regeneration unleashed great "reforming" currents and in locality after locality officials began to work out ways to "get rid of *these* Gypsies *here.*" The cumulative effect, however, was not so different than if someone in Berlin had sat down and devised a new law for the regulation of the Gypsies.

To understand the dynamic of the Gypsy persecution we have to turn then to the activities of civil servants, the mayors, town planners, welfare officers, policemen, university lecturers, members of scientific research institutes who dealt with Gypsies in the course of their normal work routine. It was in the offices of these town hall and academic racists, in the cells of the Frankfurt and Munich criminal police, on the plots of the compulsory municipal camps of the Ruhrland where Gypsy families were visited by racial scientists hunting for the gene of "asocial behavior," in the university departments of anthropology and racial health, in the "hereditary health" (sterilization) clinics run across the Reich by the city health departments and then in various concentration and death camps that *local, individual* "solutions to the Gypsy problem" were found. If we try to read all the local initiatives and approaches as the unfolding of some central plan or the inevitable consequence of structural features of Nazi rule, we will never make sense of what happened.

In the case of this despised, socially isolated minority at the bottom of the social scale, Nazi rule offered the chance to thousands of people— civil servants and party men in particular, but plenty of ordinary citizens as well—to turn their personal agendas against members of this marginal minority into state policy. The author of the most authoritative survey of the Jewish persecutions, Saul Friedlander, explains that the majority of Germans shied away from widespread violence against Jews, urging neither their expulsion from the Reich nor their physical annihilation. But in relation to the Gypsies and other marginal groups, public opinion lay not so far from Nazi policy. Images of public order, social reform, a return to a "healthy community" of productive workers, the reevaluation of the rural idyll of farmer and his family in their *hof,* and the slogan "a national community without criminals" became popular among the German electorate.

The key role of local bureaucrats in the development of the persecution of the Gypsies meant that a characteristic opposition emerged between local innovators and a conservative national civil service. While town halls improvised and innovated, in Berlin both chancellery and ministerial headquarters not only lagged behind, but actively dragged their feet. During the 1930s and even into the war, officials in various ministries committed themselves to producing a "Reich Gypsy Law" that would create a unified and consistent approach to the Gypsies and replace the old incoherent policy by which each district would expel as many Gypsies from its own territory as it could, leaving its neighbors to fend for themselves.[22] But nothing ever came of these promises.

It was at the interface of central inertia and local mobilization of new state resources that Gypsy policy developed. If we take the early development of the Gypsy camps as an example of this process, we see that what began as slightly stricter versions of municipal camps for travelers metamorphosed gradually toward ethnic internment *lager.* In fact, the appearance of continuity is deeply misleading. The *Zigeunerlager* can only really be understood in the broader context of the entire "camp system" that the Nazis were in the process of constructing. Like the scores of mini-concentration and labor camps that sprung up in 1933, the municipal Gypsy camps had a characteristically ad hoc and local nature. Above all, they had no legal basis whatsoever, not even executive decree. In creating them, each city council operated more or less as it saw fit using whatever Circular Instructions were in operation at the time. In Berlin, an instruction to establish a "manhunt day" to track down Gypsy criminals provided the pretext. In Frankfurt the same decree was used to justify the "sedentarization" of "domestic" Gypsies. In Hamburg, a year later, the mayor turned to the Decree of December 14 on "The Preventive Struggle against Crime," the provisions of which allowed closed camps for "improvement," through labor, or, helpfully, for "sundry other purposes." Just as the legal basis of the camps was determined by unchecked local power, so in the absence of any overarching set of regulations, each camp developed its own system.

If the evolution of the camp order was not planned at the outset, this does not mean it was determined entirely by chance. While the camp at Marzahn was set up to make the capital city *zigeunerfrei* for the foreign "guests" at the Olympics, almost no thought was given to how order would be maintained. Once in existence, by an almost ineluctable logic, regulations were introduced that governed an increasing number of the inmates' activities. Within a short period, a camp superintendent and a police watch had been appointed based on the following logic: What was the point of forcing all the Gypsies to live in one place if not to control their activities and to reduce the threat they posed to the surrounding population? The coming and going of residents could be restricted to departure for work (eight to ten hours) or for shopping (a much more limited time allowed for those without work). To ensure that Gypsies obeyed these rules, a register could be kept of all departures and arrivals. To enforce registration, punishment would be introduced for failure to present oneself. And what was the point of controlling the movement of the Gypsies if outsiders were allowed free entry? As this ever-sharper residential and physical segregation of the Gypsies was implemented, so also were blatant discriminatory measures introduced, followed by their gradual exclusion from the last remaining bastion where Gypsies had a place in German society: the school system. And little of this required decrees, laws, or written orders.[23]

Later on, when central orders were issued, as in the decisive Auschwitz decree of December 1942, this itself can better be seen as the outcome of a struggle between different wings of the Reich security apparatus set off by Himmler's insistence that a small minority of "pure" Gypsies be exempted from some of the regulations hitherto aimed at all Gypsies. The *Kripo*, convinced that matters were getting out of hand, used evidence from the work of racial hygienists to argue for the deportation of "the rest" of the "criminal" Gypsies, the so-called "*mischlinge.*" If this interpretation is correct, as far as the German Roma and Sinte were concerned, the most fateful decision emerged not as an effect of pure ideological or value commitment *strictu sensu*, but from the manner in which existing conditions, conceptual commitments, and political struggles intertwined at a particular conjuncture.[24]

In this sense, the fact that the decision to liquidate the Gypsy Family Camp at Auschwitz was taken, probably by Camp Commandant Rudolf Hoss, in July 1944 in order to free up space for the Hungarian Jews, rather than as part of a general plan to kill all the Gypsies, was an entirely predictable outcome. Far from demonstrating, as Gunther Lewy has perversely argued, that these Gypsies were not victims of genocidal murder, liquidation was the inevitable conclusion of the decision to place the German Gypsies in this camp of all places at this stage in the war. This was no labor camp from which reformed or broken souls might be sent back into the national fold. There were no return tickets from the Auschwitz Birkenau and the police officials who fought for the deportation decree in 1942 must have known very well what possibilities they were opening up and which they were closing down.

Prevention?

Why does any of this matter? Surveying the catalog of twentieth-century mass crimes from the Turkish killings of the Armenians in 1915, through the massacres of around one million persons in Bali in 1965, the thirty-six-year-long campaign against the Mayans in Guatemala, carried out under cover of an anti-insurgency war from 1960 to 1996, through to the horrors of Darfur today, where again a restrictive definition of genocide is allowing the Sudanese government to dispose of a troublesome minority, we can discern a clear enough pattern. Every genocide at the moment it takes place appears to outsiders to be ambiguous and inherently implausible. It is only after the event that genocides appear with certainty and without ambiguity to have taken place. It is only in their aftermath that world leaders and the peoples of the world behind them vow that they must never happen again.

More broadly, the invisibility of the Gypsy genocide teaches us something fundamental about the nature of this crime. Ever since Raphael Lemkin, the Polish-Jewish scholar who coined the term *genocide* in 1943, the scholarly and legal tradition has assumed that genocide is a crime carried out with a "special intent" and invariably involves the execution of a plan. The Romany genocide, however, shows that it is possible to arrive at a genocidal solution of a social "problem" without the political leadership or central authority of a state coming to an explicit decision or formulated "intention," as the International Genocide Convention misleadingly has it.

This matter is by no means purely academic. In 1993, a fellow anthropologist, Cornelia Sorabji, prophetically pointed out that the great powers were misrecognizing the policy of ethnic cleansing being pursued by Franjo Tudjman and Slobodan Milosevic in the former Yugoslavia against the Bosnian Muslim population. At a conference held in December of that year, eighteen months before the massacre of Srebrenica, she argued that a "holocaust" model was hampering understanding of this new genocide. She suggested that in this case a "franchise organization" had been adopted by Serbian and Croat leaders. This made the ethnic cleansing appear anarchic and decentralized.[25] (Haphazardly using schools, factories, and abandoned collective farms as their detention centers, the Bosnian Serb forces made it appear as if they were "merely" improvising, using temporary solutions for holding and neutralizing enemy combatants and their supporters.

But lack of standardization and disorderliness did not imply a lack of organization. Rather there was "organization of a different type in a different political, historical, and cultural setting."[26] One of the ex-inmates of Omarska camp in northeast Bosnia, for instance, appeared astonished when asked whether the torture there was organized: "Anyone could come there and do whatever they liked." Or, as another man detained in the same camp explained, "Omarska Camp was open for all those Serbian volunteers who had someone of 'their own' in it, some captive on whom they wanted to vent their rage."[27] The general point is that this model of genocide may in fact be the historical norm, and what one might call the "Wannsee-Auschwitz model" the exception. Predictable outcomes may arise from a persecution that has plenty of regional variations, a variety of different routes to killing, and even divergent ideological justifications for the crime.

There is another reason that the accurate reconstruction of this history matters, which is the way the historical record and its impact has on later generations. In reality, history does not repeat itself in such a mechanical fashion and, while there is little in the position of Roma in Europe to celebrate, a repeat of those persecutions seems, for the time being at least, unlikely.

But there is trouble brewing. For the past forty years, governments in eastern Europe have claimed that they are actively working toward improving the conditions of the Romany minority, but in 2009 the position of the majority of Gypsies in the region is parlous. Other taxpayers wonder aloud why they have to go on subsidizing this apparently irredeemable "social layer." The fact that under communism reform was framed within an aggressive assimilationist politics, and as such was deeply resisted by many Roma, is largely forgotten. In Bulgaria, Slovakia, and Hungary, strident, populist politicians have found that they can add a new "Gypsy card" to their pack: the Gypsy as the source of national misery, the root of social, political, and even moral corruption, the chief caller on welfare resources who drains away support from the deserving (national) poor, and increasingly of late, the Gypsy as the main obstacle to national regeneration. The role played by international NGOs in promoting human rights through taking up the Gypsies' cause has allowed populists to place this question at the heart of a nationalist-integralist politics. And now, after accession to the European Union—and the gradual integration of Romany issues into European social policies—the possibility to mobilize sizable constituencies around the "Gypsy-Globalization" alliance seems peculiarly threatening. It may be that in years to come, we look back at this decade as that in which a redemptive anti-Gypsyism took shape.

Notes

Introduction

1. Scott Straus, "An Alternative Approach to the Comparative Study of Genocide," paper presented at the American Political Science Association annual conference, August 31, 2007, p. 6.

2. Helen Fein, *Human Rights and Wrongs, Slavery, Terror, Genocide* (Boulder, Colo.: Paradigm Publishers, 2007), p. 136.

3. This is excellently analyzed by Cathie Carmichael in *Genocide Before the Holocaust* (New Haven: Yale University Press, 2009). "Russian expansion in the Caucasus," she writes, "signaled a profound change in the balance of power and threatened existing communities, many of them Muslim. The forced exodus of Circassians to the Ottoman Empire, who were joined by Muslim Abkhazians, Chechens, Laz, Ajars and Ubykhs in the 1860s signaled what Brian Glyn Williams has called 'the end of Islam on the northern Black Sea littoral'" (p. 14).

4. This is how Rummel describes their historic feats of valor: "They would reward their soldiers for every severed head they brought in from the field, whether enemy fighters or not. They would decapitate or club to death captured soldiers; they would slice off the ears, noses, hands and feet of nobles, throw them from high towers, flay them and their children to death, or roast them over a slow fire" (R. J. Rummel, *Death by Government* [New Brunswick, N.J.: Transaction Publishers, 1994], p. 46).

5. Carmichael, *Genocide Before the Holocaust*, pp. 2–19.

6. See Fein, *Human Rights and Wrongs*, pp. 133, 185.

7. Leo Kuper, *Genocide: Its Political Uses in the Twentieth Century* (New Haven: Yale University Press, 1982), p. 58.

8. Raphael Lemkin, *Axis Rule in Occupied Europe* (Washington, D.C.: Carnegie Endowment, 1944).

9. Article 3 of the UNGC reads: "In the present Convention genocide means any of the following acts committed with intent to destroy, in whole or in part, a national, ethnical, racial or religious groups as such: (a) killing members of the group, (b) causing serious bodily or mental harm to members of the group, (c) deliberately inflicting on the group conditions of life calculated to bring about its physical destruction in whole or in part, (d) imposing measures

intended to prevent births within the group, (e) forcibly transferring children of the group to another group." For a critical commentary, see Fein, *Human Rights and Wrongs*, p. 131.

10. On this last point see Benjamin Valentino, *Final Solutions: Mass Killing and Genocide in the Twentieth Century* (Ithaca: Cornell University Press, 2004), pp. 12–13.

11. Among several excellent contributions grappling with such issues, the following deserve special mention: Jacques Sémelin, *Purify and Destroy: The Political Uses of Massacre and Genocide* (London: Hurst, 2007); Alexander Laban Hinton, ed., *Genocide: An Anthopological Reader* (London: Blackwell, 2002); Adam Jones, *Genocide: A Comprehensive Introduction*, second edition (London: Routledge, 2010); Samuel Totten and Paul Bartrop, eds., *The Genocide Studies Reader* (New York: Routledge, 2009). For a brilliant exploration of the analytic problems involved in the comparative analysis of genocide, see Scott Straus's path-breaking review article "Second-Generation Comparative Research on Genocide," *World Politics* 59, no. 3 (April 2007): 476–501. In a different vein mention must be made of Jacques Sémelin's highly personal, and hugely stimulating effort to grapple with the conceptual and analytic dimensions of mass murder, "La logique monstrueuse du meurtre de masse," *Le Débat* (Paris), no. 162 (November–December 2010): 117–31.

12. Ben Kiernan, *Blood and Soil: A World History of Genocide and Extermination from Sparta to Darfur* (New Haven: Yale University Press, 2007).

13. Daniel Jonah Goldhagen, *Worse Than War: Genocide, Eliminationism and the Ongoing Assault on Humanity* (New York: Public Affairs, 2009). As Timothy Snyder persuasively argues this is only one of several flaws that raise serious questions about the author's characterization and interpretation of genocidal events, including his tendency to "reiterate the reasoning of the killers in the guise of scholarly analysis (which) risks not only naïve error but emulation of their thinking." Timothy Snyder, "What We Need to Know About the Holocaust," *New York Review of Books*, September 30, 2010, p. 80.

14. Valentino, *Final Solutions*, p. 12.

15. Israel Charny, "Toward a Generic Definition of Genocide," in George J. Andreopoulos, ed., *Genocide: Conceptual and Historical Dimensions* (Philadelphia: University of Pennsylvania Press, 1997), p. 91.

16. Ibid.

17. The definitive work on the concept, and its relationship to war crimes, is by Sévane Garibian, *Le crime contre l'humanité au regard des principes fondateurs de l'Etat moderne* (Zurich: Editions Romandes, 2010).

18. Fein, *Human Rights and Wrongs*, p. 112.

19. Ibid., p. 132.

20. George Kennan, "Introduction," *The Other Balkan Wars: A 1913 Carnegie Endowment Inquiry in Retrospect* (Washington, D.C.: Carnegie Endowment for International Peace, 1993), p. 11.

21. Lynn Hunt, *Inventing Human Rights: A History* (New York: Norton, 2007), p. 213.

22. Timothy Snyder, "Holocaust: The Ignored Reality," *New York Review of Books*, July 16, 2009, p. 14.

23. Ibid.

24. In the vast amount of literature devoted to the Armenian genocide, passing reference must be made to Donald Bloxham's outstanding contribution, *The Great Game of Genocide: Imperialism, Nationalism and the Destruction of Ottoman Armenians* (Oxford: Oxford University Press, 2005).

25. Sybil Milton, "Holocaust: The Gypsies," in Samuel Totten and William Parsons, eds., *Century of Genocide: Critical Essays and Eyewitness Accounts* (New York: Routledge, 2009), p. 163.

26. Colin Tatz, *With Intent To Destroy: Reflecting on Genocide* (New York: Verso, 2003), p. 133.

27. Bloxham, *The Great Game of Genocide*, p. 209.

28. Maurice Halbwachs, *Les cadres sociaux de la mémoire* (Paris: Mouton, 1976).

29. Phil Clark and Zachary D. Kaufman, eds., *After Genocide: Transitional Justice, Post-Conflict Reconstruction and Reconciliation in Rwanda and Beyond* (London: Hurst, 2008), pp. 65–76.

30. For a fuller discussion, see Lemarchand, "Genocide: Memory and Ethnic Reconciliation in Rwanda," in S. Marysse, F. Reyntjens, and S. Vandeginste, eds., *L'Afrique des Grand Lacs: Annuaire 2006–2007* (Paris: L'Harmattan, 2007), pp. 21–30.

31. Studs Terkel, *Race: How Blacks and Whites Think and Feel About the American Obsession* (New York: The New Press, 1993), p. 142. Quoted in Tatz, *With Intent to Destroy*, p. 142.

32. See Liisa Malkki's illuminating discussion of "the mythico-history of atrocity" in her *Purity and Exile: Violence, Memory, and National Cosmology Among Hutu Refugees in Tanzania* (Chicago: University of Chicago Press, 1995), p. 91 ff.

33. Tatz, *With Intent to Destroy* p. 142–43.

34. Pierre Vidal-Naquet, *Les assassins de la mémoire* (Paris: La Découverte, 1987).

35. Bloxham, *The Great Game of Genocide*, p. 211.

36. Thea Halo, IAGS *Newsletter*, December 16, 2007. Available at http://www.notevenmyname.com/2.html.

37. Susanne Buckley-Zistel, "Remembering to Forget: Chosen Amnesia as a Strategy for Local Co-existence in Post-Genocide Rwanda," *Africa* 76, no. 2 (2006): 131–50.

Chapter 1. Mass Murder in Eastern Congo, 1996–1997

1. While this book was in print, the UN High Commission for Human Rights published a 545-page report that confirms and details the analysis offered in this chapter (United Nations High Commission for Human Rights, Democratic Republic of the Congo, 1993–2003. *Report of the Mapping Exercise Documenting the Most Serious Violations of Human Rights and International Humanitarian Law Committed Within the Territory of the Democratic Republic of the Congo Between March 1993 and June 2003*, Geneva, August 2010). On the crimes committed by the RPA against Hutu refugees, it states that "the apparent systematic and widespread attacks described in this report reveal a number of inculpatory elements that, if proven before a competent court, could be characterized as crimes of genocide" (p. 14).

2. Johan Pottier estimates their number at 700,000, a figure consistent with the statements issued by the Rwandan government. But in an interview with one of the authors, Michael Hyden, who took part in the counting operations on behalf of the Lutheran Foundation, admitted that "no one really knows how many returned; after tens of thousands had crossed the border we just lost count," adding that anywhere between 400,000 and 500,000 would be a reasonable estimate. See Johan Pottier, *Re-Imagining Rwanda: Conflict, Survival and Disinformation in the Late Twentieth Century* (Cambridge: Cambridge University Press, 2002), p. 44.

3. Stephen Smith, *Le fleuve Congo* (Paris: Actes Sud, 2003), p. 95.

4. K. Emizet, "The Massacre of Refugees in Congo: A Case of UN Peacekeeping Failure and International Law," *Journal of Modern African Studies*, 38, no. 2 (2000): 173–79.

5. Refugees International, *Statement of Lionel A. Rosenblatt President of Refugees International on Refugees in Eastern Zaïre before the Subcommittee on International Operations and Human Rights Committee on International Relations*, U.S. House of Representatives, December 4, 1996, p. 3.

6. Philip Gourevitch, "Continental Shift," *New Yorker*, August 4, 1997, p. 45.

7. Quoted in Gaspard Musabyimana, *L'APR et les réfugiés rwandais au Zaïre 1996–1997: Un Génocide Nié* (Paris: L'Harmattan, 2004), pp. 47–49.

8. For a detailed inventory of the military hardware at the disposal of the ex-FAR and interahamwe, see Fiona Terry's outstanding discussion in *Condemned to Repeat? The Paradox of Humanitarian Action* (Ithaca: Cornell University Press, 2002), pp. 156–65.

9. Quoted in Koen Vlassenroot, "Identity and Insecurity: The Building of Ethnic Agendas in South Kivu," in Ruddy Doom and Jan Gorus, eds., *Politics of Identity and Economics of Conflict in the Great Lakes Region* (Brussels: VUB University Press, 2000), p. 274.

10. For the full text, see Manasse (Muller) Ruhimbika, *Les Banyamulenge (Congo-Zaïre) entre deux guerres* (Paris: L'Harmattan, 2001), pp. 32–33.

11. For a more sustained discussion, see Filip Reyntjens, *The Great African War: Congo and Regional Geopolitics, 1996–2006* (Cambridge: Cambridge University Press, 2009).

12. Samantha Power, *Chasing the Flame: One Man's Fight to Save the World* (New York: Penguin Books, 2008), p. 206.

13. Reyntjens, *The Great African War*, p. 53.

14. Ibid., pp. 66–79.

15. Power, *Chasing the Flame*, p. 207.

16. Howard French, *A Continent for the Taking: The Tragedy and Hope of Africa* (New York: Alfred A. Knopf, 2004), pp. 144, 145, 148.

17. Marie Béatrice Umutesi, *Surviving the Slaughter* (Madison: University of Wisconsin Press, 2004), p. 193.

18. Maurice Niwese, *Le peuple rwandais un pied dans la tombe: Récit d'un réfugié étudiant* (Paris: L'Harmattan, 2001), pp. 161–62.

19. Smith, *Le fleuve Congo*, p. 95.

20. Theophile Ruhorahoza, *Terminus Mbandaka: Le chemin des charniers de réfugiés rwandais au Congo* (Brussells: Editions Sources du Nil, 2009), p. 84.

21. William Shawcross, *Deliver Us from Evil: Peacekeepers, Warlords and a World of Endless Conflict* (New York: Simon and Schuster, 2000), p. 244.

22. Jeff Crisp, "Who Has Counted the Refugees? UNHCR and the Politics of Numbers," in Stephen C. Lubkemann, Larry Minear, and Thomas G. Weiss, eds., *Humanitarian Action: Social Science Connections* (Thomas Watson Institute of International Studies, Occasional Paper #7, 2000), pp. 53–54.

23. Ibid., p. 54.

24. Quoted in Nigel Eltringham, *Accounting for Horror: Post-Genocide Debates in Rwanda* (London and Sterling, Va: Pluto Press, 2004), p. 128.

25. Pottier, *Re-Imagining Rwanda*, p. 149.

26. Robert Gribbin, *In the Aftermath of Genocide: The U.S. Role in Rwanda* (New York: iUniverse, Inc., 2005), pp. 179, 181, 191.

27. United Nations, *Report of the Joint Mission Charged with Investigating Allegations of Massacres and Other Human Rights Violations Occurring in Eastern Zaïre Since September 1996, 2 July 1997*. Cited in Eltringham, *Accounting for Horror*, p. 131.

28. Ibid., p. 132.

29. UN Security Council, *Report of the Investigative Team Charged with Investigating Serious Violations of Human Rights and International Humanitarian Law in the Democratic Republic of the Congo*, S/1998/581, June 29, 1998, para. 96.

30. John Lewis Gaddis, *Surprise, Security and the American Experience* (Cambridge: Harvard University Press, 2004), p. 17.

31. Andrew Bell-Fialkoff, *Ethnic Cleansing* (New York: St. Martin's Griffin, 1999), p. 3.

32. Jacques Sémelin, *Purify and Destroy: The Political Uses of Massacre and Genocide*, translated from the French by Cynthia Schoch (London: Hurst and Co., 2005), p. 339.

33. See International Crisis Group, *Congo: Une stratégie globale pour désarmer les FDLR*, Rapport Afrique No. 151, July 9, 2009, p. 23.

Chapter 2. Burundi 1972

Parts of this chapter draw from some of my previous publications, notably "Le génocide de 1972 au Burundi: Les silences de l'histoire," *Cahiers d'Etudes africaines* 167, XLII-3 (2002): 551–67; "The Burundi Genocide," in Samuel Totten and William S. Parsons, eds., *Century of Genocide: Critical Essays and Eyewitness Accounts* (London: Routledge, 2009), pp. 323–41; "Burundi 1972: A Forgotten Genocide," in René Lemarchand, *The Dynamics of Violence in Central Africa* (Philadelphia: University of Pennsylvania Press, 2008), pp. 129–40. For a more "structured" and wide-ranging exploration of the subject, the reader may wish to turn to my 2008 contribution to Online Encyclopedia of Mass Violence, "The Burundi Killings of 1972", http://www.massviolence.org/The Burundi Killings of 1972. I wish to record my indebtedness to Michael Hoyt, who served as deputy chief of mission in Bujumbura at the time of the genocide, for giving me access to Embassy and State Department cables from April to July 1972. His help over the years has been invaluable.

1. Michael Bowen, Gary Freeman, and Kay Miller, *Passing By: The United States and Genocide in Burundi, 1972*, a report of the Carnegie Endowment for International Peace, 1973, p. 1.

2. In response to that question Neela Ghoshal, who served as Human Rights Watch researcher in Bujumbura before being expelled by the Burundi authorities in 2010 suggests the following explanation: "The Rwanda genocide should have provoked serious exploration about the events in Burundi in 1872, but for several reasons, it didn't. Perhaps events twenty years in the past seemed distant, and the more recent killings in Burundi in 1993, when both Hutu and Tutsi were targeted, added a layer of complexity that made it difficult to understand Burundi through the lens of genocide. During and after the Rwanda genocide, some (observers) did begin to draw connections, but parallels with Burundi may not have been convenient because they would undermine or confuse a rapidly-solidifying narrative (in relation to Rwanda) based on a characterization of 'good' Tutsi victims and 'bad' Hutu perpetrators" (personal communication).

For a more wide-ranging commentary on the connections between the two genocides, see my article "Le génocide de 1972 au Burundi: Les silences de l'histoire," *Cahiers d'Etudes Africaines,* 167 42–43 (2002), pp. 551–67.

3. Nixon's handwritten comments in Memorandum for the president from Henry Kissinger, September 20, 1972, in "Burundi, Vol. 1," Box 735, Country files, Africa, National Security Council (NSC) files. I am grateful to Christian Desroches, a former student of mine at Concordia University (Montreal), for sharing with me this extraordinary document.

4. Helen Fein, "Genocide: A Sociological Perspective," *Sociology,* International Sociological Association 38, no. 1 (Spring 1990): p. 30.

5. "Témoignages sur un génocide," *Le Monde,* Sélection hebdomadaire, May 25–31, 1972, p. 7.

6. For a more detailed discussion see Lemarchand, *Burundi: Ethnic Conflict and Genocide* (New York and Cambridge: Woodrow Wilson Press and Cambridge University Press, 1995), pp. 89–96.

7. *Génocide au Burundi,* Dossier Pax Christi, Campagne Paix 1973, Brussels 1973, p. 3; see also Jean Planchais, "Un vent de liberté au Burundi," *Le Monde,* Sélection hebdomadaire, December 23–29, 1976, p. 3.

8. *Livre Blanc sur les évènements survenus aux mois d'avril et mai 1972,* translated by the Burundi Embassy as *The White Paper on the Real Causes and Consequences of the Attempted Genocide Against the Tutsi Ethny [sic] in Burundi, Embassy of the Republic of Burundi,* Washington D.C., June 26, 1972. The full text can be found in appendix 2 of Thomas P. Melady, *Burundi: The Tragic Years* (Maryknoll, N.Y.: Orbis Books, 1974), pp. 98–103. The author served as U.S. Ambassador to Burundi from November 1969 to June 1972.

9. Jeremy Greenland, "Ethnic Discrimination in Rwanda and Burundi," in *Case Studies on Human Rights and Fundamental Freedoms: A World Survey,* ed. Willem A. Veenhoven, vol. 4 (The Hague: Martinus Nijhoff, 1976), p. 120.

10. *Livre Blanc.*

11. For a fuller review of the official propaganda emanating from Burundi authorties, see Jean-Pierre Chrétien and Jean-Francois Dupaquier, *Burundi 1972: Au bord des génocides* (Paris: Kathala, 2007), pp. 311–42.

12. Quoted in Michael Hoyt, U.S. Embassy cable to State Department, May 30, 1972.

13. Quoted in Kathleen Teltsch, "Killings Go On in Burundi," July 20, 1972, *New York Times,* p. 1.

14. Quoted in Michael Hoyt, U.S. Embassy Cable to State Department, May 22, 1972.

15. Bowen, Freeman, and Miller, *Passing By,* p. 5.

16. Roger Morris, *Uncertain Greatness: Henry Kissinger and American Foreign Policy* (New York: Harper and Row, 1997), p. 267.

17. Ibid.

18. Paul Richards, ed., *No Peace, No War* (Athens: Ohio University Press, 2005), cited in Lee Ann Fujii, *Killing Neighbors: Webs of Violence in Rwanda* (Ithaca: Cornell University Press, 2008), p. 23.

19. Liisa Malkki, *Purity and Exile: Violence, Memory, and National Cosmology Among Hutu Refugees in Tanzania* (Chicago: University of Chicago Press, 1995), pp. 191–92.

20. Augustin Nsanze, *Le Burundi Contemporain: L'Etat-nation en question (1956–2002)* (Paris: L'Harmattan, 2003), p. 218. It is a commentary on the intellectual honesty of the author that after asking me to write the preface of his book, and

having accepted to do so, he subsequently eliminated the reservations expressed in my text regarding precisely this passage of his book.

21. See Chrétien and Dupaquier, *Burundi 1972: Au bord des génocides*, p. 113.. Here are some of the extracts from the tract: "Arm yourselves and kill all the Tutsi! Let's unite to kill the Tutsi, army men or leaders! Attack Tutsi administrators and politicians and their families, and don't forget the pregnant women! No judgment for the Tutsi, all to the graveyard."

22. The two main sources are the "testimonies" of a key actor of the repression, Albert Shibura, whose mimeographed text, *Témoignages* (Bujumbura, 1996) is an extraordinary mix of palpable lies and anti-CIA rantings, and Marc Manirakiza, *Burundi: De la révolution au regionalisme 1966–1976* (Paris: Le Mat de Misaine, 1992), pp. 120–22. The authors admit that they never were able to see the tracts mentioned in either work.

23. Evariste Ngayimpenda, *Histoire du conflit politico-ethnique burundais: Les premières marches du calvaire (1960–1973)* (Bujumbura: Editions de la Renaissance), p. 451.

24. Chrétien and Dupaquier, *Burundi 1972*, p. 477.

25. Maurice Halbwachs, *La mémoire collective* (Paris: Albin Michel, 1997), p. 140.

26. Malkki, *Purity and Exile*, p. 54.

27. Only after much kicking and screaming did Rwasa finally agree to drop the Palipehutu label in order to meet the request of the government during the protracted negotiations that went through much of 2008. At first the FNL referred to the armed wing of the Palipehutu.

28. Rémy Gahutu, *The Persecution of the Hutu of Burundi*, translated from the French by Hugh Hazelton and Peter Keating (n.p., n.d.), p. 4.

29. Ibid., p. 50.

30. Agathon Rwasa, *De la crise burundaise ou la crise des Grands Lacs: La voie d'issue*, NR; R 02-017/PLPHT-FN/02m mimeo., February 2002, p. 2.

28 On the events of Ntega and Marangara—a critical watershed in the political history of the country—see Lemarchand, *Burundi*, pp. 120–27.

Chapter 3. "Every Herero Will Be Shot"

1. The first comprehensive biography of Lemkin was only recently published: John Cooper, *Raphael Lemkin and the Struggle for the Genocide Convention* (London: Palgrave Macmillan, 2008).

2. On Lemkin's perception of colonialism, see Michael A. McDonnell and A. Dirk Moses, "Raphael Lemkin as Historian of Genocide in the Americas," *Journal of Genocide Research* (2005) 4: 501–29. John Docker, "Are Settler-Colonies Inherently Genocidal? Re-reading Lemkin," in A. Dirk Moses, ed., *Empire, Colony, Genocide: Conquest, Occupation, and Subaltern Resistance in World History* (New York: Berghahn Books, 2008), pp. 81–101.

3. Raphael Lemkin, "The Germans in Africa," unpublished and undated typewritten manuscript, Jacob Rader Marcus Center of the American Jewish Archives, Hebrew Union College, Cincinnati, Raphael Lemkin Papers, Box 6, Folder 12, pp. 49–50. For an analysis of Lemkin's ambivalent perception of European colonialism, see Dominik J. Schaller, "Raphael Lemkin's View of European Colonial Rule in Africa: Between Condemnation and Admiration," *Journal of Genocide Research* 7, no. 4 (2005): 531–38.

4. Reinhart Kössler, "Sjambok or Cane? Reading the Blue Book," *Journal of Southern African Studies* 30, no. 3 (2004): 703–8. The report has recently been re-edited with commentary by Jeremy Silvester and Jan-Bart Gewald and published as *Words Cannot Be Found: German Colonial Rule in Namibia. An Annotated Reprint of the 1918 Blue Book* (Leiden: Brill, 2003).

5. Jeremy Silvester and Jan-Bart Gewald, "Footsteps and Tears: An Introduction to the Construction and Context of the 1918 'Blue Book,'" in Silvester and Gewald, *Words Cannot Be Found*, pp. xiii–xxxvii.

6. Horst Drechsler, *Südwestafrika unter deutscher Kolonialherrschaft: Der Kampf der Herero und Nama gegen den deutschen Imperialismus* (1884–1915) (Berlin [DDR]: Akademie-Verlag, 1966). Helmut Bley, *Kolonialherrschaft und Sozialstruktur in Deutsch-Südwestafrika 1894–1914* (Hamburg: Leibniz-Verlag, 1968). Helmuth Stoecker, ed., *Drang nach Afrika. Die koloniale Expansionspolitik und Herrschaft des deutschen Imperialismus in Afrika von den Anfängen bis zum Ende des Zweiten Weltkriegs* (Berlin: Akademie-Verlag, 1977).

7. Elazar Barkan, *The Guilt of Nations: Restitution and Negotiating Historical Injustices* (New York: Norton, 2000).

8. Allan D. Cooper, "Reparations for the Herero Genocide: Defining the Limits of International Litigation," *African Affairs* 106, no. 422 (2007): 113–26.

9. The Hereros' statement of claim can be found on the following website: http://www.ipr.uni-heidelberg.de/Mitarbeiter/Professoren/Hess/Hessforschung/zwang/herero.pdf (last accessed August 19, 2008). The quotation is from page 21.

10. Ibid., p. 57.

11. Jürgen Zimmerer, "Colonialism and the Holocaust: Towards an Archaeology of Genocide," in A. Dirk Moses, ed., *Genocide and Settler Society. Frontier Violence and Stolen Indigenous Children in Australian History* (New York: Berghahn Books, 2004), 49–76. Zimmerer, "The Birth of the 'Ostland' out of the Spirit of Colonialism: A Postcolonial Perspective on Nazi Policy of Conquest and Extermination," *Patterns of Prejudice* 39, no. 2 (2005): 197–219. Benjamin Madley, "From Africa to Auschwitz: How German South West Africa Incubated Ideas and Methods Adopted and Developed by the Nazis in Eastern Europe," *European History Quarterly* 35, no. 3 (2005): 429–64. For differing views on the question of continuity, see Birthe Kundrus, "Von den Herero zum Holocaust? Einige Bemerkungen zur aktuellen Debatte," *Mittelweg 36: Zeitschrift des Hamburger Instituts für Sozialforschung* 14, no. 4 (2005): 82–91. Pascal Grosse, "What Does German Colonialism Have to Do with National Socialism? A Conceptual Framework," in Eric Ames, ed., *Germany's Colonial Pasts*. (Lincoln: University of Nebraska Press, 2005), pp. 115–34. Robert Gerwarth and Stephan Malinowski, "Der Holocaust als 'genozidaler Kolonialkrieg'? Europäische Kolonialgewalt und nationalsozialistischer Vernichtungskrieg," *Geschichte und Gesellschaft* 33, no. 3 (2007): 439–66.

12. Jürgen Zimmerer, "War, Concentration Camps and Genocide in South-West Africa. The First German Genocide," in Zimmerer and Joachim Zeller, eds., *Genocide in German South-West Africa. The Colonial War of 1904–1908 and Its Aftermath* (Monmouth, UK: Merlin Press, 2008), pp. 41–63.

13. Speech by Heidemarie Wieczorek-Zeul at the commemorations of the 100th anniversary of the suppression of the Herero uprising, Okakarara, Namibia, August 14, 2004. An English version of the speech can be found on the website of the German embassy in Windhoek: http://www.windhuk.diplo.de/Vertretung/windhuk/en/03/Bilaterale_Beziehungen/seite_rede_bmz_engl_okakahandja.html (last accessed August 19, 2008).

14. Motion on the Ovaherero Genocide introduced in the Namibian Parliament by the Honourable Kuaima Riruako, paramount chief of the Ovaherero people, September 19, 2006. The text can be found on the website of the "Association of the Ovaherero Genocide in the U.S.A.": http://ovahererogenocideassociationusa.org (last accessed August 19, 2008).

15. Henning Melber, "'We never spoke about reparations': German-Namibian Relations between Amnesia, Aggression and Reconciliation," in J. Zimmerer and J. Zeller, eds., and E. J. Neather, trans., *Genocide in German South-West Africa: The Colonial War of 1904–1908 and Its Aftermath* (Monmouth, UK: Merlin Press), pp. 259–73.

16. Jan-Bart Gewald, "The Herero Genocide: German Unity, Settlers, Soldiers, and Ideas," in Marianne Bechhaus-Gerst and Reinhard Klein-Arendt, eds., *Die (koloniale) Begegnung: AfrikanerInnen in Deutschland 1880–1945. Deutsche in Africa 1880–1918* (Frankfurt am Main: Peter Lang Publishing, 2003), pp. 109–27 (114).

17. Jan-Bart Gewald, *Herero Heroes: A Socio-Political History of the Herero of Namibia 1890–1923* (Oxford: James Currey, 1999), pp. 10–26.

18. The letter dates from April 18, 1893, and is published in *The Hendrik Witbooi Papers*, National Archives of Namibia (Windhoek, 1989), 126f.

19. Theodor Leutwein, *Elf Jahre Gouverneur in Deutsch-Südwestafrika* (Berlin: Mittler, 1906), pp. 541–43.

20. Paul Rohrbach, *Deutsche Kolonialwirtschaft, Volume 1: Südwest-Afrika* (Berlin: Buchverlag der Hilfe, 1907), pp. 285ff.

21. Jürgen Zimmerer, *Deutsche Herrschaft über Afrikaner: Staatlicher Machtanspruch und Wirklichkeit im kolonialen Namibia* (Münster: Lit-Verlag, 2001), p. 9.

22. On Maharero's background and his struggle for the chieftainship, see Gerhard Pool, *Samuel Maharero* (Windhoek: Gambsberg Macmillan, 1991).

23. Jan-Bart Gewald, *Herero Heroes*, p. 108.

24. Jakob Irle, *Die Herero: Ein Beitrag zur Landes-, Volks-und Missionskunde* (Gütersloh: Bertelsmann, 1906), p. 127.

25. Proclamation by Lothar von Trotha (copy), October 2, 1904, German Federal Archive, Berlin Lichterfelde (GAF), Bestand Reichskolonialamt (R1001), 2098, 7f.

26. Ibid.

27. Letter by Lothar von Trotha to the chief of the German general staff von Schlieffen, October 4,1904, GFA, R 1001, 2089, 5. English translation in Horst Drechsler, *Let Us Die Fighting: The Struggle of the Herero and Nama Against German Imperialism* (London: Zed Press, 1980), p. 161.

28. Cited in Pool, *Samuel Maharero*, p. 251.

29. German Federal Archive Koblenz, NL 30: Victor Franke papers, diary entry of August 12,1904.

30. Ludwig von Estorff, *Wanderungen und Kämpfe in Südwestafrika, Ostafrika und Südafrika 1894–1910*, ed. Christoph-Friedrich Kutscher (Wiesbaden: Kurier Verlag, 1968), pp. 116f. English translation in Gewald, *Herero Heroes*, p. 174.

31. This interpretation has recently been called "a tenacious myth of German military omnicompetence." See Isabel V. Hull, *Absolute Destruction. Military Culture and the Practices of War in Imperial Germany* (Ithaca: Cornell University Press, 2005), p. 37.

32. Paul Rohrbach, *Um des Teufels Handschrift. Zwei Menschenalter erlebter Weltgeschichte* (Hamburg: Hans Dulk Verlag, 1953), p. 64. Theodor Leutwein came to a similar conclusion in his memoirs: Leutwein, *Elf Jahre*, pp. 525, 542.

33. Leutwein, *Elf Jahre*, pp. 511f; Bley, *Kolonialherrschaft*, p. 194; Gewald, *Herero Heroes*, pp. 167f.; Drechsler, *Südwestafrika unter deutscher Kolonialherrschaft*, p. 175.

34. Lothar von Trotha to von Schlieffen, October 4,1904, p. 5.

35. Citied in Krüger, *Kriegsbewältigung*, p. 66.

36. Lothar von Trotha to von Schlieffen, October 4, 1904, p. 5.

37. Cited in Drechsler, *Let Us Die Fighting*, p. 154.

38. Schlieffen to Bülow, December 16, 1904, GFA, R1001: 2089, 17.

39. English translation provided by German History in Documents and Images (GHDI): http://germanhistorydocs.ghi-dc.org/sub_document.cfm?do cument_id = 755 (last accessed August 19, 2008).

40. On the development of this specific German military culture, see Hull, *Absolute Destruction*, pp. 91–181.

41. Report of the *Schutztruppe* on the mortality in German concentration camps, GFA, R1001: 2140, p. 151.

42. Chancellor von Bülow to von Trotha, January 14, 1905, GFA, R1001: 2089, p. 54.

43. Joachim Zeller, "'Ombepera i koza—The Cold Is Killing Me': Notes Toward a History of the Concentration at Swakopmund (1904–1908)," in Zimmerer and Zeller, *Genocide in German South-West Africa*, pp. 64–83. Casper Wulff Erichsen, "Forced LabT in the Concentration Camp on Shark Island," in Zimmerer and Zeller, *Genocide in German South-West Africa*, pp. 84–99.

44. Cited in Zeller, "Ombepera i koza," p. 64.

45. Tecklenburg to the Colonial Office in Berlin, July 3, 1905, GFA, R1001: 2118, pp. 154f. English translation in Zimmerer, *War, Concentration Camps, and Genocide*, p. 53.

46. Lindequist to the Colonial Office in Berlin, April 17, 1905, GFA, R 1001: 2119, pp. 42f. English translation in Zimmerer, *War, Concentration Camps, and Genocide*, p. 53.

47. *Report on the Natives of South-West Africa and Their Treatment by Germany, Prepared in the Administrators Office, Windhuk [Windhoek], South-West Africa, January 1918* (London: His Majesty's Stationary Office, 1918), pp. 101f.

48. Letter of the agrarian society in Okahandja to the government in Windhoek, December 16, 1913, National Archives of Namibia, Zentralbureau (ZBU), W.III.b.1, p. 37.

49. Willem Petrus Steenkamp, *Is the South-West African Herero Committing Race Suicide?* (Cape Town: Unie-Volkspers, 1944), p. 8.

50. See, e.g., Karla Poewe, *The Namibian Herero: A History of Their Psychological Disintegration and Survival* (Lewiston, N.Y.: Edwin Mellen, 1985).

51. Drechsler, *Südwestafrika unter deutscher Kolonialherrschaft*, p. 260.

52. Gewald, *Herero Heroes*. Krüger, *Kriegsbewältigung*.

53. Jan-Bart Gewald, "The Funeral of Samuel Maharero and the Reorganisation of the Herero," in Zimmerer and Zeller, *Genocide in South-West Africa*, pp. 207–16.

54. Krüger, *Kriegsbewältigung*, pp. 201–3.

Chapter 4. Extermination, Extinction, Genocide

1. Josephine Flood, *The Original Australians* (Sydney: Allen & Unwin, 2006), pp. 58–77.

2. Lyndall Ryan, *The Aboriginal Tasmanians* (Sydney: Allen & Unwin, 1996), p. 83.

3. The Aboriginal population level at 1803 has long been disputed. Informed colonists at the time thought the number was around 6,000. Oral evidence suggests many died from disease between 1772 and 1803. Archaeologists consider 5,000 is a feasible estimate at colonization. See Flood, *Original Australians*, pp. 66–67. For later population figures, see Ryan, *Aboriginal Tasmanians*, pp. 79, 180, and 205; for transportation, see Ryan, *Aboriginal Tasmanians*, pp. 182–94, 205–21.

4. Ann Curthoys, "Genocide in Tasmania," in A. Dirk Moses, ed., *Empire, Colony, Genocide: Conquest, Occupation and Subaltern Resistance in World History* (New York: Berghahn Books, 2008), pp. 230–31.

5. Richard Broome, *The Aboriginal Australians* (Sydney: Allen & Unwin, 1982), ch. 1.

6. Richard Broome, *Aboriginal Victorians* (Sydney: Allen & Unwin, 2005), pp. 90–91.

7. Tony Barta, "Relations of Genocide: Land and Lives in the Colonization of Australia," in I. Wallimann and M. N. Dobowski, eds., *Genocide and the Modern Age: Etiology and Case Studies of Mass Death* (Westport: Greenwood Press, 1987), pp. 237–51; A. Dirk Moses, "An Antipodean Genocide: The Origins of the Genocidal Moment in the Colonisation of Australia," *Journal of Genocide Research* 2, no. 1 (2000): 89–106; A. Dirk Moses, ed., *Genocide and Settler Society* (New York: Berghahn Books, 2003).

8. Henry Reynolds, *Fate of a Free People* (Melbourne: Penguin, 1995); Henry Reynolds, "Genocide in Tasmania?" in A. Dirk Moses, ed,, *Genocide and Settler Society*, pp. 146–47; Ben Kiernan, *Blood and Soil* (Melbourne: Melbourne University Press, 2008), pp. 265–80; Curthoys, "Genocide in Tasmania," pp. 241–45.

9. Curthoys, "Genocide in Tasmania," pp. 231–32. Lemkin's draft chapter, edited by Curthoys, was published as "Tasmania," in *Patterns of Prejudice*, 39, no. 2 (2005): 170–96; John Docker, *The Origins of Violence: Religion, History and Genocide* (Sydney: University of New South Wales Press, 2008), pp. 1–11.

10. Docker, *Origins of Violence*, p. 3; Lemkin, "Tasmania."

11. Russell McGregor, *Imagined Destinies: Doomed Race Theory in Australia* (Melbourne: Melbourne University Press, 1997), pp. 134–41; *National Inquiry into the Separation of Aboriginal and Torres Strait Islander Children from their Families, Bringing Them Home* (Sydney: Australian Human Rights and Equal Opportunity Commission, 1997). The authors were Ronald Wilson, a former Australian High Court Judge, and Mick Dodson, an Aboriginal activist, lawyer, and academic.

12. Stuart Macintyre, *The History Wars* (Melbourne: Melbourne University Press, 2003); Shayne Breen, "Defending the National Honour: the History Crusaders and Australia's Past," in Andrew Gunstone, ed., *History, Politics and Knowledge: Essays in Australian Indigenous Studies* (Melbourne: Australian Scholarly Publishing, 2008), pp. 168–90; Prime Minister Kevin Rudd's apology speech was delivered in the Australian parliament on February 13, 2008.

13. For an account of Ryan and genocide, see Shayne Breen, "Fabrication, Genocide and Denial: The History Crusaders and Australia's Past," *History Australia* 1, no. 1 (2003): 73–84; Keith Windschuttle, *The Fabrication of Aboriginal History* (Sydney: Macleay Press, 2002), pp. 2, 12, 14; Robert Hughes, *The Fatal Shore* (London: Collins Harvill, 1987); Jared Diamond, *The Rise and Fall of the Third Chimpanzee* (London: Vintage, 1992), pp. 252–55.

14. Docker, *Origins of Violence*, pp. 57–59, 157–59, 161–87.

15. Curthoys, "Genocide in Tasmania," pp. 232–26.

16. Reynolds, *Fate of a Free People*, pp. 27–28; Leonie Mickleborough, *William Sorell in Van Diemen's Land, Lieutenant-Governor, 1817–24: A Golden Age?* (Hobart: Blubber Head Press, 2004), pp. 79–80, 85.

17. A. G. L. Shaw, ed., *Van Diemen's Land: Copies of all correspondence . . . on the subject of the military operations . . . against the Aboriginal inhabitants . . .* (Hobart: Tasmanian Historical Research Association, 1971); Mickleborough, *William Sorell in Van Diemen's Land*, pp. 79–87.

18. Henry Melville, *The History of the Island of Van Diemen's Land* (Sydney: Horowitz-Grahame, 1965, first published in London, 1835), pp. 79, 106–7; James Bonwick, *The Last of the Tasmanians* (Adelaide: Libraries Board of South Australia, 1969, first published in London, 1870), p. 79; John West, *A History of Tasmania* (Sydney: Angus & Robertson, 1971, first published in London, 1852), pp. 281, 330–33.

19. Curthoys, "Genocide in Tasmania," pp. 232–34; West, *A History of Tasmania*, pp. 332–33; Bonwick, *The Last of the Tasmanians*, pp. 323–32.

20. Ryan, *Aboriginal Tasmanians*, pp. 1–3; McGregor, *Imagined Destinies*, pp. 48–59.

21. Shayne Breen, *Contested Places: Tasmania's Northern Districts from Ancient Times to 1900* (Hobart: Centre for Tasmanian Historical Studies, 2001), pp. 13–22.

22. Ryan, *Aboriginal Tasmanians*, pp. 81–87.

23. N. J. B. Plomley, ed., *Friendly Mission* (Hobart: Tasmanian Historical Research Association, 1966), October 2, 1829. *Friendly Mission* contains the journals of G. A. Robinson. A new edition was published in 2008. To avoid confusion, the dates of entries are used here. West, *A History of Tasmania*, pp. 274–76.

24. Ryan, *Aboriginal Tasmanians*, pp. 66–71.

25. Mickleborough, *William Sorell in Van Diemen's Land*, pp. 69–70; James Boyce, *Van Diemen's Land* (Melbourne: Black, 2008), pp. 87–89, 99; West, *A History of Tasmania*, p. 265.

26. Plomley, *Friendly Mission*, November 3, 1830, and footnote 51.

27. Lyndall Ryan, "Abduction and Multiple Killings of Aborigines in Tasmania: 1804–1835," in Jacques Semelin, ed., *Online Encyclopedia of Mass Violence* (2008), p. 2, at http://www.massviolence.org. This section owes a considerable debt to Lyndall Ryan. Her detailed work on violent deaths forms the basis for my analysis of types of killings.

28. *Colonial Advocate & Tasmanian Review and Register*, April 1, 1830, in Ryan, "Abduction and Multiple Killings of Aborigines,", p. 6.

29. Shaw, *Van Diemen's Land*, pp. 22–26; Ryan "Abduction and Multiple Killings of Aborigines," p. 3; Reynolds, *Fate of a Free People*, pp. 108–12; Ryan, *Aboriginal Tasmanians*, pp. 91–92, 99; Ryan, "Abduction and Multiple Killings of Aborigines," pp. 3–7.

30. Reynolds, *Fate of a Free People*, pp. 108–12.

31. Boyce, *Van Diemen's Land*, pp. 269–74.

32. Ryan, "Abduction and Multiple Killings of Aborigines," p. 2.

33. Ibid., pp. 1–3.

34. Ibid., pp. 3–7.

35. Ibid., p. 2.

36. Plomley, *Friendly Mission*, October 15, 16, and 19, 1830, and footnote 16.

37. Henry James Emmett, "Reminiscences of the Black War in Tasmania," (c. 1870), MS 3311, Emmett, National Library of Australia, transcribed by Julie Gough, June 8, 2007.

38. Ryan, "Abduction and Multiple Killings of Aborigines,", p. 3.

39. Plomley, *Friendly Mission*, September 25, 1830.

40. Plomley, *Friendly Mission*, November 9, 1830; West, *A History of Tasmania*, p. 279.

41. Plomley, *Friendly Mission*, September 21, 1829; Ryan *Aboriginal Tasmanians*, pp. 124–29.

42. Ryan, *Aboriginal Tasmanians*, p. 112. For an example of press ridicule, see *Launceston Advertiser*, September 30, 1830.

43. For a discussion of the Black Line as a military exercise, see John Connor, *Australian Frontier Wars 1788–1838* (Sydney: University of New South Wales Press, 2005), pp. 93–101; for a policy discussion, see Boyce, *Van Diemen's Land*, pp. 273–76.

44. Boyce, *Van Diemen's Land*, pp. 299–304.

45. Reynolds, *Fate of a Free People*, pp. 183–89; Ryan, *Aboriginal Tasmanians*, pp. 182–94.

46. Boyce, *Van Diemen's Land*, pp. 281–84.

47. Ryan, *Aboriginal Tasmanians*, p. 186.

48. Cassandra Pybus, *Community of Thieves* (Melbourne: William Heinemann, 1991), pp. 173–88.

49. Ryan, *Aboriginal Tasmanians*, pp. 66–82; Boyce, *Van Diemen's Land*, pp. 31–35, 65–68.

50. Reynolds, *Fate of a Free People*, pp. 121–22.

51. Shaw, *Van Diemen's Land*, pp. 1–5.

52. Boyce, *Van Diemen's Land*, p. 275.

53. Ryan, *Aboriginal Tasmanians*, pp. 222–312.

54. Pybus, *Community of Thieves*, pp. 173–88; Henry Reynolds, *Nowhere People* (Melbourne: Viking, 2005).

55. Reynolds, *Fate of a Free People*, pp. 83–85; Clive Turnbull, *The Black War* (Melbourne: F.W. Cheshire, 1948); Bronwyn Desailly, *The Mechanics of Genocide*, MA thesis (Hobart: University of Tasmania, 1977). The Tasmanian Parliament unanimously apologized on August 13, 1997; compensation was announced by premier Paul Lennon in November 2006.

56. Jim Bacon, February 28, 1999, http://www.premier.tas.gov.au/speeches/080299wybalenna.html.

57. For fuller accounts of (i) the relationship between colonialism and genocide and (ii) the relationship between legal and historical approaches to studies of extermination, see Tony Barta, "Decent Disposal: Australian Historians and the Recovery of Genocide," in Dan Stone, ed., *The Historiography of Genocide* (London: Palgrave Macmillan, 2008), pp. 296–322.

58. Curthoys, "Genocide in Tasmania," pp. 245–47, makes a similar argument.

Chapter 5. Tibet

1. X. Panchen Lama, *A Poisoned Arrow* (London: TIN, 1997), pp. 52 and 70.

2. Warren W. Smith, Jr., *Tibet's Last Stand?* (New York: Rowman & Littlefield, 2010), p. 240.

3. Quoted in "Ottawa Rally Commemorates 50th Anniversary of 1959 Tibetan Uprising," press release, March 10, 2009, Canada Tibet Committee website, www.tibet.ca/en/newsroom/news_releases/162.

4. Ibid.

5. International Commission of Jurists, (ICJ), *The Question of Tibet and the Rule of Law* (Geneva: ICJ, 1959); ICJ, *Tibet and the People's Republic of China* (Geneva: ICJ, 1960); ICJ, *Tibet: Human Rights and the Rule of Law* (Geneva: ICJ, 1997).

6. Blake Kerr, *Sky Burial* (Ithaca: Snow Lion Publications, 1997).

7. Zhu Rui, *Response to the White Paper* (New Delhi: TWA, 2009), as a reply to the official Chinese white paper, "Protection and Development of Tibetan Culture," published September 2008 in Beijing. The author worked from 1998 to 2001 at "Tibetan Literature," a government-sponsored magazine in Lhasa; she later lived in Canada.

8. On this matter, Claude Arpi, in *The Negotiations That Never Were* (New Delhi-Frankfurt: Lancer, 2009), gives very useful insights.

9. José Elias Esteve Molto, *Tibet, la frustracion de un Estado* (Valencia: Tirant la Blanch, 2004).

10. Jacques Sémelin, *Purifier et détruire* (Paris: Seuil, 1995).

11. R. D. Sloane, "The Changing Face of Recognition in International Law: A Case Study of Tibet," *Emory International Law Review*, 16. no. 1 (Spring 2002): 107–86.

12. L. V. Thomas, quoted in Lowell Thomas, *The Silent War in Tibet* (Westport, Conn.: Greenwood Press, 1959), passim.

13. Raphael Lemkin, *Axis Rule in Occupied Europe* (Washington, D.C.: Carnegie Endowment, 1944).

Chapter 6. The Anfal Campaign Against the Kurds

Reprinted by permission of the Publishers from "The Anfal Campaign Against the Kurds: Chemical Weapons in the Service of Mass Murder," in *Gendered Experiences of Genocide* by Choman Hardi (Farnham, UK: Ashgate, 2011), pp. 13–37. Copyright © 2011.

The author's research was funded by the Leverhulme Trust.

1. The epigraph is quoted in Joost R. Hiltermann, *A Poisonous Affair: America, Iraq, and the Gassing of Halabja* (Cambridge: Cambridge University Press, 2007), p. 95. The Kurds are divided among Turkey, Iran, Iraq, and Syria. Their number is estimated at some 30 million, half of them in Turkey, and 5 million in Iraq, the latter heavily concentrated in the mountainous northwest region adjacent to Iran. The majority are Sunni Muslims. There is no such thing as a unified Kurdish language, but rather two main dialects.

2. Kanan Makiya, *Cruelty and Silence: War, Tyranny, Uprising, and the Arab World* (New York: W. W. Norton, 1993), p. 156.

3. Shorsh H. Resool, *Destruction of a Nation* (1990).

4. The number given by Kurdish politicians was 182,000. In response to this Ali Hassan Majeed famously said: They were not more than 100,000. Human Rights Watch was able to collect over 50,000 names and estimated the total number to be somewhere between 50,000 and 100,000. Speaking with other field researchers in Kurdistan such as Najmadeen Faqe Abdullah, Arif Ourbani, Adalat Omar and Goran Baba-Ali, I believe the number is closer to 100,000.

5. In 1983, Special Units of the Iraqi army arrested between 5,000 and 8,000 males over the age of twelve from the Barzani tribe. The incident took place in

Qushtapa, a camp to which the Barzani tribe had been relocated in 1981. The Barzani clan was particularly targeted because they were a key faction behind the Kurdish liberation movement since the 1960s. It was also retaliation for the Kurdistan Democratic Party's collaboration with Iran during the Iraq-Iran war. The victims of this attack, some of whom were only recovered and returned to the Barzan region in 2006, are now being called Anfal victims.

6. Samantha Power, *A Problem from Hell: America and the Age of Genocide* (New York: Basic Books, 2002), p. 185.

7. Cited in Hiltermann, *A Poisonous Affair,* p. 213.

8. Ibid., p. 213.

9. Joost R. Hiltermann, *Elusive Justice: Trying to Try Saddam.* International Crisis Group. *Middle East Report* no. 215 (Summer 2000).

10. Power, *A Problem from Hell,* p. 221.

11. David McDowall, *A Modern History of the Kurds* (London: I. B. Tauris, 2005), p. 362.

12. Andreas Zumach, *German Help for Iraq* (Taz Seita, December 17, 2002).

13. Hiltermann, *A Poisonous Affair,* p. xii.

14. *When The Borders Bleed: The Struggle of the Kurds,* photographs by Ed Kashi, introduction by Christopher Hitchens (New York: Pantheon Books, 1994), p. 19.

15. Power, *A Problem from Hell,* p. 187.

16. Ibid., p. 188.

17. McDowall, *A Modern History of the Kurds,* p. 362.

18. Physicians for Human Rights, *Winds of Death: Iraq's Use of Poison Gas Against the Kurdish Population: Report of a Medical Mission to Turkish Kurdistan* (Physicians for Human Rights, 1989), p. 4.

19. *Chemical Weapons Use in Kurdistan: Iraq's Final Offensive,* a staff report to the Committee on Foreign Relations (U.S. Senate, October 1988).

20. Physicians for Human Rights, *Winds of Death,* p. 5.

21. Ibid., p. 4.

22. Middle East Watch, *Genocide in Iraq, the Anfal Campaign Against the Kurds* (Human Rights Watch, 1993), p. xxvi.

23. Ibid.

24. Joost R. Hilterman, "To Protect or to Project? Iraqi Kurds and Their Future," *International Crisis Group,* Middle East Report, June 4, 2008, p. 2.

25. Gérard Chaliand, *A People Without a Country: The Kurds and Kurdistan* (London: Zed Books, 1993), p. 7.

26. Edgar O'Ballance, *The Kurdish Struggle, 1920–94* (New York: St. Martin's Press, 1996), p. 172.

27. Shorsh H. Resool, *Anfal: The Kurds and the Iraqi State* (London, 2003), (in Kurdish).

28. Middle East Watch, *Genocide in Iraq ,* p. 58.

29. Ibid., pp. 239–58.

30. Arif Qurbani, *From Um Re'an to Topzawa: The Bulldozer Driver Who Covered Some of the Anfal Victims* (Tishk Publishing House, 2004).

31. Middle East Watch, *Genocide in Iraq,* p. 93.

32. Interview with Najeeba Ahmed, Erbil, March 31, 2006.

33. Middle East Watch, *Genocide in Iraq,* p. 101.

34. Ibid., p. 118.

35. Ibid., p. 170.

36. Ibid., p. 178.

37. Physicians for Human Rights, *Winds of Death.*

38. Peter Galbraith, March 16, 2007. Anfal: The attempted destruction of the Iraqi Kurds seminar. Centre for Study of Holocaust and Religious Minorities, Olso.

39. Ellen L. Bassuk and Brigid Donelan, "Social Deprivation," in Bonnie L. Green et al., eds., *Trauma Interventions in War and Peace: Prevention, Practice and Policy* (Kluwer Academic/ Plenum Publishers, 2003), p. 34.

40. See Patricia K. R. Herbst, *From Helpless Victim to Empowered Survivor: Oral History as a Treatment for Survivors of Torture,* in Ellen Cole, Olivia M. Espin, and Esther D. Rothblum, eds., *Refugee Women and Their Mental Health: Shattered Societies, Shattered Lives* (Harrington Park Press, 1992), and Susan D. Solomon, introduction, in Green et al., *Trauma Interventions in War and Peace,*, p. 7.

41. Christine Gosden, "Why I Went, What I Saw," *Washington Post,* March 11, 1988, p. A19.

42. Fuad Baban, Adil Karem, and Christine Gosdon, *The Long Term Health Consequences of the Chemical and Biological Weapons Attack on the Civilian Population of Halabja, Northern Iraq* (Halanc. June 14, 1998).

43. Katzman and Prados, March 14, 2005, CRS Report for the U.S. Congress.

44. Hama-Saeed, May 15, 2008, IWPR.

45. Associated Press, August 22, 2006.

46. Middle East Watch, *Genocide in Iraq,* p. 349.

47. The Anfal trial, broadcast on Kurdistan TV, February 7, 2007.

48. The 40th session of the Anfal trial, Kurdistan TV.

49. Convention on the Prevention and Punishment of the Crime of Genocide, Article 2.

50. Interview with Najmadeen Faqe Abdullah, Rotterdam, August 2006.

51. Helen Fein, *Genocide, A Sociological Perspective* (New York: Sage Publications, 1993), pp. 28–30.

52. Ibid., p. 24.

53. Raul Hilberg, *The Destruction of the European Jews* (New York: Holmes and Meier, 1985), vol. 1, p. 267.

54. Mia Bloom, "The Bureaucracy of Repression: A Discussion of the Iraqi Police Files and the Anfal Campaign Against the Kurds," in Roger W. Smith, ed., *Genocide: Essays Toward Understanding, Early-Warning and Prevention* (Association of Genocide Scholars, 1999), p. 139.

55. Quoted in Power, *A Problem from Hell,* p. 242.

56. Patrick Cockburn, *Muqtada Al-Sadr and the Battle for the Future of Iraq* (New York: Scribner, 2008), p. 76.

57. Peter Galbraith, "What Went Wrong," in Brendan O'Leary, John McGarry, and Khaled Salih, eds., *The Future of Kurdistan in Iraq* (Philadelphia: University of Pennsylvania Press, 2005), p. 236.

Chapter 7. The Assyrian Genocide

1. See E. S. Drower, *The Mandaeans of Iraq and Iran: Their Cults, Customs, Magic Legends, and Folklore* (Piscataway, N.J.: Gorgias Press, [1937] 2002), pp. xviii–xxiii, 26, 40–98, 117, 121, 229–399, 408, 417; Abraham Valentine Williams Jackson, *Persia Past and Present: A Book of Travel and Research* (New York: Macmillan, 1906), pp. 12–13.

2. See Christoph Baumer, *The Church of the East: An Illustrated History of Assyrian Christianity* (London: I. B. Tauris, 2006), pp. 247–58; David Gaunt, *Massacres, Resistance, Protectors: Muslim-Christian Relations in Eastern Anatolia During World*

War I (Piscataway, N.J.: Gorgias Press, 2006), pp. 31–32; Salâhi Sonyel, *The Assyrians of Turkey: Victims of Major Power Policy* (Ankara, Turkey: Turkish Historical Society Printing House, 2001), pp. 29–41; Hannibal Travis, " 'Native Christians Massacred': The Ottoman Genocide of the Assyrians During World War I," *Genocide Studies and Prevention: An International Journal* 1 (3) (2006): 327–29; Gabriele Yonan, *Lest We Perish, A Forgotten Holocaust: The Extermination of the Christian Assyrians in Turkey and Persia* (Berlin: n.p., 1996), pp. 23–36, http://www.aina.org/books/lwp.pdf.

3. See Gaunt, *Massacres, Resistance, Protectors*, p. 93.

4. See ibid., pp. 21–28, 300–303, 406, 435; Sonyel, *The Assyrians of Turkey*, p. 14.

5. See Gaunt, *Massacres, Resistance, Protectors*, pp. 51, 62–65; Anahit Khosroeva, "The Assyrian Genocide," in Richard Hovannisian, ed., *The Armenian Genocide: Cultural and Ethical Legacies* (New Brunswick, N.J.: Transaction Publishers, 2007), p. 271; Sonyel, *The Assyrians of Turkey*, p. 87; Travis, " 'Native Christians Massacred,' " pp. 331–33, 342–43; Yonan, *Lest We Perish*, pp. 72–104.

6. See Yonan, *Lest We Perish*, pp. 72–101. Prefiguring the Nazis' aims in World War II, Ottoman Minister of War Enver Pasha planned an invasion of the Russian Empire, occupation of the oil fields of Baku, and conquest of Afghanistan and India from the British. Some Armenians and Assyrians fought with the Russians and the Persians to repel the Ottoman Third Army, which lost thousands in battle with the Russians or due to exposure to the harsh Caucasian winter of 1914–15.

7. See Vahakn Dadrian, *The History of the Armenian Genocide: Ethnic Conflict from the Balkans to Anatolia to the Caucuses* (New York: Berghahn Books, 2003), pp. 203–11, 220, 236–95.

8. See Gaunt, *Massacres, Resistance, Protectors*, pp. 65, 95.

9. See ibid., pp. 57–65, 192–56, 311–15, 447–93; Travis, " 'Native Christians Massacred,' " pp. 331–43; Yonan, *Lest We Perish*, pp. 76–99.

10. See Gaunt, *Massacres, Resistance, Protectors*, pp. 82, 106; Khosroeva, "The Assyrian Genocide," p. 271; Travis, " 'Native Christians Massacred,' " p. 343.

11. See "Massacres in Persia," *Poverty Bay Herald (New Zealand)*, March 30, 1915, p. 3.

12. See Gaunt, *Massacres, Resistance, Protectors*, pp. 141–64, 168–76, 250–56; Travis, " 'Native Christians Massacred,' " pp. 333, 336, 343–44; Yonan, *Ein vergessener Holocaust*, pp. 9–10, 29–43, 82–83, 98–105, 131.

13. See Gaunt, *Massacres, Resistance, Protectors*, pp. 164–65, 181–96; Travis, " 'Native Christians Massacred,' " pp. 332–36; Yonan, *Lest We Perish*, pp. 106–43.

14. Johannes Lepsius, quoted in Travis, " 'Native Christians Massacred,' " pp. 332–33; see also Yonan, *Ein vergessener Holocaust*, pp. 44, 204–38.

15. Quoted in Gaunt, *Massacres, Resistance, Protectors*, p. 74.

16. Quoted in ibid., p. 73.

17. Quoted in ibid., p. 75. See also ibid., p. 121; Travis, " 'Native Christians Massacred,' " pp. 333–34, 337–38.

18. Walter Holstein, German vice consul in Mosul, quoted in Travis, " 'Native Christians Massacred,' " p. 336. See also Gaunt, *Massacres, Resistance, Protectors*, p. 244.

19. See Gaunt, *Massacres, Resistance, Protectors*, pp. 76–77, 164, 181–96, 226–30, 264–67; Amill Gorgis, "Der Völkermord an den Syro-Aramäern," in Tessa Hoffman, ed., *Verfolgung, Vertreibung und Vernichtung der Christen im Osmanischen Reich* (Berlin: LIT Verlag, 2004), p. 20; Khosroeva, "The Assyrian Genocide," p. 270; Travis, " 'Native Christians Massacred,' " pp. 333–36.

20. See Gaunt, *Massacres, Resistance, Protectors*, pp. 143–46; Hannibal Travis, "The Cultural and Intellectual Property Interests of the Indigenous Peoples of Turkey and Iraq," *Texas Wesleyan Law Review* 15 (2009): 415, 436–40.

21. Quoted in Travis, "'Native Christians Massacred,'" p. 336. See also DE/PA-AA/R14093, 1916-A-24663, September 10, 1916, Chief of the Kaiser's Civil Cabinet, Valentini, to the German Imperial Chancellor Bethmann Hollweg.

22. See Gaunt, *Massacres, Resistance, Protectors*, p. 120; Travis, "'Native Christians Massacred,'" pp. 331–34, 337; Yonan, *Lest We Perish*, pp. 3–20.

23. See Baumer, *Church of the East*, p. 263.

24. See ibid., p. 263; Travis, "'Native Christians Massacred,'" p. 338.

25. See Baumer, *Church of the East*, p. 263; Khosroeva, "The Assyrian Genocide", p. 272; Travis, "The Indigenous Peoples of Turkey and Iraq," pp. 463–66.

26. See Khosroeva, "The Assyrian Genocide," pp. 267–72.

27. See Gaunt, *Massacres, Resistance, Protectors*.

28. My article drew the attention of genocide scholars to World War I–era books, journalistic articles, and government documents describing anti-Assyrian massacres, deportations, and reduction to starvation and exposure to the elements; there are many such books and reports by British and American officials, the German allies of the Ottoman empire, the Ottoman leadership, the foreign press, and the Assyrian victims of the war. See Travis, "'Native Christians Massacred.'"

29. See Adam Jones, "Genocide: A Comprehensive Introduction" (2007), http://www.genocidetext.net/iags_resolution_supporting_documentation.htm; Thea Halo, *Not Even My Name* (2007), http://www.notevenmyname.com/9.html.

30. See "Assyrian Genocide," in Samuel Totten, Paul Robert Bartrop, and Steven L. Jacobs, *Dictionary of Genocide?* (Westport, Conn.: Greenwood, 2008), pp. 25–26.

31. Israel Charny, "On the Ottoman Genocide Resolution," *International Association of Genocide Scholars Blog* (October 3, 2007), http://www.genocidescholars.org/blog/?p=88.

32. See Gavin Brockett, "Islamic 'Reaction' to the Turkish Revolution: A Framework for the Social History of the Ataturk Era (1923–1938)," master's thesis, Simon Fraser University, Burnaby, British Columbia, Canada, 1995), pp. 88–89, http://ir.lib.sfu.ca/bitstream/1892/9146/1/b17417016.pdf; Şükran Vahide, *Islam in Modern Turkey: An Intellectual Biography of Bediuzzaman Said Nursi* (Albany: State University of New York Press, 2005), p. 180.

33. John M. VanderLippe, *The Politics of Turkish Democracy: I[uf53]smet I[uf53]nönü and the Formation of the Multi-Party System, 1938–1950* (Albany: State University of New York Press, 2005), pp. 16–17.

34. See Yonah Alexander, Edgar H. Brenner, and Serhat Tutuncuoglu Krause, eds., *Turkey: Terrorism, Civil Rights, and the European Union* (London: Routledge, 2008), pp. 491–92.

35. See Amnesty International, "Turkey: 17 Years in the Balance: Lawyer Esber Yagmurdereli Returns to Prison in Freedom of Expression Case," AI Index No., EUR 44/074/1997 (November 1, 1997), http://www.amnesty.org/en/library/info/EUR44/074/1997.

36. Armenian National Committee of America, "Under Growing International Pressure Turkey Releases Assyrian Priest" (April 5, 2001), http://www.anca.org/press_releases/press_releases.php?prid=66.

37. Speros Vryonis, Jr., *The Turkish State and History: Clio Meets the Grey Wolf* (Thessaloniki, Greece: Institute for Balkan Studies, 1991), pp. 13–41, 50–57, 67–88.

38. Ibid., pp. 52, 59–63, 90.

39. Ibid., pp. 58–65, 89–115. Similarly, the Nazis characterized resistance to their genocide in Poland, the Soviet Union, and Yugoslavia as "acts of terror and sabotage in the occupied territories," for which they retaliated by killing all the men and enslaving the women. International Military Tribunal, Nuremberg, *Nazi Conspiracy and Aggression* (Washington, D.C.: U.S. Government Printing Office, 1946).

40. See Bernard Lewis, *The Emergence of Modern Turkey,* 3rd rev. ed., (New York: Oxford University Press, 2002), p. 356; Bernard Lewis, Presentation to National Press Club (2002), http://www.youtube.com/watch?v=qG70U WESfu4; Bernard Lewis, *Le Monde,* November 27, 1993; Bernard Lewis, *Le Monde,* January 1, 1994; Dalia Karpel, "There Was No Genocide: Interview with Prof. Bernard Lewis," *Haaretz,* January 23, 1998, http://www.ataa.org/reference/karpel.html; Guenter Lewy, *The Armenian Massacres in Ottoman Turkey: A Disputed Genocide* (Salt Lake City: University of Utah Press, 2005); Guenter Lewy, "Revisiting the Armenian Genocide," *Middle East Quarterly* (Fall 2005): 3–12, http://www.meforum.org/748/revisiting-the-armenian-genocide; Heath Lowry, *The Story Behind "Ambassador Morgenthau's Story"* (Istanbul, Turkey: Isis Press, 1990); Justin McCarthy, *Muslims and Minorities: The Population of Ottoman Anatolia and the End of the Empire* (New York: New York University Press, 1983); Justin McCarthy, *Population History of the Middle East and the Balkans* (I[uf53]stanbul: Isis Press, 2002); Justin McCarthy, *The Armenian Rebellion at Van* (Salt Lake City: University of Utah Press, 2006); Stanford Shaw, *From Empire to Republic: The Turkish War of National Liberation, 1918–1923,* 5 volumes (Ankara, Turkey: TTK/Turkish Historical Society, 2001). For a summary of the influence of the Institute of Turkish Studies on American universities in the 1990s, see Christopher Shea, "Turko-Armenian War Brews in the Ivory Tower," *Salon,* June 9, 1999, http://www.salon.com/books/it/1999/06/09/turkish_chairs; Roger W. Smith, Eric Markusen, and Robert Jay Lifton, "Professional Ethics and the Denial of the Armenian Genocide," in Richard G. Hovannisian, ed., *Remembrance and Denial: The Case of the Armenian Genocide* (Detroit: Wayne State University Press, 1998), pp. 271–95; Yves Ternon, "Freedom and Responsibility of the Historian: The 'Lewis Affair,'" in Hovannisian, *Remembrance and Denial,* 237–70.

41. Vryonis, *The Turkish State and History,* pp. 103–31.

42. John B. Quigley, *The Genocide Convention: An International Law Analysis* (London: Ashgate, 2006), pp. 6–9; see also Stephen Gorove, "The Problem of 'Mental Harm' in the Genocide Convention," *Washington University Law Quarterly* 1951: 174–80.

43. See Quigley, *The Genocide Convention,* pp. 5–7, 15–27, 268–69.

44. Sonyel, *The Assyrians of Turkey,* p. 197.

45. Ibid., p. 85.

46. See Raphael Lemkin, *Axis Rule in Occupied Europe: Laws of Occupation, Analysis of Government, Proposals for Redress* (Washington, D.C.: Carnegie Endowment for International Peace, 1944), ch. 9, http://www.preventgenocide.org/lemkin/AxisRule1944-1.htm.

47. Ibid.

48. Ibid., http://www.preventgenocide.org/lemkin/AxisRule1944-2.htm.

49. See Gorove, "The Problem of 'Mental Harm' in the Genocide Convention," pp. 175–87.

50. UN General Assembly, Resolution 47/121, A/47/49 (December 18, 1992), http://www.un.org/documents/ga/res/47/a47r121.htm; UN Security Council, Resolution 935, S/RES/935 (July 1, 1994), http://www.un.org/sc.

51. "China Demands Turkish Retraction," *BBC News* (UK), July 14, 2009, http://news.bbc.co.uk/2/hi/asia-pacific/8149379.stm; Republic of Turkey, Draft Resolution of the UN Commission on Human Rights, E/CN.4/1992/S-2/L.2 (November 30, 1992); "Parliament Bureau, Ecevit Defends Bank Operation," *Turkish Daily News/Global News Wire (Financial Times Information)*, December 29, 1999.

52. See Baumer, *The Church of the East*, p. 266.

53. Ann Curthoys, "Raphaël Lemkin's 'Tasmania': An Introduction," in A. Dirk Moses and Dan Stone, eds., *Colonialism and Genocide* (London: Routledge, 2007), p. 68.

54. See Gorove, "The Problem of 'Mental Harm' in the Genocide Convention," pp. 176–79.

55. See Travis, "The Indigenous Peoples of Turkey and Iraq," pp. 662–64, 676–78.

56. Sonyel, *The Assyrians of Turkey*, pp. 85, 197.

57. See Gaunt, *Massacres, Resistance, Protectors*, pp. 54–55, 65, 94–98.

58. Between 300,000 and 600,000 Germans were incinerated or otherwise killed in the fire-bombing of German cities, and up to a million German prisoners died in U.S. custody. R .J. Rummel, *Statistics of Democide* (Berlin: LIT Verlag, 2004), p. 203. This scholar describes Allied policy toward the German city of Hamburg as "blanket firebombing." See R. J. Rummel, *Death by Government* (New Brunswick, N.J.: Transaction Publishers, 1997), p. 35. Many other German cities were "turned into burning ruins" by more than 80 million Allied incendiary bombs. Jörg Friedrich, *The Fire: The Bombing of Germany, 1940–1945* (New York: Columbia University Press, 2008), p. 16. Hundreds of thousands, perhaps millions, of German women and girls were raped. Bernhard Giesen, "The Trauma of Perpetrators: The Holocaust as the Thematic Reference of German National Identity," in Jeffrey C. Alexander, ed., *Cultural Trauma and Collective Identity?* (Berkeley: University of California Press, 2004), p. 115. Some estimates of the numbers of Germans deported during and after World War II reach 15 million, with 1.8 to 3.7 million dying as a result, in addition to three to five million German military deaths from 1939 through 1945. See Rummel, *Statistics of Democide*, pp. 299, 311; Gerhard Ziemer, *Deutsche Exodus: Vetreibung und Eingliederung von 15 Millionen Ostdeutsche* (Stuttgart: Seewald, 1973). Alexander Statiev, despite being generally inclined to defend the Soviet Union from charges of a policy of extermination, argues that the Soviets deported blacklisted ethnic groups in numbers that "place[d] them in conditions that led to a genocidal attrition rate among them." Alexander Statiev, "Soviet Ethnic Deportations: Intent Versus Outcome," *Journal of Genocide Research* 11 (2009): 243, 259.

59. Travis, "'Native Christians Massacred,'" p. 340.

60. Parliament of Kurdistan in Exile, *Press Release #1* (April 23, 1995), http://www.aina.org/releases/parexile.htm.

61. Governor George Pataki, *Proclamation* (April 24, 2004), http://www.anca.org/press_releases/press_releases.php?prid=565; Governor David Paterson, *Proclamation* (April 24, 2008), http://www.ny.gov/governor/ keydocs/proclamations/proc_armenian.htm.

62. See Nat da Polis, "Erdogan Attacks the Past, Labels Kemalist Ethnic Cleansing Fascist," *Asia News*, May 25, 2009, http://www.asianews.it/index.php?l=en&art=15333&geo=1&size=A.

63. See Vryonis, *The Turkish State and History*, pp. 116–19.

64. See ibid., pp. 89–31.

Chapter 8. The "Gypsy Problem"

1. I know of no other cases like this and official ideology was opposed to the idea that people of Gypsy descent could be assimilated via socialization. Robert Ritter's main collaborator, Eva Justin, published a study that purported to show the pointlessness of raising "mixed-race" Gypsies in orphanages or German foster homes. Eva Justin, *Lebensschicksale artfremd erzogener Zigeunerkinder und ihrer Nachkommen* (Berlin: Schuetz, 1944). In Switzerland, non-Romany speaking *Jenische* traveler children were forcibly adopted out of their families in this period.

2. Romani Rose, ed., *Der nationalsozialistische Volkermord an den Sinti und Roma,* 2nd ed. (Heidelberg: Dokumentations- und Kulturzentrum Deutscher *Sinti und Roma*, 1995). 180–81. Her arrival in Auschwitz is noted in the camp register for April 1944; her departure to Ravensbruck is not noted (State Museum, 1995).

3. Interview with Else Schmidt, May 2001. Transcript and original in possession of the author. Schmidt herself talks of the teachers as "bad Nazis," but it is not clear that this teacher was such.

4. In this chapter I use the terms Roma, Gypsy, and Sinti almost interchangeably as self-referent terms for those populations the Nazis and their allies persecuted as Ziguener. I use the adjective Romany in preference to "Gypsy"—as in "the Romany peoples"—since this usage is likely to be the most acceptable to the widest range of Romany readers. For the sources from which I draw the estimated figure for losses see note 5.

5. Michael Zimmermann, *Rassenutopie und Genozid: Die Nationalsozialistische "Losung der Zigeunerfrage"* (Hamburg: Christians, 1996), pp. 381–83; also "Die Entscheidung fur ein Zigeunerlager in Auschwitz-Birkenau," in M. Zimmermann, ed., *Zwischen Erziehung und Vernichtung: Zigeunerpolitik und Zigeunerforschung im Europa des 20. Jahrhunderts,* Beitrage der Geschichte der Deutschen Forschungsgemeinschaft, vol. 3 (Stuttgart: Franz Steiner, 2007), pp. 392–424. For Yugoslavia see Dragoljub Ackovic, Roma Suffering in Jasenovac Camp (Belgrade: Museum of the Victims of Genocide, Roma Culture Center, 1995); *Jasenovac, sistem ustaskih logora smrti . . . ,*1997. Beograd, IS *"Strucna knj,"* actes en serbe d'un colloque de 1996; Dennis Reinhartz,. "Unmarked Graves: The Destruction of the Yugoslav Roma in the Balkan Holocaust, 1941–1945," *Journal of Genocide Research* 1 (1999): 81–89. For Lodz, see Lucjan Dobroszycki, ed., *The Chronicle of the Lodz Ghetto, 1941–1944* (New Haven: Yale University Press, 1984). For Romania see Andrea Varga, Andrea Nastasa, and Lucian Nastasa, eds, *Tiganii din Romania (1919–1944)* (Bucharest: Centrul de Resurse pentru Diversitate Etnoculturală, 2005).

6. For sterilization, see Hans-Jorg Reichert, *Im Schatten von Auschwitz: Die Nationalsozialistische Sterilisationspolitik gegenuber Sinti und Roma* (Munster: Waxmann, 1995).

One saga is particularly telling in its absurdity. In 1992, the German Federal Government agreed to construct a memorial to the Sinti, Roma, and Gypsies of Europe to go alongside the national monument to the Jews. They had only conceded after years of campaigning and direct action by Romany organizations. Seventeen years later, in summer 2009, the agreed location remains an ugly building site in a copse at the edge of the Tiergarten opposite the Brandenburg Gate and diagonally opposite Peter Eisenman's Memorial to the Murdered Jews of Europe. After much debate about the site itself and, more fundamentally, the purpose and meaning of such a memorial, the construction itself has been delayed to the point that at its opening, it is conceivable that no adult Romany survivors of World War II will be alive. It is true that the difficulty Romany and Sinte organizations had in agreeing on a text was a factor here, but once the German president took ownership of the problem, a solution was found.

7. The story of how, in various places and times, these families have maintained and handed down their distinctiveness has yet to be put to paper. And it is a story that when finally composed, will challenge some of the basic assumptions modern Europeans make about what constitutes "a people"—with our all-consuming model of the nation held together by a powerful sense of its own historic destiny. In the Romany world there is no book to provide a mythology of common origin, no mythology of dispersal and diaspora, not even a common faith or hieratic caste, let alone any sense of shared history. And yet the Romany peoples, as it is helpful to call them, continued to share a language, indicating some element of shared descent, and to transmit many common cultural patterns. Whenever members of this family of families happen to meet the sense of mutual recognition is tangible—even though their sense of difference and distinctiveness may be even greater.

8. The Gitanos of Spain, for instance, or the British "Gypsies" (as they call themselves) are almost certainly descended from such Romany-speaking populations, though they themselves do not speak Romany. Other populations, who probably have no historic link to Romany speakers (like the Scottish "tinkers" or the German and Swiss *Jenische*), may also be classified by outsiders as Zigeuner in part because of the similarity of their ecological niche and lifestyle to that of other Zigeuner. See Yaron Matras, *Romani: A Linguistic Introduction* (Cambridge: Cambridge University Press, 2005); and Angus Fraser, *The Gypsies* (Oxford: Blackwell, 1992), for an attempt to write a kind of national history of the Roma.

One of the secrets of Romany survival over the centuries has been the ability to hide and conceal their identity—to remain all but invisible to the world around them. The very first Romany families in Europe in the fourteenth century presented themselves as pilgrims—able thus to disappear in the great mass of devout believers who took to the roads at that time. And ever since they have played the same game. What this has meant is that even more perhaps than the Jews, these families and clans have been systematically misunderstood and misrepresented by the societies in which they lived. Henriette Asseo is currently preparing a text that will provide the first theoretically cogent and historically specific account of the history of these peoples.

9. Rose, *Der nationalsozialistische Volkermord*, p. 182.

10. Gilad Margalit, *Germany and Its Gypsies: A Post-Auschwitz Ordeal* (Madison: University of Wisconsin Press, 2002), pp. 83–142.

11. The Soviet administration was only willing to compensate victims of "fascism" and active fighters against it. Racial enemies of the Nazis were declared "passive" victims and denied compensation. Margalit, *Germany and Its Gypsies*, p. 87.

12. See Robert Gellately, *Backing Hitler: Consent and Coercion in Nazi Germany* (Oxford: Oxford University Press, 2001), p. 78.

13. See Margalit, *Germany and Its Gypsies*, p. 98.

14. Cited in Anna Mettbach and Josef Behringer, *"Wer wird die nachste sein?" Die Leidensgeschichte einer Sintezza, die Auschwitz uberlebte/ "Ich will doch nur die Gerchtigkeit" Wie den Sinti und Roma nach 1945 der Rechtsanspruch auf Entschadigung versagt wurde* (Frankfurt: Brandes & Apsel, 1999), pp. 107–8.

15. For these cases see, ZSL Ludwigsburg, 414 AR 540/83, Bd. 4, pp. 233, 799.

16. See Alfred Dillman, *Zigeuner-Buch* (Munich: K. B. Staatsministeriums des Innern, 1905).

17. Andres Wimmer, *Nationalist Exclusion and Ethnic Conflict: Shadows of Modernity* (Cambridge: Cambridge University Press, 2002), pp. 57–64.

18. See Richard Evans, "Social Outsiders in German History: From the Sixteenth Century to 1933," in Robert Gellately and Nathan Stolzfuls, eds., *Social Outsiders in Nazi Germany* (Princeton: Princeton University Press, 2001), pp. 20–44.

19. See Leo Lucassen, *Zigeuner. Die Geschichte eines polizeilichen Ordnungsbegriffs in Deutschland 1700–1945* (Cologne: Bohlau, 1996); and Thoms Fricke, *Zigeuner im Zeitalter des Absolutismus. Bilanz einer einseitigen Überlieferung : eine sozialgeschichtliche Untersuchung anhand südwestdeutscher Quellen* (Pfaffenweiler: Centaurus-Verlagsgesellschaft, 1996) for the early modern period. It is no accident that at the creation of Interpol, the pursuit of Gypsy criminals was identified as one of the specific tasks that this form of transnational cooperation would permit.

20. Richard F. Wetzell, *Inventing the Criminal: A History of German Criminology 1880–1945* (Chapel Hill: University of North Carolina Press, 2000).

21. Henriette Asseo, *Les Tsiganes: Une destinée européenne* (Paris: Gallimard, 1994).

22. See, for example, Dr. Zindel's letter to State Secretary Pfundner of March 4, 1936, and his "Thoughts on the Design of a Reich Law for the Gypsies." There we find promises of rapid new and specific proposals, but there is no further trace of these in ministerial papers. Berlin R 18, R1501 5644, pp. 215–27.

23. See Jud Newborn, " 'Work Makes Free': The Hidden Cultural Meanings of the Holocaust," unpublished Ph.D. thesis in department of anthropology, University of Chicago, 1993, especially volume 3 for an analysis of the idea of the camp as a zone of social correction, and Burleigh, *The Third Reich: A New History* (London: Macmillan, 2000), pp. 198–205, for a broad appreciation of the political logic of mass incarceration. For Marzahn in Berlin, see Frank Sparing, "The Gypsy Camps," in Fings, Karola, Heuss, Herbert, and Sparing, eds., *From "Race Science" to the Camps: The Gypsies During the Second World War* (Hatfield: University of Hertfordshire Press, 1997), pp. 55–70.

24. See Zimmermann, *Zwischen Erziehung und Vernichtung.*

25. See Cornelia Sorabji, "A Very Modern War: Terror and Territory in Bosnia-Hercegovina," in Robert A. Hinde and Helen E. Watson, eds., *War, a Cruel Necessity? The Bases of Institutionalized Violence* (London: I. B. Tauris, 1995), pp. 80–95.

26. Ibid.

27. Cited by Sorabji, "A Very Modern War," from Hukanovic, *The Tenth Circle of Hell: A Memoir of Life in the Death Camps of Bosnia* (1993; New York: Basic Books, 1996), p. 56.

Contributors

Shayne Breen earned a Ph.D. in history from the University of Tasmania, where he lectured in Aboriginal Studies for twenty years. He is the author of two books, *Contested Places: Tasmania's Northern District from Ancient Times Until 1900* (2001) and *Aboriginal Connections with Launceston Places* (2006). He is currently completing a social and environmental history of Aboriginal Tasmania from 35,000 years ago until the recent past.

Choman Hardi was born in Kurdistan (Iraq) and was educated at Queen's College, Oxford, University College in London, and the University of Kent in Canterbury where she completed a Ph.D. on problems of mental health among Kurdish women refugees. She has conducted post-doctoral field research on Kurdish women widowed during the Anfal massacre. Her findings will appear in her forthcoming book, *Gender and Genocide: Anfal Survivors in Kurdistan*. She is also a poet, author of two collections of poems in Kurdish, and one in English, published under the title of *Life for Us* (2004).

René Lemarchand is Emeritus Professor of Political Science at the University of Florida. He has written extensively on Central Africa, including a recent volume on *The Dynamics of Violence in Central Africa* (2009). His book *Rwanda and Burundi* (1970) won the Herskovits Award of the African Studies Association. He worked for six years with USAID as Regional Advisor on Governance and Democracy for West Africa in Abidjan (1992–96) and Accra (1996–98). Since retiring from the University of Florida he has served as visiting lecturer at Smith College, Brown, Berkeley, Concordia (Montreal), and at the universities of Bordeaux, Copenhagen, Helsinki, and Antwerp.

Claude Levenson (1938–2010) was trained as an Orientalist and was a leading authority on Buddhism and Tibet, which she visited on several occasions. She wrote some fifteen books on the history and culture of the people of Tibet, notably *Tibet, la question qui dérange* (2008), *Tibet d'oubli et de mémoire* (2007), and *Le Tibet* (2008), as well as a biography of the Dalai Lama, *Le Seigneur du Lotus blanc* (1987). In addition to translating into French the works of Eliade, Mandelstam, and Zamiatine, she was a regular contributor to leading French newspapers and magazines, including *Le Monde, Libération, Le Nouvel Observateur,* and *L'Express.* She was co-author, with Jean-Claude Buhrer, of *Sergio Vieira de Mello, un espoir foudroyé* (2004) and *Aung San Suu Kyi, demain la Birmanie* (2000). She died on December 13, 2010.

Filip Reyntjens is Professor of African Law and Politics at the Institute of Development Policy and Management at the University of Antwerp. He is a member of the Belgian Royal Academy of Overseas Sciences and a board member of the Institute of Tropical Medicine (Antwerp), the International Third World Legal Studies Association (New York), and the Development Research Institute (Tilburg). He is the author of a number of books and articles on Belgian Africa in English, French, and Dutch, and the co-editor of the yearly publication *L'Afrique des Grands Lacs.* His most recent publication is *The Great African War: Congo and Regional Geopolitics, 1996–2006* (2009).

Dominik J. Schaller teaches history at Ruprecht-Karls-University, Heidelberg (Germany). His research focuses on mass violence in general, European colonial rule in Africa, modern African history, and theories and methods of global history. He served as editor of the *Journal of Genocide Research* and was an editorial member of *Sozial Geschichte Zeitschrift fur historische Analyse des 20. und 21. Jahrhunderts.* Among his publications are *The Armenian Genocide and the Shoa* (2002), *Enteignet-Vertrieben-Ermordet. Betrage zur Genozidforschung* (2004), *Late Ottoman Genocides: Young Turkish Population and Extermination Policies* (2009), and *The Origins of Genocide: Raphael Lemkin as a Historian of Mass Violence* (2009).

Michael Stewart is a social anthropologist who teaches at University College London and is a frequent visiting lecturer at the Central European University in Budapest. He has worked on Romany society and history since the mid-1980s, with special emphasis on the impact of economic and social marginalization on Gypsy communities in eastern Europe. He has also carried out field research among transhumant shepherds in Romania. He is the author of *The Time of the Gypsies* (1997) and co-edited a collection of essays on marginal lives titled *Lilies of the Field* (1998).

Hannibal Travis is Associate Professor of Law at Florida International University. He graduated *magna cum laude* from Harvard Law School, and currently serves as a member of the editorial advisory board of *Genocide Studies and Prevention: An International Journal*, and an advisory board member of the Institute for Genocide Awareness and Applied Research. His publications include a chapter on genocide in Sudan in *The Top Ten Global Justice Law Review Articles, 2008*, "'Native Christians Massacred': The Ottoman Genocide of the Assyrians During World War I," *Genocide Studies and Prevention: An International Journal* (2006), and a monograph, *Genocide in the Middle East: The Ottoman Empire, Iraq and Sudan* (2010).

Index

Aborigines, 3, 5, 10; in Tasmania and Australia, 72; Aborigines Committee, 13, 76, 84; disruption of society, 71, 72; historical distortions, 76; theft of Aboriginal land, 78; abduction of, 79–80; murder, massacre and war of extermination, 79–83; assaults against colonists, 81; rewards for capture of, 81; types of killings, 81–83; capture, exile and incarceration, 84–86

Adams, John Quincy, 34

Algiers Treaty, 111

Alliance Démocratique pour le Changement (ADC), 50

Alliance of Democratic Forces for the Liberation of Congo/Zaire (AFDL), 23, 33; itinerary of, 28

Anatolia, 13

Anfal, 1, 12; meaning of, 106; verb to refer to mass murder, 107; as a synonym for Kurdish victimhood, 107; gas attacks, 107; as mass murder, 107, 108; offensives against Kurdish civilians, 113; general amnesty, 177; aftermath of, 118; role of women, 118; delayed effects of gas attacks, 119

Anfal Memorial Day, 116

Annan, Kofi, 33

Armenia, 1; controversy over genocide, 11; Turkish denialism on, 14

Armenian National Committee of America, 128

Arthur, George, 76, 80, 81, 84, 86

Assyrians, 3, 5, 6, 17, 18; estimate of population, 125; atrocities by, 157, n4; identified with other groups, 123; conversion to Judaism or Christianity, 123–124; denial of genocide, 124; cultural heritage, 124; early massacres, 125; participation of Kurds in killings, 126; human losses, 127; scholarly research, 127, 128; genocide in comparative perspective, 130 ff; a forgotten genocide, 133; problems in representing the genocide, 135, 136

Audiencia Nacional de Espana (ANE), 102

Auschwitz, 11, Auschwitz decree, 139

Australia, 71, 72; controversy over genocide, 73–75; genocide vs. extermination, extirpation, extinction, 75; immunity of settlers from prosecution, 86. *See also* Tasmania

Axis Rule in Occupied Europe, 131

Ayala-Lasso, José, 33

Ayatolla Khomeny, 108

Ba'ath party, 106, 111, 123

Bacon, Jim, 89

Balakian, Peter, 127

Balkans, 6; Balkan wars, 10

Bantu, 4

Banyamulenge, 22, 24

Banyarwanda, 23

Barkan, Elazar, 53

Barril, Maurice, 34

Barta, Tony, 73

Beijing, 15

Berlin conference, 55

Bigirimana, André, 49

Bismarck, Otto von, 57

blame-the-victims construction, 13

Bloxham, Donald, 14, 158, n24

The Book of Gypsies, 147

Boutros-Ghali, Boutros, 24

Boyes, G. W. T., 87

Breaux, John, 108